EMITOWN

05.2009 TO 04.2010

EMITOWN VOL. ONE. FIRST PRINTING. NOVEMBER 2010. PUBLISHED BY IMAGE COMICS, INC. OFFICE OF PUBLICATION - 2134 ALLSTON WAY, 2ND FLOOR BERKELEY, CA 94704.

PRINTED IN SOUTH KOREA. ISBN: 978-1-60706-318-6

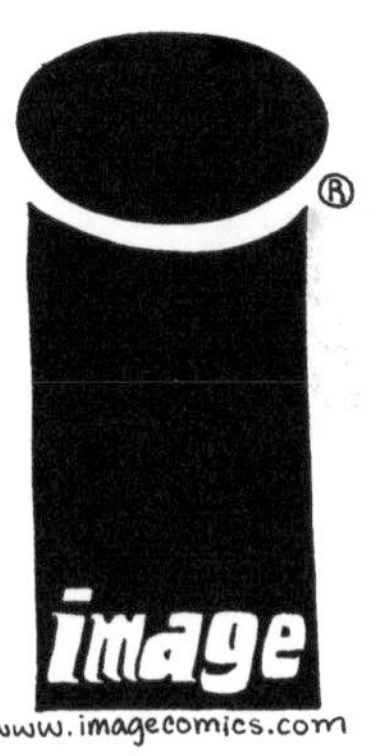

INTRODUCTION
BY JAMIE S. RICH

I HAD READ EMI BEFORE I HAD EVER SEEN HER, AND I SAW HER BEFORE I MET HER.

I WAS GOING TO A PARTY AT BRETT WARNOCK'S HOUSE. BRETT IS ONE HALF OF THE TOP SHELF COMICS TOP BRASS, AND HE THROWS THE BEST PARTIES. HIS COCKTAILS HAVE BEEN KNOWN TO KNOCK MY BRAIN SIDEWAYS ON MORE THAN ONE OCCASION, AND IF I CAN GET AN INVITE TO VISIT HIS HOME, I MAKE AN EFFORT TO BE THERE.

IN THIS CASE, I TOOK THE BUS ACROSS TOWN AND WHEN I GOT TO MY STOP, DECIDED TO TAKE A DETOUR TO A PLAID PANTRY CONVENIENCE STORE TO PICK UP SOME GINGER ALE. AS I CROSSED THE PARKING LOT TO GO INSIDE, A CUTE GIRL WITH DARK HAIR AND TAN SKIN WAS EXITING. SHE WAS DRESSED ALL IN BLACK, AND SHE LOOKED HAPPY, LIKE SHE WAS ENJOYING A PRIVATE JOKE. I DID A BIT OF A DOUBLE TAKE. WHAT WAS A GIRL LIKE THAT DOING IN NE. PORTLAND? ONCE YOU GET USED TO SEEING WHITEBREAD HIPSTERS EVERYWHERE, YOU TEND TO NOTICE PEOPLE WITH A LITTLE PERSONALITY.

AFTER BUYING MY GINGER ALE, I WENT TO BRETT'S HOUSE. I WAS THERE FOR A FEW MINUTES BEFORE, LO AND BEHOLD, THE GIRL FROM THE CONVENIENCE STORE WALKED IN. WAS THIS SOME STRANGE KISMET? HOW WAS THIS POSSIBLE? SHE WAS INTRODUCED TO ME AS TOP SHELF'S NEW INTERN. "I SAW YOU AT THE PLAID PANTRY," I SAID. "BUT WHERE THE HELL DID YOU GO? YOU WERE WALKING THE OPPOSITE DIRECTION WHEN WE PASSED."

"THE GUY BEHIND THE COUNTER WAS BEING REAL CREEPY," SHE SAID. "I DIDN'T WANT HIM TO SEE WHICH WAY I WAS REALLY GOING, SO I WALKED UP THE BLOCK AND CIRCLED AROUND."

THIS SOUNDED A LITTLE CRAZY TO ME, AND MAYBE SUGGESTED THAT THIS GIRL WAS A TAD BIT FULL OF HERSELF, BUT THEN I REMEMBERED THAT I HAD BEEN CHECKING HER OUT, TOO, AND I QUITE POSSIBLY HAD ONLY ADDED TO THE SKEEVY VIBE IN THE AIR. OOPS.

THE CONVERSATION CONTINUED, JOINED BY WRITER PAUL TOBIN AND HIS OCCASIONAL CARTOONING PARTNER COLLEEN COOVER. (THEY ALSO HAPPEN TO BE HUSBAND AND WIFE.) THEY TALKED TO THIS GIRL ABOUT TIME SHE HAD SPENT WITH THEM AT PERISCOPE STUDIO AND ALSO ABOUT HER WEBCOMIC, A PERSONAL DIARY THAT SHE HAD BEEN KEEPING AND HAD ONLY STARTED PUTTING ONLINE RECENTLY.

"WAIT," I ASKED, "WHAT'S YOUR NAME AGAIN?"

"EMI."

"WAIT! ARE YOU EMITOWN? I READ YOUR COMIC! IT'S GREAT. I'M JAMIE RICH. YOU LEFT A COMMENT ON MY BLOG WHEN I LINKED YOU."

SHE CHUCKLED -- THOUGH SOMEWHAT HESITANTLY -- AND WE REDID INTRODUCTIONS, AND THEN, SEEING AN OPENING FOR AN INAPPROPRIATE JOKE, I SAID, "BOY, YOUR BOOBS AREN'T NEARLY AS BIG AS YOU DRAW THEM IN YOUR COMIC."

WITHIN SECONDS, DARK HORSE EDITOR SIERRA HAHN JUMPED IN BETWEEN US AND PUT HER HAND ON MY MOUTH AND WAS INSISTING THAT I HEAD OFF TO A QUIET CORNER. HALF THE PEOPLE LAUGHED, AND HALF OF THOSE DID SO NERVOUSLY; THE OTHER HALF WERE SILENT, NOT QUITE SURE WHAT TO THINK OF ME.

BUT EMI LAUGHED. MY SPIDER-SENSES HAD TINGLED CORRECTLY, I KNEW SHE'D GET THE WRONGNESS OF THE JOKE AND THAT BY VIRTUE OF BEING SO WRONG, IT HAD COME ALL THE WAY BACK TO BEING FUNNY AGAIN. IT'S SO OBVIOUS! SUCH IS THE LIFE OF JAMIE RICH, NOT EVERYONE GETS ME HALF AS WELL AS I GET MYSELF.

SUCH IS THE LIFE OF EMI LENOX. ANY OF THE ABOVE COULD HAVE BEEN AN EPISODE OF EMITOWN. HER DIARY CHRONICLES HER OWN ODD BEHAVIOR, AS WELL AS THE OFTEN OFFENSIVE AND BAFFLING BEHAVIOR OF OTHERS. NOTHING IS CLEAR-CUT IN EMITOWN EITHER. THOUGH OTHER DIARISTS CHRONICLE LIFE IN A STRAIGHT-AHEAD FASHION, EMI WILL WALK AROUND THE BLOCK, PURSUED BY THE UNCOMFORTABLE TRUTH, LOOKING FOR A PLACE MAKES SENSE TO HER. YOU MAY NOT GET IT RIGHT AWAY, THIS ISN'T A COMIC STRIP WHERE YOU CAN READ ANY ONE RANDOMLY AND CHUCKLE AT HOW EMI HATES MONDA AND DEVOURS BREAKFAST BURRITOS LIKE A ROLY-POLY ORANGE CAT BURYING HIS FACE INTO LASAGNA. THE TRUE JOY OF EMITOWN IS IN THE CUMULATIVE EFFECT, AS YOU BEGIN TO SPOT PATTERNS, BOTH HUMOROUS AND EMOTIONAL, AND CRACK AT THE CODE THAT EMI HAS CREATED FOR HERSELF. WHAT STANDS EMITOWN APART FROM THE COMPETITION, BESIDES THE INCREDIBLY SKILLED AND OFTEN ADORABLE CARTOONING, IS THE PERSONAL ICONOGRAPHY THAT EMI HAS ESTABLISHED. THE BLACK HEART AND THE WHITE HEART, THE ARMY OF CATS, OCEAN GIRL AND OCTOZOID: THESE ARE THE THINGS THAT CAN CONFOUND READERS WHO FIND THEM OUT OF CONTEXT, BUT THAT MAKE PERFECT SENSE ONCE YOU'VE SETTLED IN. LIKE A NOVEL OR ANY OTHER FICTIONAL NARRATIVE, YOU HAVE TO FOLLOW THE THREAD. EACH STITCH BUILDS ON THE LAST, AND THE NEXT THING YOU KNOW, YOU'VE GOT A CRAZY QUILT OF CARTOONS.

YOU CAN SEE WHAT EMI CHOSE TO TELL US ABOUT THE PARTY. IT'S THE JUNE 26 STRIP. NEWSFLASH: I DIDN'T MAKE THE CUT. INSTEAD, EMI WENT WITH STARS IN HER EYES AND SHOWED CRAIG THOMPSON EATING CORN OFF THE FLOOR OR SOMETHING LIKE THAT. I WAS SO DISAPPOINTED WHEN I SAW IT. "BUT... BUT... I WAS FUNNY!" I EVENTUALLY DO SHOW UP A LITTLE BIT LATER, AND YOU WILL FIND ME IN VARIOUS SPOTS AFTER. I WAS EVEN HANGING OUT WITH EMI LAST NIGHT, AND I'M ANXIOUSLY AWAITING IF I DID ANYTHING COMIC-STRIP WORTHY THAT WILL GET ME IN VOLUME 2. THIS ALSO IS LIFE AROUND EMI LENOX, WONDERING JUST WHAT WILL MAKE THE PAGE FROM DAY TO DAY. JUST WHAT WILL I READ ABOUT TOMORROW?

– JAMIE S. RICH
MAY 2010

JAMIE S. RICH IS THE AUTHOR OF VARIOUS NOVELS AND COMIC BOOKS, BUT HE IS PERHAPS BEST KNOWN FOR HIS COLLABORATIONS WITH ARTIST JOËLLE JONES ON BOOKS LIKE YOU HAVE KILLED ME AND 12 REASONS WHY I LOVE HER. THEIR MOST RECENT RELEASE IS SPELL CHECKERS WITH NICOLAS HITORI DE. BOTH JOËLLE AND NICO SHOW UP IN THIS COLLECTION, AND EMI ONCE GRACIOUSLY DREW A GUEST STRIP JAMIE WROTE FOR MARC ELLERBY'S ELLEBISMS WEBCOMIC (10/9/09 IN THE ARCHIVE). YOU CAN SEE JAMIE'S OTHER WEB-BASED MUSINGS AT CONFESSIONS123.COM.

A VISITOR'S GUIDE TO EMITOWN

THE WHO, WHAT, WHY BY EMI LENOX

I DON'T KNOW ABOUT YOU BUT WHEN I GET SAD OR MAD,

I DRAW.

THAT'S WHY I STARTED EMITOWN.

EMITOWN BEGAN IN 2008 AS A WAY FOR ME TO WORK THROUGH A LOT OF EMOTIONAL STRESS IN MY LIFE. IT WAS A PERSONAL RECORD OF EVERYTHING GOING ON IN MY WORLD, GOOD AND BAD, SO I HAD SOMEWAY TO REMEMBER IT ALL WHEN WHATEVER WAS GOING ON HAD PASSED. IT WAS FOR ME AND ME ALONE.

BUT THEN I MET BRETT WARNOCK.

IN EARLY 2009, I BEGAN TO INTERN FOR TOP SHELF PRODUCTIONS AND CO-PUBLISHER BRETT WARNOCK SAW WHAT I WAS WORKING ON AND ENCOURAGED ME TO PUT IT ONLINE. BETWEEN HIS SUGGESTION AND TOP SHELF MARKETING FELLOW LEIGH WALTON DOING THE SAME, I PUT EMITOWN UP FOR THE ENTIRE INTERNET TO SEE.

IT WASN'T EASY.

I WASN'T COMFORTABLE. EMITOWN WAS MORE OR LESS MY DIARY. YET WITH THEIR PERSISTENCE AND SUBSEQUENT NUDGING ON BEHALF OF MY OTHER INTERNSHIP AT PORTLAND'S PERISCOPE STUDIO, I CAVED IN.

I'M GLAD I DID.

SOME OF MY FAVORITE COMICS ARE AUTOBIOGRAPHICAL. THINKING ABOUT IT, THE REASON I ENJOY THEM IS BECAUSE OF HOW MUCH I WAS ABLE TO RELATE TO HOW SOMEONE ELSE DEALS WITH SIMILAR TRIALS AND TURMOIL IN LIFE. I THOUGHT IT MIGHT BE NEAT IF MAYBE I COULD DO THE SAME FOR SOMEONE ELSE! RIGHT?

I HAD A HARD TIME WITH THE TITLE. IN FACT, EMITOWN CAME AFTER A LONG STRING OF HORRIBLE NAMES, ONE OF WHICH WAS CENTERED ON POOP. HOWEVER, I THOUGHT OF A NICKNAME I JUST GAVE MY BEST FRIEND, JAMIE, JAMESTOWN AND OPTED TO MODIFY IT FOR ME.

SO EMITOWN WAS ESTABLISHED! WHOO!

IT'S A LITTLE WEIRD HAVING A SELF-NAMED TOWN NAMED AFTER ME, BUT I LIKE TO THINK IT'S NOT SOME BIG METROPOLIS, BUT A SMALL ONE-HORSE TOWN WHERE ANY OF MY FRIENDS CAN VISIT. THEY'LL SIT ON THE PORCH, HAVE A NICE COLD BREW AND TALK ABOUT THE DAY.

I CAN'T SAY I'VE BEEN TOTALLY COMFORTABLE IN EMITOWN. PUTTING MY LIFE ONLINE FOR THE WORLD TO SEE COMES WITH CERTAIN CHALLENGES. IT'S HARD TO GET TOO PERSONAL WHEN ANYONE FROM MY MOM TO ANY NUMBER OF STRANGERS CAN FIND OUT ALL MY INTIMATE DETAILS. YOU'LL FIND OUT I HIDE A LOT OF THINGS WITH CAT METAPHORS.

EVEN STILL, I HOPE YOU ENJOY THIS TRIP THROUGH MY TOWN.

♥ EMI LENOX

FACES OF EMITOWN

HERE ARE SOME REGULAR CITIZENS OF EMITOWN!

EMI
EMI HERSELF! SHE HATES BEARS BUT LOVES A LOT OF THINGS STILL.
JAMESTOWN
EMI'S BESTEST FRIEND AND FASHIONABLE SOUL SISTER!
HENRY
EMI'S FIRST DOG AND CURRENT PET. HE'S A BASSET NOT A BEAGLE...
WHITE HEART/BLACK HEART
THE POSITIVE AND NEGATIVE THINKING ON LOVE AND LIFE. THE OPTIMIST AND THE PESSIMIST.
OCEAN GIRL
OCEAN GIRL NEVER LOSES! OCEAN GIRL WILL PREVAIL! OCEAN GIRL CAN'T SWIM!
ARMY CATS
TO HELP FIGHT ON THE BATTLE FIELD OF LOVE. OOOOH YEAH!

MAY 2009

5/13 "A SOUL SINGER IN A SESSION BAND"
-BRIGHT EYES
5/20 "CLINT EASTWOOD"
-GORILLAZ

M-$192
S-$100
CC-$57
HAVE-$442
DELL-$750
SWINE FLU HITS PORTLAND
4.30.2009
SHOULDN'T DRINK THIS WEEKEND... CAN'T LET IMMUNE SYSTEM WEAKEN...
DARN THAT APOCALYPTIC BOOK I READ A COUPLE MONTHS AGO ABOUT A PANDEMIC THAT WIPED OUT THE WORLD WHICH CAME FROM PIGS!
UH OH... BLAZERS LOST SHOULDN'T HAVE DRAWN THAT YESTERDAY..
CAN I CALL IT OR CAN I CALL IT?!
WEEKEND IS GOING TO BE BUSY... I CAN'T WAIT FOR A NON BUSY WEEKEND IN WHICH TO RELAX...
1) HENRY GROOM
2) TOPSHELF HELP
3) PAQUIAO / HATTON FIGHT
4) BUNNY TIME
5) JAGODA COME
6) NATURE WALK W/ JAMESTOWN
7) GROCERY SHOP
8) EMITOWN
9) PAINT
9) ROBBIE COMIC?
PLANE TIX $280
BUT I WAIT... I REGRET LATER?
5.01.2009
I SALIVATE LIKE I NEED TO VOMIT... I BLAME THE SAUSAGE EGG MCMUFFIN
DROOL...
I WENT STRAIGHT HOME AFTER WORK AND PASSED OUT
FRIDAYS IS WHEN ALL THE LACK OF SLEEP CATCH UP TO ME... IT BLOWS... RUINS MY FRIDAY NIGHT...

5.02.2009
I DROVE THROUGH SOME
SERIOUS
APOCALYPSE RAIN.
MAD FLASH FLOOD RAIN, WIND, HAIL, LIGHTNING... IT WAS SCARY....
MET AND PET BUNNIES FOR THE FIRST TIME.
2 ROUND KNOCK OUT!!
POW
TOOK HENRY TO THE DOG PARK AND GOT SLIMED THREE TIMES BY SOME STRANGER'S DOG... EW x 3.
Drool
WATCHED THE PAQUIAO VS HATTON FIGHT. IT WAS PRETTY EPIC... I HOPE PAQUIAO FIGHTS MAYWEATHER NEXT!
I HATE THE DRUNK SMOKING PEOPLE FROM THE BARS NEXT DOOR HANGING IN FRONT OF THE DOOR TO MY APT...
....
I SMOKE WHERE I WANTA!
HE WORE DUMB GOLD CHAINS...
...SO THEN I PUSHED HIM

DOLLAR TREE IS OPEN
5.03.2009
TOILET BRUSH $1
BONE
DOG BONES $1
HAND SOAP
HAND SOAP $1
DUSTER $1
TOILET BOWL CLEANER $1
SAMMICH BAGS $1!
BYE JAGODA! DO NOT FEAR THE BORDER
JAGODA, JAMESTOWN, AND I w/ THE DOGGIES ON A NATURE WALK!
IT WAS A WONDERFUL SUNNY DAY
EXCUSE ME YOUNG LADIES
RUN?! OR NO RUN?
(JERK) STICKS
WE GOT BUSTED BY THE MAX FARE BUSTERS FOR NOT PAYING FOR ONE MEASLY STOP... OUTSIDE OF FARELESS SQUARE... HOW UNLUCKY.
PRICE TO PAY $115.00
NOT TOO BAD CONSIDERING HOW MUCH I'VE SAVED OVER THE YEARS...

$
$
$
REMEMBER RENT DUE TOMORROW!!!
BUILD MY OWN BUNNY CAGE
5.04.2009
DOOR
FLOOR
(BED?) FLOOR
MAT?
LITTER BOX
DOOR
HAY THINGIE
WATER
• 3 ACROSS
• 1 WIDTH
• 2 HIGH...
(SMALL → MED BUNNY)
FINALLY BOUGHT PLANE TIX.
$219!!
NOT TOO SHABBY. MAY BE SWINE FLU MADE COST GO DOWN?
STOP CALLING ME MULTIPLE TIMES A DAY WAMU! I AM NOT MARIA
PORTLAND RAIN
HOLE
THE BOOTS WERE NICE EXCEPT THE HOLE

4.05.2009
WHAT IF I USED A DIFFERENT PEN FOR THIS JOURNAL...
BE BETTER? MORE DYNAMIC? OR NO...
WOULD MAKE FOR GOOD PRACTICE FOR CONTROL...
MAYBE NOT... I NO LONGER HAVE FUN AND THE INK BLEEDS FROM THE PAPER AND MARKER.
RENT CHECK
PARK CHECK
TIME TO PAY UP.
MAYBE I SHOULD SELL MY OLD INTUOS WACOM TABLET... IT'S HUGE AND I WANT A SMALLER ONE!
BUT I ♥ YOU
I COULD GET A SMALL BAMBOO WACOM FOR $70...
HMMM...
BLISS..
IS IT SAD HOW OFTEN I THINK OF SLEEP? WIERD THAT AS A KID I WOULD CRY WHEN I HAD TO... NOW, I LOOK FORWARD TO IT... FANCY HOW LIFE IS.
OR... I USE THIS BRUSH PEN.... YES? NO... OR STICK WITH THIS PEN FOR CONSISTENCY
BUT IT MUDDIES THE MARKER...

5.6.09

THIS MORNING AT 3AM, HENRY BARFED UP HIS MILK BONE...

HENRY'S CRATE

BAARF

NEW FLU STRAIN? BASSET FLU

I FEEL THE PRE SIC
BODY ACHES... I AI
SO TIRED AND SLE
AT WORK... PLEASE
DON'T LET ME BE
SICK

TOMATO UPDATE!

THEY ARE GROWING WONDERFULLY!! ♥ ♥ ♥
I HOPE I DIDN'T PUT TOO MANY IN THE POT THOUGH... IT WILL TAKE FOREVER FOR MY CHERRY

TOMAYTOES

MY BOX OF BOOKS
DONT SCOOT AWAY WITH THOSE BOOK

I HAD TO CARRY A HEAVY BOX OF BOOKS TO READING FRENZY (TOPSHELF ORDER) AND AN OLD MAN OFFERED TO SCOOT IT THERE WITH HIS SCOOTER THING. THOSE THINGS

CAN MOVE!

I THOUGHT HE WOULD SCOOT AWAY WITH THEM
I WONDERED WHAT I'D DO IF HE DID... THOUGHT ABOUT RUNNING AFTER HIM... BUT THEN WHAT? HE'S AN OL MAN! PEOPLE WOULD BE ON HIS SIDE! MAN...
OLD MAN SCOOTER PEOPLE WOULD ALWAYS WIN...

5.7.2009
MAN, THERE IS NO ONE TO TALK TO... I'M HIGH ON COFFEE AND I REALLY WANT TO TALK 200 MPH BUT NO ONE HERE TO DO THAT TO THAT WOULDN'T BE MAD OR SCARED...
COFFEE RUSH.
TODAY IT WAS FREE! I HAD COUPON
R- 275
M- 200
S- 130
P- 750
CC- 250
MAX- 115
I CAN DO IT!!!
SHAGGY LOOKING GUY ASKED ME HE COULD BUY A CIG OFF OF ME WHEN I SAID I DON'T SMOKE REPLIED "NICE TEETH"
KITTY
SQUEEZE.

5.8.200
$35
TODAY I BOUGHT NEW HEADPHONES EVEN THOUGH ITS PRICEY, ITS ESSENTIAL FOR LIVING!
FINALLY GOT THE DRESS TO WEAR AT THE WEDDING THIS FRIDAY! BUT I STILL NEED SHOES!
CORAL ORANGE
$50
SANDALS?
HEELS?!
FLATS?
FRI DAY
BEST DAY!
GIRLS OUT FOR THE SUMMER! GIRLS OUT FOR-EVER!
I NEED A DRINK

5.9.2009

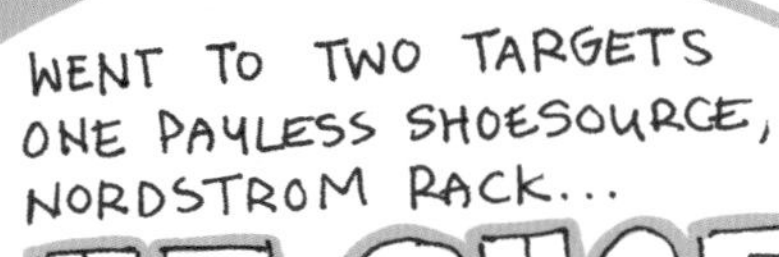
WENT TO TWO TARGETS
ONE PAYLESS SHOESOURCE,
NORDSTROM RACK...
NO SHOES
... ALSO WENT TO A
PETCO BUT THERE WAS NO
BUNNIES... HMMPH!

TOOK HENRY ON A SUPER
WALK ARMED WITH CANTEEN.
AWW. CANTEENS BRING BACK
OLD CAMPING MEMORIES WITH THE
BOY SCOUTS....

TOOK A NAP
Z

WENT TO DRINK AND DRAW...
UT HAVE TROUBLE DRAWING
ROUND OTHERS...

PONIES

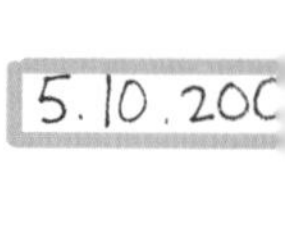

HELF
HELPED PACK LETTERS TODAY... IT WAS FUN... I LIKE MORPHING INTO A MACHINE....

COFFEE HOUSE NORTHWEST MAI
THE BEST WHITE MOCHA (ICED)
EVER. I LITERAL
QUIVER WITH GLEE...

I HATE HOW SOME MUSIC CAN BE RUINED BY BAD MEMORIES...

I REALLY MISS VIDEO GAME
SOMETIMES....

PSHAW!!

I'M TIRED AND MY BELLY

I'D BE DARN LUCKY IF I GOT OVER 4 HOURS OF SLEEP LAST NIGHT... I REALLY CAN'T STAY UP PAST 11PM ON SATURDAYS...
5.11.2009
SO SLEEPY...

I HAVE SOOOOOO MUCH TROUBLE FALLING ASLEEP ON SUNDAY... ERRRGH! SURVIVAL!

MAMA MADE MENTION OF HOW I SHOULD MAKE A COMIC ABOUT BEING HALF JAPANESE... BUT I DON'T THINK IT'S THAT UNIQUE OR DIFFERENT THAN MOST...

THANKS FOR PEARL HARBOR! EAT DOGS!

OTHER THAN THE RACIAL JOKES AT MY EXPENSE (WHICH I HATE) AND NOT UNDERSTANDING HALF MY FAMILY....

I THINK MY FRECKLES ARE MORE VISIBLE... PERHAPS FROM MY SUPERWALK IN THE SUN ON SAT.?

YUCK!

TRIM ASAP

MY NAILS ARE TOO LONG... THEY MAKE GROSS CLICK CLACKY NOISES.

STARTED TO WEAR MY OLD PUMA TRACK COAT I GOT AT A THRIFT STORE IN S.F. A LONG TIME AGO... I FORGOT HOW PLEASANT IT FEELS (LIKE PINK PAJAMA!) BUT WHEN I WALK AROUND IN IT I CAN'T HELP BUT STROKE IT AND IT MUST LOOK LIKE I'M FEELING MYSELF... OR ITCHY...

PILOT PRECISE EXTRA FINE VS PENTEL BRUSH PEN

I THINK I'M GOING TO STICK WITH THE BRUSH PEN... ITS GETTING TOO BORING WITH THE OTHER ONE... AND MAYBE A NEW COLOR?!

5.12.20
YEAH! LAST PAGE OF BOOK 2!! GOOD JOB!
I RULE!
I HATE YOU!!
I WANT A NEW JOB.
• PAID HOLIDAYS
• VACATION
• 401K (MAYBE)
• SECURITY (MAYBE)
WHY
• COMIC PLACE/CO.?
• WAITRESS?
• SECRETARY/ ADMIN ASSIST?
WHERE/WHAT
I'VE BEEN HAVING A LOT OF HAT
DREAMS LATELY ABOUT A CERTAIN
PERSON... UNRESOLVED ISSUES? I
DON'T REALLY HATE... RIGHT?
HIRE ME PLZ!
UPDATED MY RESUME AND WORKED ON SOME COVER LETTERS
GAME ON
BLOG IDEAS
• INTERNING
• COMIC OPINION
• COMIC REVIEW
• MOVIE REVEW
• ONLINE COMICS
HMM
LAST NIGHT I GAMBLED WITH JAMESTOWN AND OL GOLD CHAINS FROM 5.02.2009 WAS THERE
YOU'RE GONNA WIN A MIL! YOU'RE GONNA LOSE!
WANT TO PUSH
GOT MY SHOES!
GOLD
$35
KITTEN HEEL
STEVE MADDEN SHOES... I THOUGH
HE WAS A FOOTBALL GUY... WTF

5.13.2009
LAST NIGHT MISSING CAT GUY OFFERED ME THE PASSWORD TO HIS WIFI! TOO BAD MY APT IS TOO FAR TO PICK UP THAT SIGNAL.... AWWW.
HOW NICE
BUT THATS NOBODY'S FAULT.
you MEAN NOTHING TO NO ONE
TODAY I TRIED MACDONALDS ICED MOCHA
NOT VERY GOOD...
$2.99!
ALLERGIES, HI.
AND yet ANOTHER RAIN DAY
I ALREADY TORE OUT A PAGE... FIRST PAGES ARE SO INTIMIDATING...
MOVIE EXTRAS
1-800-
1-800-
GOV. JOBS
800- EX.
AMERICAN DATA GROUP
EX.
JOBS
WHAT ABOUT THE NAVY?!
PA WOULD BE PROUD

5.14.2009
1
2
BANDANA
COWBOY HAT
GRIMY LONG HAIR
COWBOYISH COAT
JEANS
BOOTS
PIRATE HAT
HOOP EARRING
LONG HAIR
OLD BLACK COAT W/ BIG CUFFS.
SNEAKERS
JEANS
YESTERDAY ON MY WAY TO PERISCOPE I SAW A COWBOY (#1)
THEN ON MY WAY HOME FROM PERISCOPE, I SAW A PIRATE... THOUGH THE PIRATE WORE JEANS AND SNEAKERS. HE DID HAVE BELLS ON HIS SHOES...
YES!
I GET TO HELP LAYOUT A BOOK FOR TOP SHELF! AND GET CRED?!
SO COOL
000000
000001
I PUT UP A HIT COUNTE ON MY BLOG TODAY...
$ 137.90
- 20.00 PA
- 15.00 GAS
- 15.00 FOOD
$ 87.90
- 30.00 HEN
$ 57.90
$157.90
$137.90
CC - $ 293.20
PA - $ 750.00
OR - $ 115.00
PGE - $ 17.00
THE SHACK
WILLIAM P. YOUNG
I'M ALMOST DONE READING THE SHACK AND I'LL TELL YOU WHAT...
ITS NO WHERE NEAR WHAT I THOUGHT IT WOULD BE ABOUT...
HOW DOES SOMEONE WRITE A BOOK LIKE THAT?
WEDDING IS TOMORROW! I GUESS I'LL JUST TAKE A TAXI...

5.15.2009
FLOYD MAYWEATHER JR VS. JUAN MANUEL MARQUEZ IN JULY.
I'VE BEEN TRYING TO CUT BACK ON THE COFFEE... ITS NOT EASY.
IT DOES NOT FEEL LIKE ITS FRIDAY.
HOW
I WANT TO PLAY SCRABBLE ALL THE TIME! :(
KARAOKE
$135.00
- 15.00 GAS
- 15.00 FOOD
$105.00
- 50.00 MACYS
$ 55.00
MADONNA STYLE
THE WEDDING WAS BEAUTIFUL. I TEARED UP... AND HAD THREE DRINKS.
I DON'T KNOW WHAT I DID WRONG TO DESERVE THIS TREATMENT... I THOUGHT I WAS NOTHING BUT NICE AND FRIENDLY...
I'M SAD PEOPLE CAN'T JUST GET ALONG... AND SAD THAT CERTAIN PEOPLE MAY NOT BE WHAT THEY SEEM...
YEESH...
OH WELL... GUESS I CAN'T EXPECT EVERYONE TO LIKE ME.... :(
SO BEAUTFUL...!

5.16.2009

LOOK! EMI MADE A MESS!

WHAT DID YOU DO EMI?

TOOK MAMA AND JAMESTOWN TO SWEET TOMATOES WHERE I DROPPED THE SOFT SERVE ICE CREAM ON THE FLOOR... JAMESTOWN TOLD ON ME... MY MOM WAS EMBARASSED....

HOORAY! I GOT THE KITTY PRYDE POSTER BY BARNABY WARD! I WANTED THIS! THANKS BEN!

JAMESTOWN

DOOX

EMI

THE GIRLS HANGING OUT! IT FEELS LIKE FOREVER! I TRULY TREASURE. BRINGS BACK OLD O'BRIENS HILLSBORO MEMORIES...

THE SUN MAKES ME SO TIRED

5.17.2009

WENT W/ JAMESTOWN AND THE DOGS FOR A HIKE IN THE GORGE. IT WAS BREATHTAKINGLY BEAUTIFUL AND A BEAUTIFUL DAY.

I LOVE OREGON

PHOO
I HIKE GOOD.

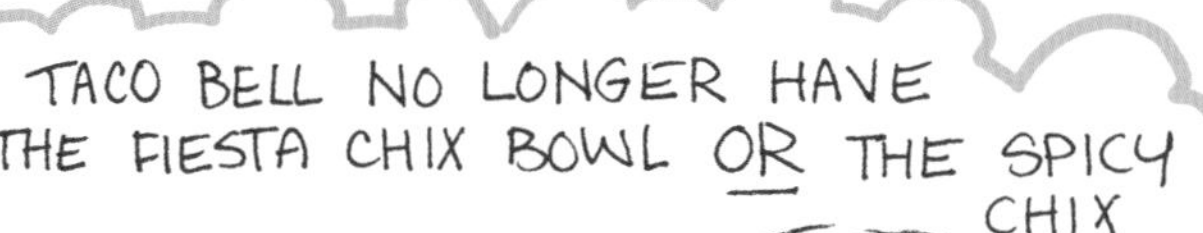

TACO BELL NO LONGER HAVE THE FIESTA CHIX BOWL OR THE SPICY CHIX TACOS.
RIP

WHY ARE ALL THE FAST FOOD PLACES DISCONTINUING MY FAVORITES ?!
.. DON'T SAY THE ECONOMY!

I THINK THE POT IS TOO SMALL FOR THE TOMATOES... MAYBE NOT?

I AM UNCERTAIN WHAT TO THINK ABOUT THAT... ERRRM... HUH...
I DON'T THINK I'M READY...

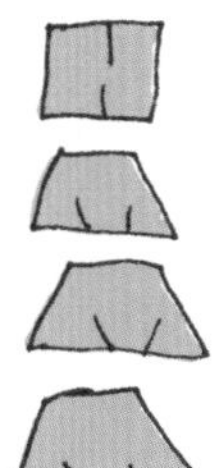

5.18.2009

LUNCH

BLT W/ RANCH 5 DOLLAR FOOTLONG... LIKE THE CHIX BACON RANCH... JUST W/O THE CHIX...

I AM ONLY ALLOWING MYSELF TWO COFFEES THIS WEEK...

STUPID HENRY SWALLOWED A MACDONALD'S BURGER WRAPPER HE FOUND ON THE GROUND THIS MORN... THERE'S ALWAYS SO MANY BUT THIS IS THE FIRST TIME HE MANAGED TO SWALLOW ONE...

I NEED TO MAKE CURRY.

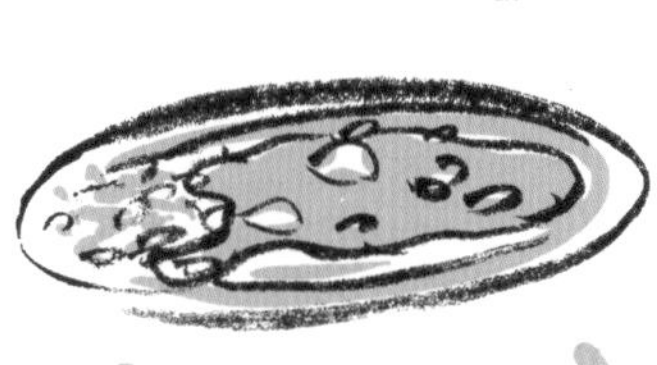

SOMETIMES I DREAM OF HAVING TONS OF COMIC SUBSCRIPTIONS... BUT THEN I REALIZE I CAN'T AFFORD IT AND WHAT WOULD I DO WITH THEM? BEST STICK WITH TRADES & GRAPHIC NOVELS...
WHEN IS THE SECOND CASTLE WAITING OUT?...

I HAVEN'T FORGOTTEN ABOUT BUNNIES...

5.19.2009
DOWNSIDE TO FREEZING A FULL WATER BOTTLE? WAITING FOR IT TO MELT SO YOU CAN ACTUALLY DRINK IT...
LOPSIDED WATER BOTTLE....
NO
MEOW
CAT
YESTERDAY I PHYSICALLY STOPPED AND LOOKED AT KITTY LITTER IN FRED MEYER AND REMINISCED ABOUT WEENIE... ITS BEEN HALF A YEAR SINCE I HAD TO PUT HIM DOWN....
OUCH!
I'M NOT SUPPOSED TO HAVE CRAMPS ANYMORE!!
I FEEL LIKE PEOPLE KEEP LOOKING AT THE DIRT SPOT ON MY PANTS... IT LOOKS LIKE POOP.
NOT POO!

5.20.2009
LESS FAT
GLUTEN FREE
WHOLE GRAIN
riceWORKS
Salsa Fresca
$1
THE MACHINE RAN OUT OF CHEESE-ITS SO I GO ON A LIMB AND BUY SOME HEALTH CHIPS... IT COST A DOLLAR AND THERE IS LIKE ONLY
10 CHIPS
INSIDE!!! AND ITS NOT THAT GOOD...
OUTRAGE!!
MAYBE I SHOULD BE POSITIVE...
YOU CAN DO IT!!!
REMEMBER:
PROCEED WITH
CAUTION
I'M USELESS BUT NOT FOR LONG THE FUTURE IS COMIN ON
IS IT SUNNY OUTSIDE? CAUSE I DON'T KNOW... I'M IN A CUBICLE....
YESTERDAY:
GIGGLE FEST
?
DELL
I SAT CROSS LEGGED AND MY PANTS RIPPED IN THE CROTCH... DUMB CHEAP JEANS
THIS HAS NOT BEEN A GOOD WEEK FOR PANTS
WOAH. PLANE TIX IS BACK UP TO $300 FOR SD... I BOUGHT RIGHT AT THE BEST TIME! $219!
GO ME!
PLAYING SCRABBLE AND ERRUPTING IN MULTIPLE SILENT GIGGLE FESTS IN PUBLIC IN A COFFEE HOUSE... I REALLY NEED TO GET INTERNET AT HOME...

5.21.2009
I MISSED ALL THE CONCERTS I REALLY WANTED TO SEE NOW THERE IS NOTHING COMING UP... YANN TIERSON MARGOT & THE NUCLEAR SO & SO'S COLD WAR KIDS...
$190.42
- 20.00 PA
- 15.00 GAS
- 30.00 DOG
- 20.00 FOOD
$115.42
INTERNET IN BED. I LOVE INTERNET IN BED
THANKS
KRIS! YOU'RE THE BEST!
① DISHES
② TRASH
③ VACCUM ...VACUUM?....
I HAVE HAD NO TIME TO CLEAN THE APT... ITS GROSS... MUST DO
HOW DO I DO THIS W/O BEING MEAN?
DO NOTHING?
THATS MEAN!
ACK! I DID IT! ITS NOT MEAN IS IT? I WORRY SO MUCH! I JUST WANT TO BE A GOOD PERSON...
I MISS JAMESTOWN! SO BUSY! CAN'T WAIT FOR THE PAC WALK!
I DID SO GOOD... THIS MY FIRST COFFEE ALL WEEK!
I SURE DRAW GIRLS FALLING A LOT IT SEEMS... FALL DOWN! DOWN! DOWN! DOWN! DOWN!
CRAZY COFFEE ATTACK! AT LEAST NOT SAD COFFEE ATTACK...

5.22.2009
WENT TO CHEMOWA AND GOT ME MAGIC PILLS!
GRIFFIN 2009
THIS IS LIKE THE 4TH TAPE ADAPTER I HAVE BOUGHT! THIS ONE BETTER
LAST!
FINISHED THE COMIC FOR THE TOP SHELF BLOG. UGH COLORS!
OMG... DATING... I FORGOT HOW SCARY IT IS... I'VE ONLY REALLY BEEN WITH FRIENDS... NOT REALLY NEW PEOPLE... ITS BOTH EXCITING AND UGH AT THE SAME TIME. I HOPE I'M READY..
HAD A BEER WITH BEN... WAS NICE BUT HE ALWAYS GIVES ME REASONS TO WORRY...

5.23.2009

HIT HENRY'S QUICK WHEN TRIMMING HIS NAILS LAST NIGHT... CLEANING UP HIS BLOOD OFF THE FLOOR WAS A TASK TO BE DONE... **DID!**

!!!!

ON MY DATE I WENT TO A BURRITO PLACE WHICH SHARED A BATHROOM TO A STRIP CLUB... I SAW A BUTT.

DOOR #1 DOOR #2 DOOR #3

?

GOT LOCKED OUTSIDE AND FORGOT WHICH DOOR WAS MY DATE'S. IT FELT LIKE A GAME SHOW... **WHICH DOOR?**

MY LEFT EYE HURT BY THE END OF THE NIGHT... IT FELT LIKE MY PUPIL WAS A SQUARE AND THE CORNERS KEPT POKING MY SKULL...

SO I WENT TO BED...

5.24.2009

CHIX

ICE CREAM

WENT TO THE ROSE FESTIVAL WHERE I GOT CHICKEN ON A STICK! ALSO GOT AN AIRBRUSH TAT ON MY BICEP OF A MARINE THING.... LOOKS LIKE THIS:

OH, THE THINGS YOU DO WHEN YO LONELY...

ON THE WALK WITH HENRY, I NOTICED A TELEPHONE POLE SMOKING... I TOLD PEOPLE... THEY PUT OUT THE FIRE

CAUSED BY SUN?

THE BLUE DONG DOESN'T BOTHER ME NONE...

SAW THE WATCHMEN FINALLY LAST NIG

5.25.2009
WE'RE GONNA DIE !!
WHAT?
ON THE WALK ... WELL... AT THE LUCKY LAB, JAMESTOWN REPORTED TO ME THE THREAT THAT EMERGED AGAIN W/ N. KOREA AND THIER NUKES... OH SHIT... BUILD BOMB SHELTER NOW!!
YAH.
OH NO
IT BEGINS... IT STARTS
OH NO OH NO OH DEAR OH MY.
WATCH IT, EMI!
DEFENSE
ARMOR
ON!

SO DELETING THAT PERSONAL'S AD...

5.26.2009

DALEEEET

I REJECT ONLINE DATING.

GETTING UP AT 5:15AM IS NOT EASY AFTER A FOUR DAY WEEKEND...

AND FINALLY SENT THE CHECK IN FOR THE MAX FINE... $115.00

BLOWFEST

GRUMBLE

I WILL TURN YOUR HEART

B L A C K

5.27.2009
SOMETHING TASTES FRIGHTFULLY WRONG IN MY ICED COFFEE TODAY...
THO...
THE SAUSAGE EGG MACMUFFIN TASTES JUST RIGHT!
GOT A LOT DONE ON MY RELATIONSHIPS PROJECT!
I FEEL
PROUD
SNIFFF
I SMELL FRENCH BREAD! SOMETHING ITALIAN...
LORD
I LOVE
SMELLS
GOOD ONES OF COURSE!
CUCUMBER
BROCCOLI
TOMATOES
CARROTS
CHEESE!
TOOTHPASTE
SHAMPOO
CONDITIONER
RAMEN
GUAC
CHIPS
CURRY
POTATOES
JUICE
YOGURT
SKIP
MARUCHAN
RAMEN
BEEF
RAMEN: THE POOR MAN'S LUNCH...
I REALLY REALLY NEED TO TAKE OFF ALL THE BRIGHT EYES ON MY IPOD... ITS SIMPLY NOT
TOLERABLE!

5.27.2

OH...AND IN LIFE, THE BUM DID NOT LOOK LIKE EINSTEIN. I DON'T KNOW

BUMS IN PORTLAND ARE MEAN...ONE THREATENED ME WHEN I TOLD HIM TO BACK OFF CAUSE JAMESTOWN DOESN'T HAVE ANY CIGGS FOR HIM... SOON AFTER, I GOT TO WAVE DOWN COPS CAUSE THE BUM TRIED TO FIGHT SOME GUY WHO PHYSICALLY PROVOKED HIM...

D'OH

YOU KNOW ITS TOO EARLY WHEN YOU COMPLETELY MISS WHEN TRYING TO TAKE A DRINK OF WATER...

RICE... SPAM!

I GET PAID AND MONEY GOES BYE WISH I GOT MORE "OBAMA DOLLARS"

$244.35
- 50.00
194.35
- 30.00 FOOD
- 15.00 GAS
- 20.00 PA
$129.35
50.00 PEA
$79.35

N. KOREA... OH NO... WHAT WILL HAPPEN?

05.29.2009
JAMESTOWN AND I ARE GOING TO ROOSTER ROCK TOMORROW... IT WAS BROUGHT TO MY ATTENTION THAT IT'S A NUDE BEACH...
WHAT?
(I RESEARCHED AND ITS TRUE... BUT THERE IS A CLOTHED SECTION A DECENT DISTANCE AWAY... SO I WON'T HAVE TO WORRY ABOUT SEEING HAIRY SAGGY BUTTS)
JUICE!
JUICE
XXX
LIQUOR!
BEACH TOWEL
SUN BLOCK
COOLER?
CHIPS
CHIPS
SAMMICHES?
DOG WATER BOWL
WATER
TO BRING TO ROOSTER ROCK
I WEAR A BUBBLE DRESS FOR NIGHT IN THE PEARL DISTRICT...
BUBBLEY
JAMESTOWN AND I HAD QUITE A NIGHT
-2 COSMOS
-1 JAGER BOMB
-2 BEERS
-1 LEMON DROP
EACH!

SWIM!
TRIED TO SEE IF HENRY WOULD SWIM
HE DID NOT...
TOO HOT
I HATE.
JAMESTOWN LOVES...
DR MARIO RULES
SUSHILAND...
TABLE FOR ONE
STILL YUMMY!
SAW UP!
THIS MOVIE WAS SO GOOD AND TOUCHING...
I'D SEE IT AGAIN.

5.31.2009
HE STUPID SUN
UCKS OUT ALL
HE ENERGY FROM
MY BODY...I DO
OTHING ALL DAY
HEAT
UCKS.
PGE
CHIGGERS
THIS
EW
I HATE WHEN I HAVE
TO SCRATCH BELOW MY
NECK THAT I FEEL THE
CLAVICLE...
VACADO
SHAMPOO
CONDITIO
CARROTS
BROCCOLI
TOOTH PASTE
COLGATE
CUCUMBER
BRIE
BLU CHEESE
NOODLES
SOMEN
MOUTH WASH
ACT
AG.
CURRY
NINTENDO POWER
MILK 1%
GRAPE JUICE
POTATOES
CURRY MIX

JUNE 2009

6/8 "TILL KINGDOM COME"
- COLDPLAY
6/9 "CALENDAR GIRL"
-STARS
"AS TALL AS CLIFFS"
- MARGOT AND THE NUCLEAR SO AND SO'S
6/11 "MACHINE"
- ENIAC
6/16 "JEN IS BRINGING THE DRUGS"
- MARGOT AND THE NUCLEAR SO AND SO'S
6/18 "A SEA SHANTY OF SORTS"
-MARGOT AND THE NUCLEAR SO AND SO'S

6.01.2009
15¢
YOU KNOW I'M TIRED WHEN I WAS TOO LAZY TO PICK UP 15¢ ON MY WAY TO MY CAR THIS MORNING...
LONG ARM
SUMMER MAKES ME CONSTANTLY HUNGRY FOR
SUSHI
HAI!
I WAS TOLD IF I WAS AN ANIMAL, I'D BE A PANDA BY SEVERAL DIFFERENT PEOPLE...
RACIST?
HA HA
I REALLY MISS THE OLD OLD DAYS....
WHEN IT WAS GOOD, IT WAS PRETTY GOOD...
EVERYONE GETS LONELY SOMETIMES, RIGHT?
SIGH
OR
THE HEAT MAKES ME CONTEMPLATE GETTING MY HAIR CUT SHORT AGAIN...
THO... I COULDN'T WEAR IT CURLY IF I HAD IT SHORT...

6.02.0
ZZZ
DONE PASSED OUT LAST NIGHT... SO ~~ TIRED!
ONE DOOR CLOSES... OPEN A NEW ONE!!!
I KEEP TOSSING THE POOP BAGS TOO HIGH OVER THE WALL THAT INSTEAD OF GOING INTO THE TRASH, THEY GET STUCK IN THE TREE.
I PLAY CUPID!
I SET UP JAMESTOWN! I HOPE I DID
GOOD JOB!

6. 3. 2009
WHERE IS MY LETHALLY CUTE BUNNY?
COME TO MY DESK THIS MORNING TO FIND THAT
Y CO-WORKER LEFT THE CUTEST BUNNY
ICTURE ON MY DESK FROM HER DAILY CALENDAR.
THERE IS A SMALL CAFE ACROSS THE STREET OF MY WORK. GOT A BREAKFAST BURRITO $ A COFFEE NO MORE FAST FOOD!! PLUS ITS CHEAPER!!
OW DID I TAY AWAY ROM COFFEE OR SO LONG (1 WEEK) FEEL LIKE MILLION DOLLARS!
GOT AN EMAIL AT WORK ABOUT SIGNING A SCROLL
A SCROLL?
??
ARISTOCRAT
INK
WHATEVER IT IS, I CAN'T IMAGINE THAT TEMPS ARE A PART OF IT...
LIKE THIS FOR REAL!!
WHEN I WAS STARING AT MY MONITER AT WORK I SUDDENLY SAW STARS.. TWO OF THEM. THIS NEVER HAPPENED BEFORE.
WHAT DOES THIS MEAN?

6.04.2009
$123.01
- 15.00 GAS
- 10 FOOD
$98.01
$80 ~ PA
$75 CC
$342.95
- 200.00
142.95
- 30.00 PA
112.95
IT HURT TO WALK
LAST NIGHT I HAVE NO IDEA HOW I HURT MY FOOT BUT IT FELT LIKE A HUGE MARBLE WAS UNDER THE SKIN...
AWWW... NO BUNNY THIS WEEKEND.... WHEN WILL MY TIME COME?! BISQUICK!!!
GROUND KONTROL W/ CORN TODAY! CAN'T WAIT TO PLAY DR. MARIO
MAO?
SPIRIT HUG!
IT TURNS OUT CUPID-EMI MADE A DIRECT HIT W/ HER ARROW... I DID GOOD JOB!!
TODAY IS HUG YOUR CAT DAY
LAUNDRY TIME

6.5.2009
LAST NIGHT
YOU'RE AWESOME!
RAZOR!!
SO I WAS FEELIN A LITTLE BUMMED WHEN I HEARD A RUMOR THAT "HE" WAS ENGAGED. BUT THEN I HAD TO RAZOR SCOOT TO GROUND KONTROL TO CLOSE MY TAB... I WANTED TO JUST GET IT THE NEXT DAY BUT THEY CHARGE 25% TIP IF YOU DO... NO WAY
PEOPLE ON THE STREET LOVED THE SCOOTER. AM I COOL? AM I BRINGING BACK THE RAZOR? MAYBE NOT...
RAZOR
YESTERDAY THERE WAS TORNADO WARNINGS IN HILLSBORO!! WHAT? AL GORE RIGHT? WILL BE LIKE THAT MOVIE DAY AFTER TOMORROW?!!
SO... INCREDIBLY SCARY...
I FEEL SO DESENSITIZED TO LOVE.
MAYBE I DON'T WANT TO BE LOVED.
SO WHY DO I KEEP TRYING?! AH, LIFE... SO MUCH FUN SOMETIMES..
ROCK BAND TONIGHT!!
RAWK

HELLO?!
HELLO!!!
WHATS GOING ON?!!
6-6-2009
ARE YOU GOING TO BE OKAY ??
I GOT A CALL THAT SAID IT WAS FROM THE CORRECTIONAL FACILITY AND IT WAS B... BUT I COULDN'T TALK TO HIM CAUSE THERE WAS SOME SORT OF ACCOUNT I NEEDED TO HAVE... HE WAS IN JAIL FOR DUI... IT WAS FOUR IN THE AFTERNOON...
JUST BE GOOD.. LEARN AND GET BETTER !! PLEASE!
DELISH!
SILVER DOLLAR PIZZA...
HUNG OUT W/ PEEPS AND NEW PEEPS... IT WAS ALRIGHT... I WAS STILL OH-SO-WORRI
Z!
DAY BE OVER NOW..

6-7-2009
H
I GOD
LEAK
MY TIRE WAS SLIGHTLY FLAT SO SOME DUDE HELPS ME OUT AT THE GAS STATION AND PUTS AIR IN IT... FIVE MIN LATER I COULD HEAR AIR LEAKING OUT! MOST TIRE PLACES ARE CLOSED ON SUNDAY SO IT WAS LIKE SPEED OR SOMETHING DRIVING TO SOMEWHERE TO FIX IT BEFORE THE AIR RUNS OUT!
LUCKILY I PULL INTO AN OIL CHANGE PLACE WHERE THEY PUT ON MY SPARE, TOLD ME I NEEDED THE VALVE STEM REPLACED AND WHERE THE ONE TIRE PLACE OPEN WAS...
WHINE WHINE
HANK GOODNESS HAPPENED ON NDAY AND NOT ON WORK DAY...
LEAK
T THE NON-BBQ GOT TO JUMP ON TRAMPOLINE... N'T REMEMBER THE ST TIME I DID THAT
O
UN!
TRIED TO WATCH CONAN 'O BRIEN ON HULU BUT MY SLOW CONNECTION MADE IT HARD...
SO SAD...
I ♥ CONAN

6-08-2009
ZZ
SKITTER
I DREAMT THAT I DIDN'T CLEAN MY ROOM AND COCKROCHES APPEAR WITH THE HOPPING AND SKITTERING NOISE LIKE IN ANIMAL CROSSING...
STOMP TO KILL!
I WISH COMPUTER DEATH
GRRRRRR
GOT LOCKED OUT OF EVERYTHING! OWL, EXPLORER, AND WINDOWS AS A WHOLE
AARGH!
THE WHEELS JUST KEEP ON TURNING
THE DRUMMERS BEGINS TO DRUM
I DON'T KNOW WHICH WAY I'M GOING
I DON'T KNOW WHICH WAY I'VE COME.
FOR YOU I'D WAIT 'TIL KINGDOM COME. UNTIL MY DAYS... MY DAYS ARE DONE..

06.09.2009
THE ENEMY... IT APPROACHES
BATTLESTATIONS READY.
LOVE IS A BATTLEFIELD...
IF I AM LOST FOR A DAY TRY TO FIND ME. BUT IF I DON'T COME BACK THEN I WON'T LOOK BEHIND ME.
ALL OF THE THINGS THAT I THOUGHT WERE SO EASY. JUST GOT HARDER AND HARDER EACH DAY.
HENRY EATS HEALTHY. I GIVE HIM BROCOLI AND CARROTS...
NOW
GOING TO SEE
THE
HANG
OVER!
I should be leavin Tonight....

6-10-20

30"?

TOMATO UPDATE!! SO... THE BIGGEST ONE IS AROUND 24" TO 30" TALL... BUT STILL NO FLOWERS! FROM WHAT I UNDERSTAND, NO FLOWERS MEAN NO FRUIT... IS IT STILL TOO EARLY FOR FLOWERS?!

NUM NUMS!

THIS WEEKEND IS A DOUBLE B-DAY WEEKEND! LAURA ON FRIDAY... STEPHAN'S ON SATURDAY BUT ITS AT THE BEACH CHINOOK WINDS STYLE... I WANT TO GO BUT WHAT ABOUT HENRY?!

OH MAN!

WHO WILL TAKE CARE OF HENRY FOR A NIGHT?!

NOT THE BEST... BUT WHEN POOR I DRINK WHAT I GOTZ...

I'M HAVING A HUGE SHOPPING THIRST... ONLY.. I HAVE NO DOLLARS... MAAAAAAAAAN... THIS SUCKS.

THIS MORNING WHEN I TOOK HENRY OUT TO PEE A BUM WALKED BY SAYING/SINGING WHAT SOUNDED LIKE "HELLLOOooOo" SO WITH A SMILE I SAY "HELLLLOooo0o" AND HE STOPPED DEAD IN HIS TRACKS IN FRONT OF ME AND ACCUSED ME OF MAKING FUN OF HIS SUPPOSED SINGING IN MONGOLIAN AND POLISH? I TOLD HIM 'NO, I THOUGHT YOU WERE TRYING TO DISTRACT MY DOG' AND HE YELLED "NO ONE GIVES A @$#:! ABOUT MY DOG." THAT THE 'WORLD DOESN'T REVOLVE AROUND MY DOG." I SHOUTED BACK "OH! MAYBE IT SHOULD, HUH?!" AS WE WALK OFF IN OPPOSITE WAYS, HE STARTED SINGING GOBBLEDY POOP SILENT NIGHT...

SOMEDAY I WILL DIE BY A BUM. I CAN'T HOLD BACK MY SASSY MOUTH WHEN THEY ARE RUDE. UGH!

292 OKL

NOT ACTUAL #...

SO MY LICENSE PLATE THAT WAS STOLEN IN DEC HAS TURNED UP! AN OFFICER CALLED MY PARENTS HOUSE SAYING THEY FOUND AN ABANDONED 2004 SATURN WITH MY PLATE ON IT. COOL!

I ATE MY BREAKFAST BURRITO W/ SIRACHA HOT SAUCE... LATER RUBBED MY EYE.

THAT BURN OOO!

ARE YOU SOMEONE THAT I REALLY NEED OR JUST SOMETHING TO FILL SOME HOLE IN ME TEMPORARILY.

MAN... I'VE BEEN FEELING DOWN LATELY... I DON'T HAVE A REAL REASON TO BE. OTHER PEOPLE ARE GOING THROUGH REAL HARD TIMES... MAYBE ITS LACK OF SLEEP... I DON'T KNOW... I HOPE IT GOES AWAY SOON.
VIDEO GAMES LIVE NOV. 7, 8 7:30, 3PM SCHNITZER CONCERT HALL BALCONY $25-$45 TICKETMASTER.
6.12.2009
YAYS: · JAKE · ME
I HAVE $75 TO LAST ME UNTIL NEXT THURS... CAN I DO IT?!
NO... NO YOU CAN'T
DID I MENTION: I HATE MONEY
I SCOOTED TO PERISCOPE FOR A VISIT. I KINDA LIKE THIS SCOOTER... I THINK I WILL MAKE IT MY MODE OF TRANSPORTATION IN THE CITY.
YOU MAKE ME SICK YOU'RE A COWARD IN YOUR SIN. I HOPE I NEVER SEE YOU AGAIN
FOR DOOX'S BIRTHDAY, THEY ARE HAVING A GIN PARTY... I DON'T RECALL ENJOYING THAT PARTICULAR SPIRIT... BUT I'LL GIVE IT ANOTHER GO.
BEN SAID HE'LL CHECK IN ON HENRY WHEN I'M AT THE BEACH/CASINO
YAY!

CASINO
BEACH

6.13.2009

WENT TO LINCOLN CITY FOR STEPHAN'S BIRTHDAY. STAYED AT CHINOOK WINDS CASINO WHERE CRAZINESS ENSUED...

TONS OF ALCOHOL, A GOOD NUMBER OF PEOPLE, AND NO RAIN... MAKE FUN TIME...

ROULETTE KICKED MY ASS... I LOST $20

SIGH

WHAT KIND OF QUESTION IS THAT? HUH?!

CHING!

THEN AROUND 6AM MAYBE? STILL AWAKE AND SOMEHOW ALIVE, JOINED STEPHAN AND 3RIT FOR A DOUGHNUT (I HAVE NO IDEA WHERE) WHERE I ISCOVER A HUNDRED DOLLAR ILL IN MY BACK POCKET. EING COMPLETELY SLAMMED, HAD ABSOLUTELY NO IDEA HERE IT CAME FROM.

GAVE A WINNING # IN A OULETTE GAME AND GOT SOME DOLLARS FOR THE LUCK METHINKS)

A GUY (WHOM I LATER IN THE EVE END UP HANGIN W/) ASKED ME IF MY FRIEND WAS GOING TO BE ON THE SLOT MACHINE ALL NIGHT... THIS CONFUSED ME.

LORD I AM SO DENSE.

WHAT DID YOU DO?! WHERE DID YOU GET IT?!
?

RIP...
I LOST MY BEDAZZLED FLASK!
OH NO

6.14.2009

WOKE UP ON THE FLOOR OF THE HOTEL ROOM FEELING REALLY WOOZY. THINKING 'WHAT IN HEAVEN'S NAME HAPPENED?!"

Z

DO YOU REMEMBER WHO YOU ARE?

MAZATLAN BREAKFAST! WHO DOES THAT?! WE DO... I ATE LITTLE AND STRUGGLED TO SURVIVE WHILE WE WERE THERE.

STOPPED INTO THE MATADOR BECAUSE I HEARD A RUMOR THEY WERE HAVING A BEACH PARTY COMPLETE WITH WATERSLIDE... ERR... I MEAN A SLIP & SLIDE... AMAZING... IT WAS ALL TRUE.

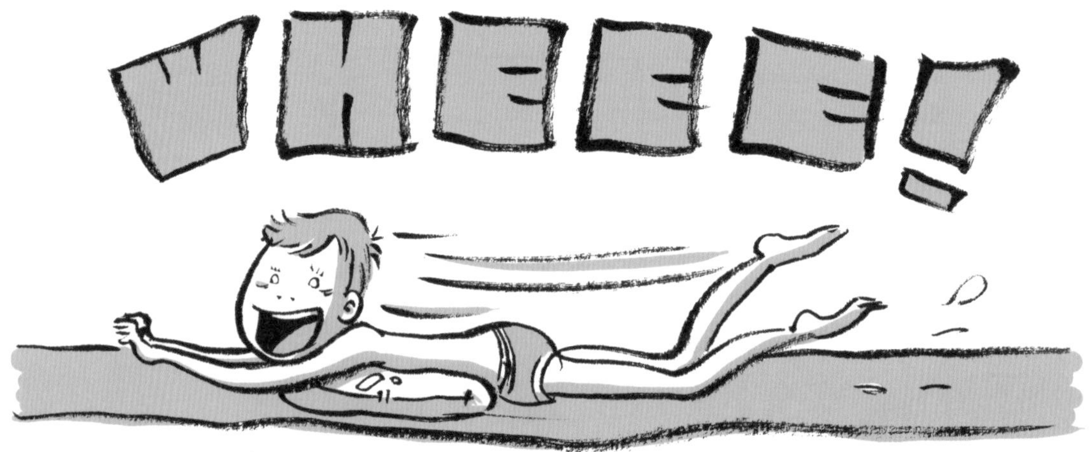

6.15.2009

UH OH... THE "ENEMY" APPROACHED FROM A COMPLETELY DIFFERENT DIRECTION THEN I HAD EXPECTED!

BLIND SIGHT-ED!
LAUNCH AND EXCECUTE PLAN
B!

I DO NOT REGRET NOT GOING INTO WORK

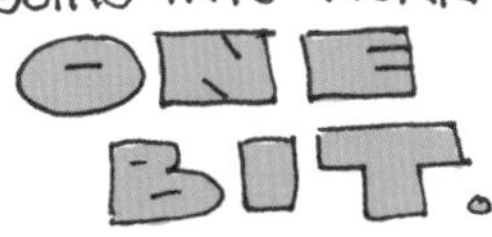
ONE BIT.

I MISS JAMESTOWN

JAMESTOWN IS IN CALIFORNIA! NOES! SHE WILL BE TAN AND MAKE ME SEEM PALER... CAUSE... YOU KNOW... THATS ALL THAT MATTERS... COME HOME NOW! KTHNX.

I FEEL LIKE ALL I DID TODAY WAS LAY IN BED... I DID FINALLY GET OFF MY BUM AND CLEAN THE APT AND DO THE DISHES.

CLEAN

I FEEL LIKE THIS PAST WEEKEND WAS A DREAM AND NOW I'M BACK TO MUNDANE REALITY... THINGS LIKE THAT DON'T HAPPEN... UNREAL... DON'T LET IT FOG UP YOUR BRAIN! WAIT... MY BRAIN IS ALREADY FOGGY. CURSES

6.16.2009

THE FEAR
I COME IN TO WORK TODAY AND A COWORKER THOUGHT I WAS LAYED OFF SINCE I WASN'T HERE YESTERDAY. I GUESS THEY LET GO A BUNCH OF PEOPLE FRIDAY.
OH MAN.
I SURVIVED ANOTHER CUT.. FEELS LIKE THAT GAMESHOW
SURVIVOR
DAIMLER TRUCKS OF N. AMERIC
OH MAN... THE ANXIETY! I FEEL LIKE MY HEART IS PRESSING UP ON MY LUNGS AND I HAVE TROUBLE BREATHING... HEART... HURTING... WHY DO I DRINK COFFEE?! CAUSE THROUGH THE STRUGGLE OF BREATHING, I AM AWAKE. YOU ARE A DEADLY BUT NECESSARY DRINK, COFFEE. YOU ARE.
I'M READY TO GO SOMEPLACE WHERE NOBODY WILL HAVE A CLUE WHERE I AM.
DRINK MEEEEE.
+
=
COFFEE....
CA...CA... COME BACK!
OH GOD, CHUT UP... YOU'RE SO STUPID... GET REAL..
BLACK HEART EMI
HMMPH

6.17.2009
THE GOGOLS ARE DOING GOOD!
UND OUT YESTERDAY THAT MY BEDAZZLED
ASK WAS FOUND! I GUESS IT WAS IN THE
OTEL ROOM! THANK GOODNESS
W TWO PEOPLE
ING KITES AT
STARBUCKS
OSS THE
STREET.
PGE PARK
BEAVERS
TACOMA
I WANNA FLY A KITE. NOT ALONE LIKE CHARLIE STYLE THO.
GOOD GRIEF!
I HAVE NOT BEEN SLEEPING WELL LATELY... IT SUCKS... IT REALLY DOES... AND I LOVE SLEEPING...
I DIDN'T DRINK COFFEE TODAY SO NO CRAZY ANXIETY SMASHING MY LUNGS... HOPEFULLY, THAT SHOULD DO THE TRICK!
SIGH

GRRRR
HEY PIPSQUEEK. WHERE'S YOUR 'RENTS. HUH? GO HOME.
6.18.200
WHEN I WENT TO GET M
BURRITO AND COFFEE FR
THE PLACE ACROSS THE ST.
THERE WAS A LITTLE DOG
HANGING OUT IN THE
OFFICE PARK. NO ONE IN
SIGHT... HE KEPT GROWL
AT ME AND IT WAS 7A
I JUST LEFT HIM.
SOMEONE IN THE OFFIC
MUST OWN HIM... STILL
IT FELT SO RANDOM.
MY FIRST GELATO!! IT WAS TASTY UNTIL IT TURNED INTO SOUP!
yumm!
A WOLF IN A SHEEPSKIN COAT
THE WEATHER IS JUST FINE
WE'VE GOT TO LIVE THE BEST WE KNOW HOW TO
DR. DARIO TIM

6.19.2009
SO I DUMBLY TAKE A CURVE OFF THE FREEWAY AFTER FRESH RAIN AND SPUN OUT. I SPUN AT LEAST 2.5 TIMES! AMAZINGLY, NO CARS HIT ME COMING OFF THE FREEWAY AND I DIDN'T HIT ANY THING AT ALL. THE CAR, SUZY AND I CAME OUT SHAKEN AND COMPLETELY UNHARMED.
LESSON LEARNED!
BOUGHT HENRY DOG FOOD AND WAITED FOR A CERTAIN SOMEBODY TO ARRIVE FROM THE MYSTERIOUS LAND UP NORTH.
OCEAN GIRL AND OCTOZOID
SPOTTED PAINTING THE CITY OF PORTLAND RED.

6.20.2009
THE HANGOVER
EVERY-THING WILL BE OKAY.
SAW THE HANGOVER AGAIN! THAT MOVIE IS COMEDIC GENIUS... STILL FUNNY THE SECOND TIME.
OMG... WHAT IS HAPPENING WHAT... IS... HAPPENING? SO... SCARY... IS GOOD? IS BAD? UGH.
YAY! ♥
JAMESTOWN HAS RETURNED FROM HER CALIFORNIA TRIP!! AND SHE BROUGHT ME A KNITTED BLANKET HER MOM MADE FOR ME.

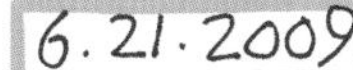
6.21.2009

SO GO ON, LOVE. LEAVE WHILE THERE'S STILL HOPE FOR ESCAPE. YOU GOTTA TAKE WHAT YOU CAN THESE DAYS.
YOU KILL ME, YOU ALWAYS KNOW THE PERFECT THING TO SAY. I KNOW WHAT I SHOULD DO BUT I JUST CAN'T WALK AWAY
WENT TO THE PARENT'S HOUSE FOR FATHER'S DAY AND FOUND THESE OLD DRAWINGS WHEN I WAS IN ELEMENTARY SCHOOL. I DREW LOTS OF DINOS.
DINOS RULE!
WORK TOMORROW. OH YAY.
OCEAN GIRL
IS ALONE... WHAT PERILS AWAIT FOR HER?

6.22.200
YESTERDAY ANOTHER STARBUCKS PALM TREE WAS ON FIRE. THATS THE SECOND TIME! WHATS UP WITH THAT? IT WASN'T EVEN HOT YESTERDAY...
FIRE!
PACK WALK WITH JAMESTOWN! ITS BEEN TOO LONG SINCE MY LAST LUCKY LAB SUPER DOG IPA ♥
yum yum!
KEEP YOUR HEAD UP WHEN YOU'RE WALKING DOWN THE STREET. TRY TO SMILE MORE THINGS ARE BETTER THEN YOU THINK.
ON THE WORK PHONE LIST I'M ON THERE UNDER WARRANTY DEPT. OPERATIONS. COOL. IS THAT WHERE I BELONG NOW?
LEAVE MY SOU
ALONE...
ACK!
OCTOZOID! WHERE ARE YOU?
SIDEKICKS AREN'T SUPPOSED TO LEAVE YOUR SIDE!!!
I NEED YOU SO MUCH CLOSER.
OH. DARN.

06.23.2009
I WAS SITTING AT MY DESK WHEN I FELT A GREAT WAVE OF PRIDE. I'VE COME SO FAR SINCE LAST YEAR. I NEVER THOUGHT I'D BE DOING THE THINGS I AM NOW OR KNOW THE PEOPLE I DO NOW PARTICULARLY IN THE COMICS BIZ. HERE'S A PAT ON MY BACK!
KEEP ON TRUCKIN!
DON'T GIVE UP!
PAT!
SUZY HASN'T BEEN DRIVING THE SAME SINCE SPINNING OUT. OH MAN, MAY THERE BE NOTHING WRONG WITHHER.
I HAVE TO GET MY BLOOD DRAWN TOMORROW!! UGH!!
NOT EXCITED
AND IT'S STARTING TO GET WARM AGAIN!
Yay
MY TOMATOES FINALLY GOT ITS FLOWERS! AT LEAST TWO OF THE FOUR PLANTS.
OCEAN GIRL DEFEATS GHOST!

6.24.2009

TO DO
- HENRY SHOTS
- SUZY OIL CHANGE

JUST BE YOURSELF. IT DOESN'T MATTER IF ITS NOT GOOD ENOUGH FOR SOMEONE ELSE

GOT THE 'OL VEIN TAPPED INTO TODAY. IT WASN'T **THAT** BAD... BUT THE ANTICIPATION KILLS! AND WOOZINESS IS STRANGE TOO... I DO FEEL REALLY PROUD THAT I SURVIVED ONE OF MY FEARS!

NO... MARLEY.. YOU WERE A GOOD BOY!

PANASONIC

I'M NOT **STUPID**

WATCHED MARLEY AND ME LAST NIGHT... TOTALLY A BORING CRAPPY MOVIE BUT THE END... THE END MADE ME CRY LIKE A BABY!

OCTO SIGNAL

6.25.2009

$94.84
20.00 OIL
74.84

EK!$
TIGHT

HENRY APP.
SUNDAY
12:20AM
$117.70
TIME TO MAX OUT THE 'OL C.C.

①

③

WAS FEELING WAY
OOZY AND WEIRD
IS MORNING. I ATE
THREE
NUTS! I HAD NO
EA I WAS CAPABLE.

OH NO

MICHAEL JACKSON DEAD AT 50 DUE TO CARDIAC ARREST.

TONIGHT! TINY COCKTAIL PARTY AT BRETT'S! OMG CRAIG THOMPSON AND FAREL DALRYMPLE WILL BE THERE! THO IT WAS SPECIFIED NO GUSHING ALLOWED. CHECK!
STAY TUNED!
BE GOOD!

SO SAD. HE WAS ONE OF FIRST HUGE MUSICAL MEMORIES FROM MY CHILDHOOD.

THE POP STAR OF OUR TIME.
RIP.

BANDS I WANT TO SEE.

- WINTERSLEEP
- MARGOT & THE NUCLEAR SO AND SO'S
- JIMMY EAT WORLD
- STARS

6.26.200
LAST NIGHT WAS A BLAST! WISH I COULD HAVE STAYED LONGER BUT WORK IN THE AM CALLS. MET COOL PEOPLE, SAW COLLEEN AND PAUL FROM PERISCOPE & LEARNED TONS AND HOPEFULLY THE PEOPLE I CHATTED W/ I CAN NOW GO "HEEY! WHATZ UP?!" NEXT TIME I SEE THEM.
CRAIG THOMPSON PICKED UP MY DROPPED CORN!
EATING CORN DRUNK.
CORN I DROPPED
I MAKE FRIENDS? HOPE SO!
COFFEE IS IN ORDER.
GIVE ME THAT TOXIC DELISH DRINK!
THIS 2 THIS
HI HI HI HI
HI HI HI HI
WHEEEZE
HI HI HI HI
HI HI HI
HI HI
HI
BLESS THEE, COFFEE, BLESS THEE TO HELL.
BILLIE JEAN IS NOT MY LOVAH ~♪
WENT VOICEBOX KARAOKE WITH CAT, RON, AND TALLY. SO MUCH FUN! WE EVEN SANG BILLIE JEAN IN MEMORY OF RECENTLY PASSED MJ.
BOOM BOOM BOOM BOOM
BOOM BOOM BOOM
THE WOLF COMETH....

6.27.2009
LOOK AT ALL THE ALGAE...
NO, ITS PLANKTON.
NT TO THE ZOO TODAY! WHERE I CALLED
GAE PLANKTON, A KID GRABBED MY BUTT,
OTHER KID SHOT ME FIVE TIMES, ONE
THOUGHT I WAS LYING ABOUT SEEING
DUCKLING, AND ONE WAS AMAZED ABOUT
DOOR... CHILDREN... SUCH STRANGE CREATURES.
THINK I'LL PROBABLY HAVE ONE SOMEDAY...
I SAVE DOOX BY HELPING HER GET INTO HER APT WHEN SHE DIDN'T HAVE HER KEY!
I'VE PLAYED FINAL FANTASY...
BEAM
HAVING PLAYED FINAL FANTASY EARNS A HUNDRED POINTS IN EMI'S BOOK...
BUSTER SWORD!
WENT TO GROUND KONTROL
PLAYED = DR. MARIO (DUH)
TETRIS
TMNT
RUISIN USA
DDR (DRUNK!)
OUBLE DRAGON
TEKKEN
AMES + BEER = HAPPY FUN FUN TIMES.
TASTES LIKE BEER!
THIS STRANGE BUT NICE GUY TRIED NATTO FOR THE FIRST TIME AT SUSHILAND THE ICKY NATTO "ALIEN" SLIME STRUNG FROM HIS MOUTH... IT WAS AWESOME.
NATTO

I TOTALLY SAW AN EYE BUBBLE ON HENRY... AND
IT POPPED!
IN HIS EYE!
HOW SICK IS THAT?

TAKE ME WITH YOU...

I FINALLY WATCHED BIG. NOW I UNDERSTAND ALL THOSE GIANT PIANO REFERENCES IN VARIOUS SHOWS AND MOVIES. IT WAS A WONDERFUL FILM. MOVIES JUST DON'T SEEM AS WHOLESOME ANYMORE.

2 KABOB SKEWERS
+
PAINTING TAPE
=
TOMATO STABILITY!
FINALLY MADE POLES FOR MY TOMATO PLANTS WHICH HAVE GROWN SO TALL THEY LEAN...
THEY'RE NOT THE STRONGEST POLES BUT THEY'LL DO, I HOPE!

WOKE UP A LITTLE HUNG OVER... WHICH IS STRANGE CONSIDERING I DIDN'T DRINK AS MUCH AS I HAVE IN THE PAST... AH WELL...

SO I PARKED IN A SPOT WHERE WE'RE SUPPOSED TO PARK IF SOMEONE IS IN OUR SPOT AT THE LOT I RENT... AND MONDAY (WHEN I FINALLY GO TO MY CAR) THERE IS A VEHICLE TOWING NOTICE FROM FRIDAY... BUT I WASN'T TOWED... AND THE REASONS MARKED DON'T EVEN MAKE SENSE... I **DO** HAVE A VALID REGISTRATION STICKER AND IT **WASN'T** A FIRE LANE.. I REFUSE TO TAKE THIS SERIOUSLY.. MAYBE THATS WHY I WASN'T TOWED...

PFFFFT.

WHATEVER.

6.29.2009

OIL CHANGE
$30
GAS
$15.

HENRY GOT HIS SHOTS AND STUFF. $175.00. JEEZ... HIS WONKY LEG WAS LOOKED AT TOO... SAID WORSE CASE SCENARIO HIS LEG WOULD HAVE TO BE AMPUTATED! OH NO! BUT IT MIGHT BE FINE... JUST HAVE TO KEEP HIM TRIM.

LOVE EVERYONE BUT KEEP THEM FAR FROM YOUR SOUL

WHILE DRIVING ON TWISTY SKYLINE DR., HENRY SHOCKED MY FACE WITH HIS NOSE. SCARED THE CRAP OUT OF ME!

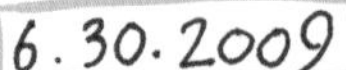

SURVIVED

MOTHS
VULNERABILITY
DETERMINATION
CONCEALMENT
ATTRACTION
SUBTLETY
INTUITION FAITH

1 2 3

THIS MORNING I SAW THREE MOTHS. A SMALL ONE IN THE ELEVATOR (ODD), A HUGE RED ONE IN MY APT, AND ANOTHER SMALL ONE ON THE WAY TO MY CAR.
I HOPE THE HUGE RED ONE IS GONE WHEN I GET HOME... UGH... GIANT MOTHS... I WON'T TOUCH OR KILL IT... SO UNPREDICTABLE HOW THEY FLITTER!

ANOTHER ROUND OF DTNA LAYOFFS... THATS 2 WEEKS IN A ROW! I'M FEARING...

OH PLEASE DON'T LET ME GO!

AWMAN
ITS GONNA BE ONE OF THOSE DAYS TODAY, I THINK...
POO...
SIGH

PACK WALK & BEERS WITH JAMESTOWN. YAY!

LIKE A CRYSTAL ON A SILVER PLATE ♡

ON MY DESK IS A PIECE OF BROKEN GLASS ON A CANADIA QUARTER... PRETTY!

WORKING ON THE PROMO CARD FOR EMITOWN JUST GOT FUN! THE RESPONSES TO MY QUOTE REQUEST SURE MADE MY DAY BETTER... AND FULL OF BLUSHES

THANKS GUYS ♡

LIGHT UP, LIGHT UP AS IF YOU HAVE A CHOICE. EVEN IF YOU CANNOT HEAR MY VOICE, I'LL BE RIGHT BESIDE YOU, DEAR.

JULY 2009

7/15 "A SEA SHANTY OF SORTS"
-MARGOT & THE NUCLEAR SO & SO'S
"BIG CASINO"
-JIMMY EAT WORLD
7/17 "WHAT SARAH SAID"
-DEATHCAB FOR CUTIE
7/21 "HANNAH HOLD ON"
-THE GET UP KIDS
7/28 "LAY ON THE RAILS"
-THE NEW AMSTERDAMS

I GOT A BREAKFAST BURRITO EVEN THOUGH I DIDN'T REALLY WANT ONE 100%... I FEEL LIKE LOUIE C.K. AND THE CINNABUNS...

7.1.2009
JULY!
BIRTHDAY & COMICON MONTH FINALLY HERE!
26
COMIX

THE BANE OF MY EXISTENCE...
BUT THEY ARE JUST SO
GOSH-DARN TASTY

GOALS FOR THE FOUR DAY WEEKEND!

1. GET ANOTHER SKETCHBOOK
2. FINISH PROMO CARD
3. GET INK
4. WIKIPEDIA
5. TOP SHELF BOOK ORGANIZATION
6. PAINT (FINISH ONE PAINTING)
7. GOODWILL FOR FRAMES?
8. CLEAN APT
9. GROCERY SHOP
10. CLEAN CAR
11. HAIR CUT?

TRUST ME, ITS FOR THE BEST
NO! IT WON'T WORK! THE HEART IS TOO STRONG!
BLACK

ACTUALLY TRIED TO USE EARPLUGS FOR A NAP CAUSE THE TIMBERS GAME WAS SO LOUD!

OH SHIT! 7.2.09
ERK!
GOT A RUM AND DIET (DIET?!) AT THE MATADOR LAST NIGHT AND THERE WAS HARDLY ANY SODA! I GUESS THATS ALL FINE AND DANDY BUT IT WAS
GROSS!
TANK
SHORTS
JEAN MIN
PLAID SHIRT♥
BIKINI TOP & BOTTOM
INK CART-
2 SKETCH BOOKS
TOMBO BRUSH PENS
CLEARANCE SHOPPING!!
DON'T EVEN WANT TO THINK ABOUT HOW MUCH I SPENT (WASN'T TOO B
BUT I'LL MAKE IT WORK!
ON BANNER "ANIMAL LIBERATION"
I FIND IT COMEDIC TO OWN A TANK TOP THAT SAYS "ANIMAL LIBERATION" WHEN I'M A HARDCORE CARNIVORE. WHY DO I HAVE IT? IT WAS HOT AT A FESTIVAL AND THEY WERE SELLING TANK TOPS...
I HAVE A KILLER BUG BITE ON MY LEG... IT HAS TO BE A SPIDE BITE... MY GOD... A SPIDER WA ON.. MY... LEG..
HI, SIR! ♥
I WAS WAITING FOR A SUPER DUPER LONG TIME IN LINE FOR CHECK OUT AT A STORE AND A DUDE WHO JUST PLOPPED IN AND WAITED FIVE MIN WAS HELPED BEFORE ME AND HE GOT A DISCOUNT FOR WAITING?!! I WASN'T EVEN OFFERED ONE UNTIL I MENTIONED. IT... MAYBE I HAVE TO BE OLD AND GRUMPY TO GAIN IN THIS WORLD!
HMMMPH!

7.4.2009 3
HUNG OUT WITH AN OLD HIGH SCHOOL FRIEND! WENT TO BLUE MOON WHERE I HAD A RUBY AND A CAPTAIN NEON BURGER! YUM!!
SAVE MONEY NIGHT
STAYED IN WITH JAMESTOWN AND WATCHED MOVIES AND DRANK CHEAP CHAMPAGNE...
TOO HOT!
1
(LAST NIGHT)
FINALLY GOT TOP SCORE ON THE DR. MARIO MACHINE AT GROUND KONTROL... GRANTED THE MACHINES ARE REBOOTED I THINK OFTEN, MY NAME WAS ON TOP FOR AT LEAST ONE NIGHT... I BEAT THE TOP SCORE BY 50,000 POINTS!
ROCK!

7.4.20

BEEN SLEEPING IN UNTIL 11:30AM EVERDAY! MAN, MONDAY IS GOING TO SUC WILL I BE ABLE TO GET UP AT 5:30AM?!

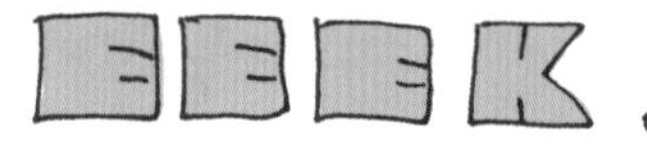

I FEEL LIKE I ATE A TON! OH, FOOD COMA...

RICE KRISPEE TREA

CHIPS

BURGER ♡

MAC SALAD

CRACKERS & SEAFOOD DIP...

OK... THIS MAY NOT SEEM LIKE MUCH... BUT IT FILLED MY TUMMY!

SPENT THE FOURTH WITH THE BOOTHS, ERIC, STEPHAN, AND BRITTNAY. AND ELAINA... IT WAS PRETTY CHILL. DIDN'T DRINK SINCE I HAD TO DRIVE HOME... THOUGH, DRINKING WITH A FOOD COMA COULD ONLY WORSEN THE CONDITION... SO MAYBE IT WAS A GOOD THING ON MULTIPLE LEVELS...

7.5.2009

DISHES

VACUUM

LAUNDRY

I DID SOME CLEANING... ACCOMPLISHED SOMETHING.

TARTED THE GREAT TOP SHELF STOCK
EORGANIZATION PROJECT... SO MUCH
EFT TO DO! SO MANY TITLES! WHEW!

KABOB STICK TOMATO POLE VERSION 2.0!

THE TOMATO PLANTS WERE FALLING OVER WITH MY FLIMSY STICKS SO I MAKE BETTER ONES

THIS TIME WITH THREE KABOB STICKS TO ADD STRENGTH AND EXTRA STABILITY

CLEVER!

COOL

MET WITH JAMESTOWN FOR A BEER AND SHE SAID MY TAN MAKES ME LOOK NATIVE AMERICAN

7.6.200

VIRGINIA WOOF W.

VIRGINIA WOOF E.

3:30 PM

FRI $25-35
SAT $30
SUN-5-7PM

WANT A BREAKFAST BURRITO SO BAD BUT CAN'T. TRYING TO CUT BACK FOR HEALTH AND FINANCIAL REASONS... I CAN ONLY DREAM... WAH!

HENRY GETS SCREENED TO SEE IF HE IS KENNEL WORTHY!

NOT EVEN ANY MONEY IN THE PIGGY BANK...

I WILL SURVIVE! I WILL!

I HAD A DREAM THAT MY FLASK WAS BACK... SEEMED SO REAL...

ALSO HAD A DREAM IN WHICH SOMEONE TOLD ME KEANE WAS THE MOST TALENTED BAND EVER.

AVE IN AND GOT A BREAKFAST
URRITO... NO COFFEE THO. SO HAPPY!
S IT SAD THAT HAM, HASHBROWNS, EGG,
ND CHEESE WRAPPED IN A WARM TORTILLA
AN JUST MAKE MY DAY?
NMMMMM
7.7.2009
I'M JUST GONNA PUT MY HEART ON MY SLEEVE... BE BOLD! YOUR WAY IS TOO STRESSFUL. IT WILL BE WORTH IT SOMEDAY. I KNOW IT!
WAT?! SO STUPID!!
"PUT THE GO IN GO-FOR-IT"
REMEMBER MATES, TOSS BACK THE PUNY ONES. WE BE NEEDIN THE BIGGEST AND TENDEREST OF HEARTS!

7.8.20

TYPE
NUMERICS
TYPE

JIFFY

TO HELP KICK MY BURRITO HABIT, I HAVE STARTED EATING PEANUT BUTTER SANDWICHES IN THE MORNING.

MORE TOP SHELF ORGANIZING...
PHEW

AMERICAN ELF
AMERICAN ELF

MAN, ACTUAL FIVE DAY WEEKS KILL NOW... I'M SO SPOILED... AND REMOVING 7,460 VINS (OFF CONTRACTS) IS NOT MY IDEA OF FUN... ITS 12:35 AND I HAVE REMOVED 965. YAY!

ITS BEEN SO LONG
OR HAS IT REALLY
SHORE FEELS LIKE FOREVER
ACK! DO SOMETHING!
COME DOWN HEEEERE...
PLEASE.

COMIC CON IS ALMOST ONLY 2 WEEKS AWAY! I SURE DID A PISS POOR JOB OF SAVING MONEY.... OH WELL, THIS YEAR ISN'T ALL ABOUT THE SHOPPING!

LEVEL SLOWLY RISING.

OH GOD, I HAVE TO GO ON A PLANE... ONCE A YEAR... THOSE DAMN PLANES!!

SCHEDULE HENRY'S BOARDING!

2 WEEKS TO SAVE SOME MONEY TO SURVIVE

I STILL NEED TO FINISH THAT POSTCARD!

7.9.2009

I KNOW I WRITE ALOT ABOUT COFFEE BUT I AM TAKING A STAND AGAINST IT FOR REAL! NO MORE EVER. THE ANXIETY IS SIMPLY TOO MUCH.

" YOU COFFEE!

ICK!

THERE WAS AN ART OPENING AT COFFEEHOUSE NORTHWEST. DROPPED BY TO CHECK IT OUT. THE PAINTINGS WERE WHIMSICALLY BEAUTIFUL.

MEDICINE FRIDAY! SHANGHAI TUNNEL HAPPY HOUR = WIN!!!!

7.10.20
HALF OFF WELL DRINKS! CHEAP!!

HUNG OUT W/ RON AND CAT FOR HAPPY HOUR AT SHANGHAI TUNNEL! THEN WENT TO PIZZA... THEN MET UP W/ FRIENDS AT GROUND KONTROL. KIDS... BOOZE IS <u>NOT</u> THE ANSWER!

NO REASON TO HAVE SUCH A BLACK HEART ANYMORE... LOCK IT AWAY...

BLACK HEART IS SO STUPID ANYWAY.

PORTLAND SUMMER WEATHER HASN'T BEEN FEELING SO... SUMMERY...

7.11.2008

FOR BEN'S B-DAY WE ALL WENT TO A CAJUN PLACE WHERE I GOT TO TRY CRAWFISH FOR THE FIRST TIME. I GOT **REAL** GOOD AT RIPPING THOSE SUCKERS APART!

IT WAS A TRIPLE B·DAY DAY

COLLEEN

HAPPY B-DAY! ♥

RICH

IT SMOKES BECAUSE ITS A SMOKER!

HAPPY B-DAY!

BEN

HAPPY B-DAY!

WENT TO A STRIP CLUB SO HIS GF COULD GET HIM A STRIP LAP DANCE... I DON'T REALLY LIKE STRIP CLUBS (ITS WEIRD) BUT WATCHING BEN UNCOMFORTABLE ON STAGE HANDCUFFED TO A POLE WHILE TWO CHICKS SHOVED THEIR CROTCHES AND BOOBS IN HIS FACE WAS PRICELESS. HAVEN'T LAUGHED SO HARD IN A LONG TIME... AND I WASN'T EVEN DRUNK!

CAUGHT UP WITH JAMESTOWN FOR AN HOUR...
RECAPPED EACH OTHER'S WEEKEND ADVENTURES.

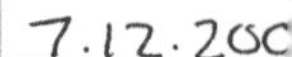

$19.95
-15.00 GAS
4.95

FACK... MAYBE $10.00 FOR GAS...

SAW THE SADDEST WEINER DOG THAT JUST HAD BACK SURGERY... ALL THESE STAPLES DOWN ITS BACK! :(

LAZY DAY... SPENDING TIME CATCHING UP ON EMITOWN AND THEN WALK WITH HENRY.

7.13.2009

409.00 ON THURS
-134.00 RENT
275.00
- 30.00 (DOG)
- 20.00 (FOOD)
- 15.00 (GAS)
210.00 (-20)
(-20 PGE) $190
(-75 CC)
(-25 PA)

ERE WILL BE NO
N DOLLARS...
VILL EAT CEREAL.
Y ONLY PRESENTS.
EED FLASK TO SAVE
AT BAR ACTIVITIES.

KIX

@!!$# YOU! YOU $!#!!
SHOPPING CART NOISE

HAVING TROUBLE SLEEPING... DON'T KNOW IF ITS DUE TO LATE WEEKEND NIGHTS, WARM NIGHTS WHERE I LEAVE WINDOW OPEN, OR TOO MANY THOUGHTS... I GOT 4 HOURS OF SLEEP LAST NIGHT... I THINK ABOUT TRYING THE EAR PLUGS BUT WHAT IF I DON'T HEAR MY ALARM?! OH LOSE...

EW...

I REALLY NEED TO TRIM HENRY'S NAILS... HE HATES THE CLIPPERS... I HATE HIS NAILS!

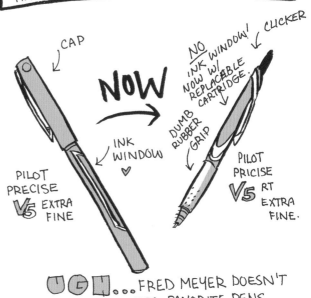

HMMMM...

I NEED NEW TUNES FOR THE OL' IPOD... BUT I KNOW NOTHING BECAUSE ALL I LISTEN TO IS THE IPOD. I LOSE.

CAP

INK WINDOW ♥

PILOT PRECISE V5 EXTRA FINE

NOW

CLICKER

NO INK WINDOW! NOW W/ REPLACABLE CARTRIDGE.

DUMB RUBBER GRIP

PILOT PRICISE V5 RT EXTRA FINE.

UGH... FRED MEYER DOESN'T CARRY MY PRIZED FAVORITE PENS... NOW THEY HAVE SOME CLICKER PEN I HOPE PILOT DIDN'T DISCONTINUE THE OLD ONES FOR THIS ONE!

SO WHEN I WAS GETTING MY COFFEE (I KNOW I GAVE IN!) AND WAITING FOR MY B. BURRITO, I CHECKED OUT ESQUIRE MAG WHICH I THOUGHT WAS ODD AT THE ASIAN COUPLE OWNED CAFE...
7.14.2009
I LEARNED THE FOLLOWING:
① NOD
HOW TO HEAD NO
IT LITERALLY HAD DRAWN OUT PICTURES ON HO
TO DO VARIOUS NODS...
② THE 5 PLACES IN THE U.S. TO FIND LOOSE WOMEN.
OH HAI
EVIDENTALLY PORTLAND, OR IS ONE OF THOSE PLACES?! THANKS, ESQUIRE.... MAN SLUTS WILL COME FOR A LAY AND HELP PUSH DISEASE AROUND.
GROSS.
IF YOU CARE, OTHER PLACES WERE:
UTAH, LA, MI, AND WASHINGTON D.C.
IN CA...
③ WHAT MOVIES/SHOWS W/ THE THEME OF REVENGE
VIOLENCE! YAY!
AND LASTLY
I SAW SOME BOOBIES.
MEN'S MAGAZINE'S ARE FUNNY.
BRIAN DESPAIN
ROQ LA RUE
2312 2ND AVE.
SEATTLE, WA 98121
NOV. 13
1PM-6PM
WED~SAT
MUST REMEMBER TO SEE BRIAN BEFORE HE MOVES FAR AWAY AND I WON'T GET TO ANYMORE! AND HIS LOVELY PAINTINGS ♥
1
2
3
DETONATE!!!

7.15.2009

AND I CAN'T BREATHE WITH THE DUST OF RETREAT.

FROM HELL
AMERICAN ELF
AMERICAN ELF
BLANKETS
SWALLOW ME WHOLE
THAT SALTY AIR

TOP SHELF ORGANIZING TODAY
I CAN DO IT!

I'VE BEEN WATCHING ALOT OF BAND OF BROTHERS LATELY... I LIKE WAR MOVIES... ESPECIALLY ABOUT OLD WARS... ♡ FASCINATING

A TEXT!!

WHO IS IT FROM?!

DON'T GIVE UP YOUR HOPES

1 NEW MESSAGE

IS IT OCTOZOID?!

WHAT DOES IT SAY?!!

I LOVE GETTING TEXT MESSAGES!
IT MEANS SOMEONE THOUGHT OF YOU!
EXCEPT A MASS TEXT... YOU'RE JUST
ONE OF THE HERD...
AND YEAH... THATS MY SWEET
RAZR... JEALOUS? MMMHMM

$165
- 15 GAS
- 10 FOOD
- 30 DOG
$110
7.16.2009
EW DRIP!
TOO HOT TO COOK!
I EAT VEGGIES ON A PLATE FOR DIN.. CUCUMBER, TOMATOES, BROCCÓLI AND CARROTS
I SUN ON MY FIRE ESCAPE AND A TRAIL OF SWEAT BEGAN AND WENT ALL THE WAY DOWN MY ARM... I WAS DISGUSTED...
I DIDN'T GIVE A SHIT ABOUT MONEY! I TREATED JAMESTOWN AND I TO A PITCHER! IT WAS A LONG WEEK...
PITCHER!
OCTOZOID! COME IN! COME IN, OCTOZOID!
SEATTLE
MEDFORD
COMMUNICATION WITH OCTOZOID IS DOWN. WHAT WILL OCEAN GIRL DO? PROBABLY SIT AND STUFF...

7.17.2009
YAY!
EMITOWN
THE CARDS I WILL HANDOUT AT COMIC CON HAVE ARRIVED! THEY LOOK ALRIGHT... THEY SHALL DO.
LOVE IS WATCHING SOMEONE DIE
WHO'S GONNA WATCH ME DIE?!!! OH, MAN.......
I HEAR THIS DEATHCAB SONG CALLED "WHAT SARAH SAID" AND THIS LINE MADE ME TEAR UP WHILE I WAS DRIVING... AT FIRST I WAS WAS ALL 'WHAT DOES THAT EVEN MEAN?!' THEN I THOUGHT ABOUT IT... MAYBE IT MEANS THAT WHEN SOMEONE YOU LOVE DIES OR IS DYING, YOU'RE THERE SO THEY AREN'T ALONE... NO MATTER HOW MUCH IT WILL HURT TO SEE THEM DIE, YOU DO IT ANYWAY CAUSE YOU LOVE THEM SO MUCH... AND THEY CAN LEAVE KNOWING THEY ARE LOVED... THE LAST THING THEY SEE BEFORE DEATH IS LOVE...
ATE WITH MAMA ON HER BREAK AT THE RESTARAUNT SHE WORKS AT... GOT A FREE CHIRASHI DONBURI! YUM!!
TIME FOR MEDICINE (BOOZE) FRIDAY!! TIME FOR FUN

B•DAY★CELE★DAY

7.18.200

FOR MY BIRTHDAY STEPHAN TOOK ME TO DIN AT THE OUTBACK STEAKHOUSE. STEAK, RARE WITH GARIC MASHED POTATOES AND GRILLED ONIONS = GOLD! BRITTNEY GOT NOODLES?! AWW.

7.20.200

STUPID BIRTHDAY DEPRESSION STARTING TO SETTLE IN... I DON'T KNOW WHY I GET SAD ON MY BIRTHDAY... BUT I DO... TONIGHT I WILL PUT A CANDLE ON A SLICE OF PIE AND MAKE MY WISH.

SOMEONE IS EATING TUNA FOR LUNCH AT WORK... IT SMELLS JUST LIKE THE SQUISHY FOOD WEENIE LOVED. WEENIE MEMORIES CAME FLOODING BACK. :(

MY BIRTHDAY IS ALSO OCEAN DAY THIS YEAR IN JAPAN. STRANGE COINCIDENCE... I AM OCEAN GIRL!

WHERE ARE MY POWERS

I DROPPED MY CURRY RICE AND BROKE A BOWL... OH WOE.

SPILLED

7.21.2009

H NO...
M BEING REPLACED!
HAT IS NEXT
STEP?
IT TIME
LREADY?
DON'T THINK
M READY...
HAT 2DOWHAT 2D
STILL HAVE TIME
FIGURE IT OUT...
BIRTHDAY DONE AND OVER.
YAY!
UNTIL NEXT YEAR...

ELECTRONICS
ARE FAILING MEEEEEEE...
KAPUT.
MY DVD PLAYER BROKE...
I'VE HAD IT FOR 6 YEARS...
I GUESS IT WAS TIME.
THEN MY IPOD STARTING HAVING ISSUES... ITS NOT EVEN A YEAR OLD... OR IT IS... THE BUTTONS STOPPED WORKING. I RESET IT AND ITS FINE NOW... NO MORE SCARES!
YAY!!
DO YOU EVER HAVE ONE OF THOSE DAYS WHERE YOU'RE IN THE BEST MOOD FOR NO REASON? THATS TODAY... IT RULES.
YOU ONLY DISSAPPOINT THE ONES WHO DON'T BELIEVE.
THE WAR IS NOT OVER, BOYS!!!

ANOTHER CASUALTY! DAMN YOU! WE'RE LOSING TOO MANY! WE'RE LOSING THIS WAR! CURSES!!!
7.22.2
ZzzzZ
MY SCHEDULE AT WORK GOT CHANGED FROM 6AM-2:30 TO 8:00AM ~ 4:30PM..... IT WILL BE NICE NOT HA TO WAKE UP AT 5:30A
SPIDERS = NO!
PORTLAND
· DARKHORSE
· ONI PRESS
· TOP SHELF
SEATTLE
· FANTAGRAPHICS
OAKLAND
IMAGE
WHAT IS MY NEXT STEP? I PREFER TO STAY IN PORTLAND BUT I WOULD LOVE TO BE AT FANTA-GRAPHICS... HOW? I NEED MORE CONNECTIONS? WHAT DO I DO NEXT?!
MUST... GET... COMIC... JOB... MUST!
DON'T GIVE UP!!!
GLASS!
HENRY HAD A DINGLEBERRY AND SCOOTED ON THE SIDE WALK DANGEROUSLY CLOSE TO BROKEN GLASS. LUCKILY, HE CAME OUT UNCUT.

HANDMADE SOME BUSINESS CARDS SINCE I REALIZED I SHOULD HAVE SOME JUST IN CASE... BETTER SAFE THAN
SORRY!
WRITE
SCRIBBLE
LAST MINUTE PACKING
SMART
TO DO
• DEPOSIT $
• BUY SHOES
• DROP OFF HEN
• PACK HEN FOOD
• TOY
• BED
• SHOWER
• PACK
• EMITOWN
• HANG W/ JAMIE
• SLEEP!
DONT FORGET
CELL
CHARGER
CHARGER
PROMO CARDS
DEODERANT! (IF ONLY ALL CON GOERS HAD IT...)
SKETCH
BUSINESS CARDS
$ 600
$ 178.70
$ 90 DOG BOARD
WHEN I CHECKED MY MAILBOX I FOUND A PIECE OF A BROKEN MIRROR... NOTHING ELSE... WHAT DOES THIS MEAN? WHY DID SOMEONE PUT IT THERE? ITS LIKE A SIGN OF BAD THINGS TO COME.
WAT

SDCC DAY ONE
7.24.20
SHOES OF DEATH
WORE NEW SHOES TO CON... HOW DUMB AM I?
I WANTED TA LOOK GOOD!
BLISTER 1
2
3
4
MENTAL NOTE... DO NOT BOOK A FLIGHT AT 6AM CAUSING YOU TO WAKE AT 4AM AND BEING TIRED AND MISERABLE ALL DAY... AT A COMIC CONVENTION...
THE BIG COMIC CONVENTION
SIGH
OCEAN GIRL GAINS SILVER SHELL OF POWER!
THANKS BATTLENUN!
WEREWOLVES & VAMPS GOT NOTHIN ON ME!!
AT THE SUSHI PLACE AND TEMPURA BANANAS
I GOT ICE CREAM WITH A CANDLE
HAPPY B-DAY EMI
FOR MY B-DAY! (LAST MON) AWWW! MY PALS EVEN SANG HAPPY BIRTHDAY TO ME! SO SWEET!
?!!
OOOF
IN THE GAS LAMP DISTRICT, A DRUNK COUPLE REFUSED(?) TO LET GO EACH OTHERS HAND AND WALKED THROUGH ME HITTING ME (QUITE HARD) IN THE STOMAC
THEN CLAIMED THEY DIDN
WHEN I SHOUTED IN DESPAIR.
HOW CAN YOU NOT REALIZE YOUR FISTS MADE CONTACT TO ANOTHER HUMAN BEING?!
HOW?!

7.25.2009
WHILE PIMPIN EMITOWN AND HELPING AT THE TOP SHELF BOOTH, SOMEONE ACTUALLY ASKED ME TO DRAW IN THEIR SKETCHBOOK.
WHOAH... DUDE, I'M NOT EVEN PUBLISHED... I FELT SPECIAL.
?!
EH?
DUDE, WHATS UP WITH YOUR BOW?
?
I TUCKED PART OF THE BOW INTO MY PANTS ON ACCIDENT AT THE HYATT PARTY. OH GOD... BLUSH!
FACE TOUCH! IS BAD?
DRUNKENLY MADE A FOOL OF MYSELF IN FRONT OF JEFFREY BROWN AND JEFF LEMIRE... AND POSED TOO CLOSE TO GABRIEL BÁ FOR A PIC AT THE HYATT... THANKS FOR INTRODUCIN' ME, JOE!!
THE HYATT WAS THE BEST! HUNG OUT WITH JOE, FORUM BUDS, AND PERISCOPE PEEPS! ♥♥♥♥
$20!
BOOP!
$200?
SPARE ANY CHANGE?!
I DON'T EVEN HAVE THIS MONEY!!
I DRUNKENLY ENTERED TOO MANY ZEROS INTO THE ATM AND WITHDREW $200 INSTEAD OF $20. A BUM CONVENIENTLY STOOD NEAR THE ATM AND ASKED FOR MONEY. I MAY HAVE FLIPPED OUT A LITTLE BIT.

7.26.200

I FELT SO HUNGOVER AT THE AIRPORT... I MUST HAVE LOOKED PATHETIC WITH MY BLISTERED FOOT CAUSING AN ODD LIMP PLUS MY ATTEMPTS TO BREATHE AND NOT BE SICK.

GIMP LEG

DUMB...

WHY THEY PU THIS HERE? IT MAKES THE SEA SOOOO UNCOMFORTABLE!!

THE SWAG

I DIDN'T DO AS MUCH SHOPPING THIS YEAR... BUT HERE IS WHAT I CAME HOME WITH:

1. DEREK HUNTER'S PIRATE CLUB!

pirate club

2. TED MATHOT'S CORA: PART TWO

CORA Part Two

3. TOKIDOKI KITTY VINYL CHARACTERS

a. CARINA

b. ~~BURRITINO~~ BURITTINO

4. T-SHIRT FOR A B-DAY PRESENT FOR A FRIEND

5. THE NEW JAME JEAN POSTER BOOK! PROCESS RECESS WAS SOLD OUT. :(

KINDLING

6. ASSORTED BUTTONS.

7. AGE OF BRONZ BY ERIC SHANOWER

8. BUTTON

NOT TOO SHABBY!

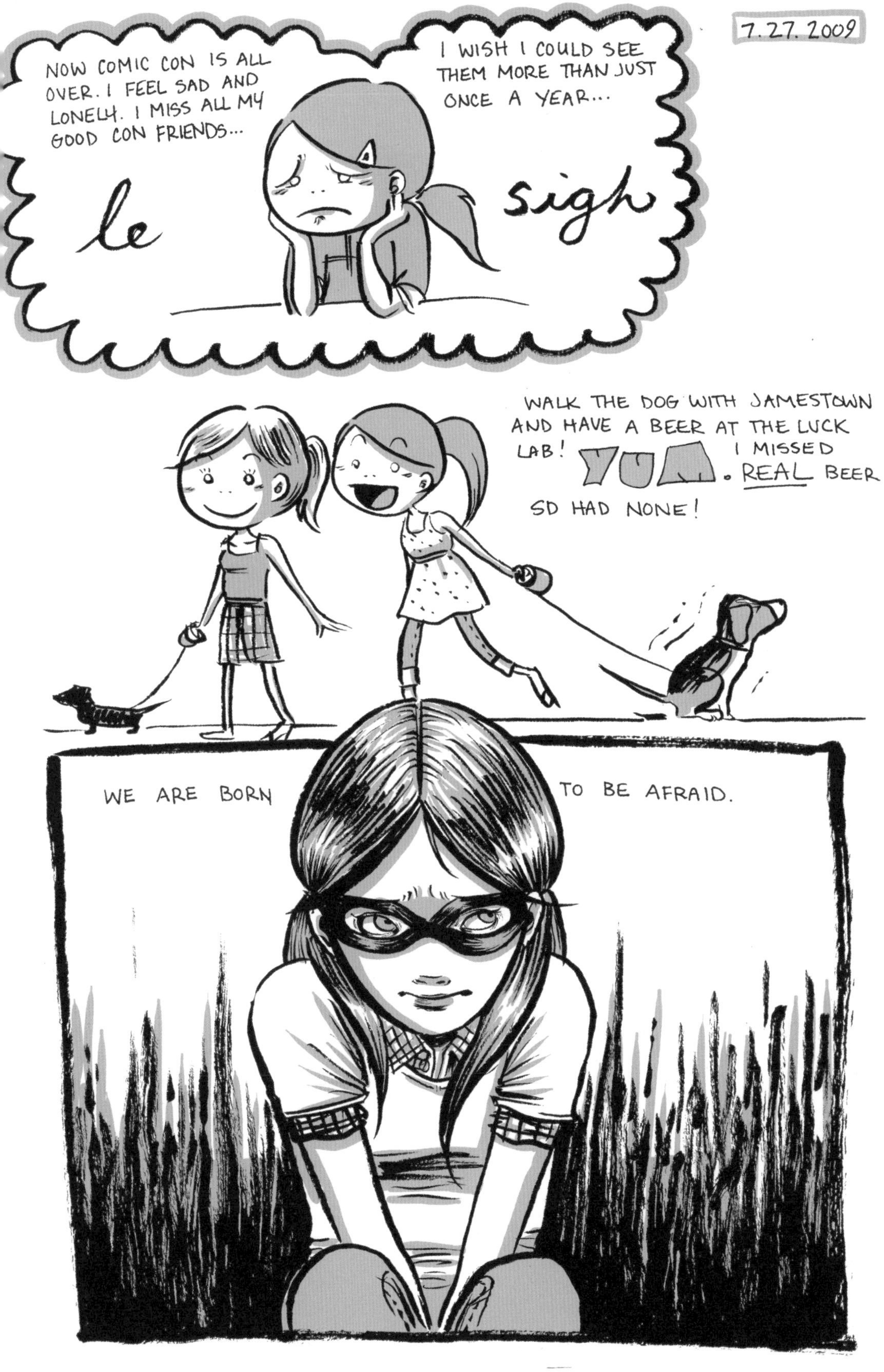

WALK THE DOG WITH JAMESTOWN AND HAVE A BEER AT THE LUCK LAB! YUM. I MISSED REAL BEER SD HAD NONE!

WE ARE BORN TO BE AFRAID.

I WISH I HAD A YARD... I'D TOTALLY GET A KIDDIE POOL AND SIT IN IT... WITH A BEER. I KNOW... IF I'M WISHING, WHY NOT JUST WISH FOR A REAL POOL? *SIGH* I DUNNO.

7.29.2009
URK
!!
ON THE WAY TO MY CAR THIS MORNING, I STEPPED INTO DOG POOP... WHAT A MIGHTY FINE WAY TO START MY DAY. TODAY WILL BE
AMAZING
I AM SURE...
DO YOU SMELL HAT? SMELLS...
DOG DOO
SOMETIMES I LIKE TO TYPE LYRICS TO SONGS WHILE I LISTEN... ITS TYPING PRACTICE...
TYPE
TYPE
AND I DO IT FOR FUN!
AM I WEIRD?
I'M A LESBIAN AND PROUD OF IT!
GIGGLE YEAH... YOU LOVE GOING DOWN ON CHICKS! *GIGGLE*
I WANT TO GET A JAR TO PUT ALL THE PIECES OF PRETTY BROKEN GLASS I FIND ON THE GROUND... WHEN ITS FULL, IT WILL BE LIKE A JAR FULL OF MAGIC CRYSTALS!
JAMESTOWN SAID SHE WAS A LESBIAN TO THIS DUDE WHO KEPT HANGING AROUND. SO INCREDIBLY FUNNY. HE TOTALLY FELL FOR IT. OH JAMESTOWN, YOU'RE SUCH A RIOT.

7.30.2009
HOORAY
I AM SO HAPPY TODAY IS MY "FRIDAY" THIS WEEKEND SHOULD AND BETTER BE
AWESOME
OH SHIT STRESS
AFTER A FIVE WEEK ABSENCE OF OCTOZOID, OCEAN GIRL HEADS NORTH TO THE STRANGE LAND TO SEE HIM AT HIS OCTO-LAIR...
MAP...
MY IDEA OF A RELAXING EVE
CONAN O'BRIEN AND A MIRROR POND PALE ALE
EMI SLEEPS WITH AIR CONDITIONIN
THIS NIGHT! EAT IT, HELLISH HEAT OF PORTLAND!!

7.31.2009
[S]AVED!
[T]ODAY I SAVED A BEE FROM [D]ROWNING IN THE LAKE... I [SP]ITE BEES BUT NON-SWIMMERS [G]OTTA LOOK OUT FOR EACH OTHER!
I GOT TO DRIVE THE OCTO-BOAT AROUND THE LAKE...
IT RULED!
FLOATING IN A LAKE
MIRROR POND (I LOVE IT!) AND
EQUALS A GOLDEN TIME...
GUESS WASHINGTON ISN'T THAT BAD...
I LEARNED FEELING LIKE YOU
DON'T
FIT IN
AND DRINKING IS NOT A GOOD MIX. DUH, RIGHT? AH, WELL. WE ALL MESS UP SOME-TIMES....
I MADE A DUCK FRIEND. I NAMED HIM LLOYD.
GOOD
DUCK
LLOYD →

AUGUST 2009

8/3 "FOR THE WIDOWS IN PARADISE"
-SUFJAN STEVENS
8/5 "IN THE BEDROOM AFTER THE WAR"
-STARS
8/6 "SUCH TRAGIC STORIES"
-ASPHALT THIEVES
8/11 "DON'T BE AFRAID TO SING"
-STARS
8/12 "SMILE AT ME"
-ARCHER AVENUE
8/15 "LO SIENTO BAMBINO"
-ARCHER AVENUE
8/16 "WE'LL BE FINE"
-MATT PRYOR
8/17 "PIGLET"
-ARCHER AVENUE
8/22 "80 WINDOWS"
-NADA SURF

8.01.2009
ON THE DRIVE HOME FROM WASHINGTON, SOME DOLT DIDN'T CHECK HIS BLIND SPOT AND STARTED TO GET INTO MY LANE. I HAD TO SWERVE OUT OF THE WAY. AT 75 MPH, IT WAS A BIT SCARY. SECOND TIME THIS HAPPENED TO ME! JEEZ PEOPLE!!
HAPPY B-DAY JAMES TOWN!
TODAY I LEARNED I SUCK AT PING PONG
QUITE A BIT ACTUALLY.
DRINKING JAGER STRAIGHT FROM THE BOTTLE ON THE STREETS OF SOUTH EAST PORTLAND...
ROCK STAR

8.02.2
WHEN YOU RU
OUT OF CLEAN
UNDERWEAR, IT
LAUNDR
TIME
THE PAST IS TOLD BY THOSE WHO WIN.

WHAT IF THEY'RE RIGHT?

OH DARUMA-SAN, WILL I EVER GET TO DRAW IN YOUR OTHER EYE?

WHEN YOU HAVE A DARUMA DOLL, YOU MAKE A WISH AND DRAW IN ONE EYE... WHEN IT COMES TRUE, YOU DRAW IN THE OTHER. THIS IS FROM 8.10.2008... I THINK HE WILL HAVE ONE EYE FOREVER

8.03.2009
DATA BOOK CODES TOWING WAE-003 WA1-013 SUSPENSION AXLES WAG-001
BREAKFAST BURRITO MONDAY. I ALWAYS GO THROUGH A WHOLE BOTTLE OF WATER DUE TO THE FIERY HELL SRIRACHA SAUCE PUTS ME THROUGH.
I AM SO HAVING A CASE OF THE MON-DAYS...
I BELIEVE YOU'D GET YOUR ASS KICKED SAYIN' SOMETHIN LIKE THAT, MAN.
I WAS DRESSED IN EMBARRASSMENT, I WAS DRESSED IN WHITE. IF YOU HAD A PART OF ME WOULD YOU TAKE YOUR TIME. EVEN IF I COME BACK, EVEN IF I DIE, IS THERE SOME IDEA TO REPLACE MY LIFE.

MFNW
$60.
SUNNY DAY REAL ESTATE · ARTIC MONKEYS · THE GET UP KIDS · BLAH · BLAH · OTHER BANDS... ETC · ETC.
SEPT 16-20
WHAT?! GET UP KIDS ARE PLAYING A SHOW? BUT THEY BROKE UP! WILL THEY PLAY THEIR OLD GOOD SONGS?! BUT SO NOT WORTH $60 FOR JUST ONE BAND... DRAT MUSIC FEST NORTHWEST. CURSE YOU TGUK!
FREE DONUT!
8.04.200
LEFT OVER CHIPS FROM JAMIE'S B-DAY
NO CAFFINE
SPRIT
MY BREAK FAST.
SODA.
I NEVER DRINK SODA BUT I WANTED A CARBO SWEET BEVERAGE... I STI COULDN'T EVEN FINISH
· BAND OF HORSES MCDONALD THEATRE (EUGENE!) 9/1 (TUES?)
· KEANE ROSELAND 9/9 (WED)?!
AND WHY IS IT ALL THE BANDS I WANT TO SEE PLAY FAR AWAY AND/OR ON A WEEK NIGHT?! A WORK NIGHT?! CURSE MUSIC.
OCEAN GIRL ALWAYS WINS!
I WAS READING MY OLD EMITOWN FROM 2008 (MOST ISN'T POSTED) AND ON ONE PAGE DESPITE HOW HARD THINGS WERE ALL I WANTED WAS TO BE THE BEST ME POSSIBLE AND RADIATE HAPPINESS AND JOY TO ALL.
HOW EASY IT IS TO FALL FROM THAT MINDSET. THINGS AREN'T BAD AT ALL RIGHT NOW... I NEED TO GET BACK TO ♡ RADIATING ♡
BE HAPPY
BE PEACEFUL

LAST NIGHT:
8.5.2009
WTF!!
OCEAN GIRL, OCTOZOID IS MY SIDEKICK. YOU SHOULD KNOW. PICS TO PROVE: FROM: XXX
I LIKE TO BE A SIDEKICK TO OTHERS TOO. ITS NORMAL! JUST HAVING FUN! I CARE AND LIKE YOU THOUGH!
NO! NOT NORMAL! ITS BEEN ALMOST 2 MONTHS. OCEAN GIRL ISN'T LOOKING FOR A PART TIME SIDEKICK! IF YOU CAN'T DEDICATE THEN OFF WITH YOU!
PLAYBOY-O-ZOID
CAN I STILL TALK TO YOU?
NO WAY
OCEAN GIRL DOES NOT NEED THIS.
SHE CAN FIND A BETTER SIDEKICK.
THERE IS ONLY ONE OCEAN GIRL!
OCEAN GIRL DESERVES HONESTY AND
RESPECT. IS THE CODE DEAD THESE DAYS?
WHERE IS THE DECENCY?! THE CONSIDERATION?!
P.S. IRON MAN THINKS YOU'RE A DOUCHEBAG.
YOU SHALL NOT MISLEAD ME ANYMORE.
ODAY... AS CRAPPY THINGS TEND TO OCCUR IN
UMBERS, SOMEONE LET THE AIR
UT OF MY TIRE.. AND SOME-
NE ELSE'S ON MY LOT.
ANDALS! I HAD HELP
O PUT ON THE SPARE... BUT
DID GET THE LUG NUTS OFF!
ND I TOTALLY COULD HAVE
HANGED IT MYSELF IF THE JACK WASN'T SO POORLY DESIGNED
WAKE UP. SAY GOOD MORNING TO THAT SLEEPY PERSON LYING NEXT TO YOU. IF THERE'S NO ONE THERE THEN THERE'S NO ONE THERE. BUT AT LEAST THE WAR IS OVER.
LIFT YOUR HEAD UP AND LOOK OUT THE WINDOW. STAY THAT WAY FOR THE REST OF THE DAY AND WATCH THE TIME GO.
AT FIRST THEY WOULD NOT BUDGE.
I STILL THINK THIS YEAR WILL BE TOTALLY AWESOME!

8.6.200

SEEMINGLY EVERY OTHER DAY OR SO, WHEN I RIDE THE ELEVATOR DOWN TO TAKE HENRY TO POTTY, IT IS FULL OF BEER KEGS. I HIJACK THE ELEVATOR WHEN THE BEER DELIVERY GUYS ARE LOADING KEGS TO CARRY THROUGH THE APT. BASEMENT TO THE BAR NEXT DOOR.

IS IT STRANGE THAT ITS NORMAL FOR ME TO RIDE IN AN ELEVATOR FULL OF KEGS?

THROW IT BACK. ITS NOT WHAT WE HOPED. DON'T WORRY THOUGH, MATE. SOMETIMES ITS HARD TO TELL...

YOUR STRUGGLING EFFORTS. NOTHING YOU'VE EVER DONE HAS BEEN THAT CONVINCING OR BEEN WORTH DEFENDING
YOU'RE SUCH A BAD ACTOR. BEST TAKE YOUR EFFORTS. ITS NOT THAT CONVINCING. ITS SO SELF DEFEATING...

8.7.2009
1
2
3
SANDRA
DEB
CONNIE
ON MY WALK I FOUND THREE COOL ACORNS. THEY LOOK LIKE THREE SISTERS... I ALSO FOUND SIAMESE TWIN ACORNS BUT ONE BROKE AWAY.
MAYBE SOMEDAY SOMEONE WILL GET ME AN AUTHENTIC WWII HELMET....
OH MAN...
I WOULD ♥
HELLO, EBAY...
MEDICINE FRIDAY!!
WITH CAT & REUBEN!
① SHANGHAI TUNNEL HAPPY HOUR!
② SUSHILAND!! ♥
③ BEN AND JERRYS!
COFFEE ICE CREAM!
THEN I WENT TO A SHOW OF A BAND I DIDN'T KNOW AND SCOOTED HOME. FOR THE MOST PART IT WAS ONE OF THE BEST MEDICINE FRIDAYS!
I RAZOR SCOOTED MY WAY HOME FROM THE BAR DRUNK AND WAS KICKING SOME SERIOUS ASS. FEELING CONFIDENT, I ATTEMPT A TRICK FOR THE FIRST TIME IN THE GRASS BY THE HIGHWAY ONRAMP (I'M SO COOL! NOT!) AND FAILED EPICALLY. HIT MY LEG... IT WAS OUCH.
SWING!!
PAIN!

8.8.2009

TODAY WAS A FUN FUN DRAW DAY.

FIRST DRAW GROUP WITH ANGIE W. AND TALLY ♡
MY FAVORITE PART WAS DISCUSSING STUMPTOWN PLANS!

THEN THE THREE OF US WENT TO DRINK AND DRAW. WHICH WAS TONS OF FUN! I ATE ONE OF THE BEST BURGERS EVER!!
PBR ↑ ...EW
SO GOOD! NO JOKE!
TAKE A REST, WHITE HEART. YOU BEEN THROUGH ALOT THE PAST TWO YEARS. I'LL TAKE CARE OF THINGS!
I NEED TO GO TO GOODWI
AND GET FRAMES....
I NEED TO JUST
BE HAPPY

8.9.2009

BOUGHT THE COMIC EVERYONE HAS BEEN TALKING ABOUT. LITTLE PRICEY BUT I DON'T REMEMBER THE LAST BOOK I BOUGHT! ITS DUE TIME TO TREAT MYSELF.

ASTERIOS POLYP BY DAVID MAZZUCHELLI

ALSO BOUGHT 2 PACKS OF INK CARTRIDGES FOR MY BELOVED BRUSH PEN... AND A NEW SKETCH BOOK FOR EMITOWN! AUG. 7 WAS THE LAST PAGE OF THE THIRD BOOK! THIS IS THE FOURTH! I'VE NEVER IN MY ENTIRE LIFE FILLED THREE WHOLE SKETCHBOOKS BEFORE.

"EXPECTATIONS LEAD TO DISAPPOINTMENT, SOCRATES. THATS WHY I TRY NOT TO HAVE THEM" -BRISCO COUNTY JR.

I HAVE SOME OPPORTUNITIES POP UP WHICH I REALLY SHOULD TRY FOR TO DO A FULL COMIC... BUT I FEEL SO UNINSPIRED... I CAN'T THINK UP ANY STORIES! UGH... I WISH I DIDN'T HAVE A DAY JOB... I'D HAVE MORE TIME TO DO COMIC THINGS...

8.10.2009

COMIC IDEA Birthing....

LIVE!!

CRACK!

MUST NURTURE SO IT GROWS INTO SOMETHING DECENT!!

OH SHIT... THAT WAS GOOD.

ASTERIOS POLYP

I WEAR THIS DRESS... I THINK IT LOOKS LIKE A SLIP

IT'S NOT!!

FINISHED ASTERIOS POLYP... I DON'T REMEMBER WHEN A COMIC MOVED ME SO MUCH... IT HAS BEEN AWHILE... BUT THIS IS WHAT I LIVE FOR IN REGARDS TO COMICS. AHH! I CAN'T GET OVER IT.

BEAR NIGHTMARES ARE BACK. THEY STARTED TWO OR THREE YEARS AGO. BEAR ALWAYS SINGLES ME OUT AND KILLS ME... LAST ONE I HAD WAS LAST YEAR I THINK AND FOR THE FIRST TIME THEY JUST LEFT ME ALONE... UNTIL LAST NIGHT! IN MY DREAMS I'VE LEARNED TO SENSE WHEN THEY COME... THIS TIME I FOUND A HIDING SPOT IN SOME ROCKS BUT HAD NO TIME TO WARN THIS GIRL AND SHE WAS ATTACKED... I HEARD IT FROM MY HIDING SPOT. WHAT IS DIFFERENT IS THE BEAR DIDN'T GET ME THIS TIME... OH GOD, I HOPE THE BEAR DREAMS AREN'T GONNA BE A REGULAR THING AGAIN.

I WON'T PRETEND THAT I CAN SEE THE END BUT ITS FAR AWAY. ITS IN THE DISTANCE.

DENTIST SAYS THE WISDOM TEETH AND THE BABY HAVE TO GO!!!

SO I EAT OUT TO FEEL BETTER...

BETWEEN KAIZER AND PORTLAND I GET FOOD... A BLT & T TO BE EXACT. I RELAX WITH A BOOK IN A SHABBY BAR AND GRILL IN WILSONVILLE ...NO BEER THO...

8.12.2009
GOAL FOR MY DAY OFF FRIDAY. GET HAIR CUT... TRIM AND LAYER PLEASE
SNIP SNIP
LONG HAIR
YOU ARE NOT HELPFUL. JUST STOP PLZ...
IT RAINS IN PORTLAND... IT'S A NICE CHANGE OF PACE... AH, RAIN. ♥
DO YOU THINK YOU'LL SURVIVE. YOU'RE A FOOL KID, THEY'LL EAT YOU ALIVE. WHEN YOU'RE LONELY, THEY COME OUT AT NIGHT WITH THOSE FANGS.
CREAM
DECAF
REG COFFEE
I FIGURED OUT I CAN DRINK COFFEE! I CAN STILL FEEL IT BUT NOT TO THE POINT WHERE IT DESTROYS MY MIND AND LIFE.
SO SMART
KINDA...

THIS HAPPENED TO ME TODAY... WELL... IT HAPPENS OFTEN... I DON'T KNOW IF ITS MY HEARING OR IF I HAVE **THAT** BAD OF AN ATTENTION SPAN...

8.14.2009

HAIR
↖ BOUGHT A SCARF...
SO PRETTY! DARK GREEN,
BLUE, AND PLUM. SCORE!

CUT!
HAIR CUT ACCOMPLISHED!
– $30.00

AT SKETCH GROUP TODAY, I GOT AN ITALIAN SODA! I HAVEN'T HAD ONE FOR A LONG TIME! THEY ARE SO GOOD! AND THEY DON'T DESTROY MY LIFE LIKE COFFEE DOES.

IS IT LIKE IN THE MOVIES?
SORORITY GIRL →
TALLY SAID SHE'D TAKE ME TO A FRAT PARTY SOMEDAY. OMG HOW FUNNY WOULD THAT BE?! WILL I HAVE THAT LIFE EXPERIENCE?! BEER BONG!!!!

THEN I WENT TO MEDICINE FRIDA
AND A SHELTER RED SHOW AT
THE ASH ST... MUCH DRINKING...

PERHAPS TOO MUCH? UGH.

8.15.2009

HAD TO WALK ALL THE WAY TO ASH ST. TO GET MY FORGOTTEN DEBIT CARD. ON THE WAY, I SAW TWO PEOPLE DRESSED AS WALDO...
WHAT THE HECK IS UP WITH THAT?!

TREATED MYSELF TO SUSHI AT SUSHILAND BUT I WAS SO HUNGOVER I ONLY ATE THREE PLATES... BUT I WAS THERE FOR LIKE AN HOUR... IT AT LEAST FELT LIKE AN HOUR...

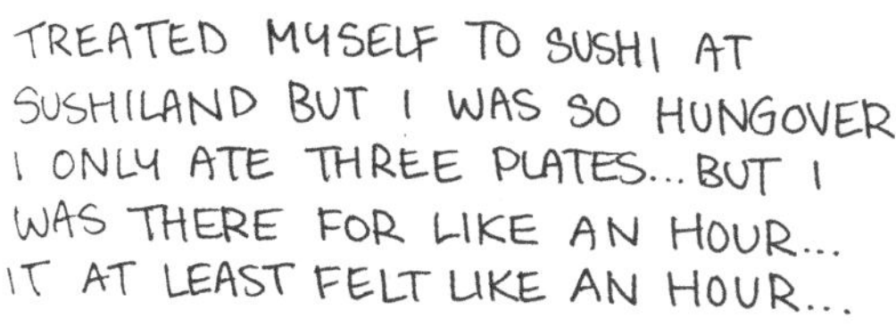

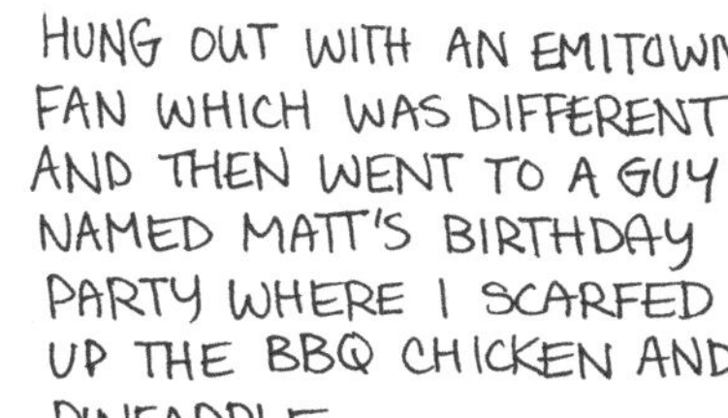

I AM MOVED BY NO ONE AND NO ONE MOVES ME.

HUNG OUT WITH AN EMITOWN FAN WHICH WAS DIFFERENT AND THEN WENT TO A GUY NAMED MATT'S BIRTHDAY PARTY WHERE I SCARFED UP THE BBQ CHICKEN AND PINEAPPLE.

QUESTION

SONG: "FUNK DAT" SAGAT

AND ALL I CAN THINK ABOUT IS SOME WEIRD SONG MATT WOULDN'T STOP REPEATING

QUESTION

8.16.2009

I SLEPT UNTIL NOON TODAY WHICH I HAVEN'T DONE IN A LONG LONG TIME... I GUESS THATS WHAT HAPPENS WHEN YOU'RE UP TIL 3AM

WE ALL HAVE A DARK SIDE THAT IS OURS AND OURS ALONE.

8.17.2009

ON ONE LEVEL BECAUSE OF WHERE I WORK...

I JUST WANT TO BE THE WORLD'S BEST ME... BUT I DON'T FEEL LIKE I HAVE BEEN LATELY... THAT SUX. WHAT DO I DO?

I FEEL A BIT DISAPPOINTED IN MYSELF

I PUT EXTENDED COVERAGE ON SEMI TRUCKS...

WHAT?! WHY?!!

I FEEL ASHAMED TO TELL MY ART FRIENDS WHERE I WORK... I KNOW I DON'T BELONG AT THIS JOB... THEY ARE ALWAYS SURPRISED TO FIND OUT MY JOB IS NEITHER WITH COMICS OR EVEN CREATIVE... I WANT OUT OF HERE SO BAD BUT I FEEL STUCK... WHAT TO DO... WHAT TO DO... PLUS THIS JOB EATS UP SO MUCH TIME THAT I COULD BE USING CREATIVELY... UGH...

PICK YOUR BATTLES CAREFULLY CAUSE THEY'LL HUNT YOU WHEN THEY THINK YOU'VE GONE TO SLEEP. AND THEY'LL TEAR AWAY YOUR HEART IF THEY CAN.

8.18.2009
EMITOWN
SCREW YOU REAL LIFE... I GOT MY DAYDREAMS...
AND I'M DAMN GOOD AT DAYDREAMING!!
JUST DO WHAT YA GOTTA DO, EMS.
AT WORK THEY ARE MOVING ME TO THE FRONT DESK BY THE RECEPTIONIST. I WILL DO MY USUAL WORK PLUS BE BACKUP TO ANSWER CALLS...
UGH... IT COULD BE LIKE THE PREZ OF THE COMPANY CALLING...
HARRO? DAIMLER...
IT WILL BE WEIRD TO HAVE TO TALK TO PEOPLE AGAIN...
I MAY GET TO BE IN
POPGUN 5 ANTHOLOGY!
I CAN DO IT!

SO... I'M BACK ON FULL TILT POKER... I HAVEN'T BEEN ON FOR 2 YEARS OR SO... I DON'T PLAY REAL MONEY BUT I FORGOT HOW FUN IT IS... MAYBE... NO! NEVERMIND

8.20.2005

A DRUNK GUY CALLED JAMESTOWN'S DOG STUPID TO HER FACE SO NATURALLY I REACTED AND SAID "YOU'RE STUPID... WITH YOUR STUPID SUNGLASSES, STUPID SHIRT, AND ABNORMALLY SMALL FEET." HE THEN SAID "WELL... YOU'RE A GOOK"... JAMESTOWN LOST HER MIND AND I SHOT BACK "THATS NOT EVEN THE RIGHT RACIAL SLUR, THATS HOW STUPID YOU ARE!" AS HE WALKED AWAY... I DON'T GET THOSE COMMENTS OFTEN BUT SOMETIMES THEY DO HAPPEN... FIRST TIME IT WAS A YOUNGER GUY THO... HMMMPH!

R.I.P
EMI L.
1983 ~ 2043 ISH
HAD A CAT NAMED WEENIE WHO IS ALSO DEAD... LIVED AWESOMELY! ROCK!

MY FRIEND CARRIE READ MY PALM AND SAID I'LL LIVE TO 60 ~ 65... COOL... IT COULD CHANGE THO.

SAW LEIGH AND CHECKED OUT THE PANDER BROS TASTY BULLET BOOK RELEASE AND KARAOKE PARTY AT VOICEBOX. HAD A DRINK, SANG A SONG, AND DIDN'T WIN THE RAFFLE...

8. 21. 2009
GOT A REAL COFFEE FROM MY NEIGHBORHOOD COFFEE PLACE:
COFFEE HOUSE NORTH-WEST
OH AND A CARROT AND ZUCHINNI BREAD THINGIE.
YUM!
THESE DAYS AT WORK ALL I DO IS WATCH THE CLOCK TICK BY... THOUGH THE COMPUTER CLOCK DOESN'T EXACTLY TICK... OR TOCKS...
THIS IS MY JOB LIFE...
3:59
RON
CAT!
TALLY
MATT
PARTY!
PARTY AT RON'S!
HAD SANGRIA AMONG OTHER DELISH DRINKS.
LIMBED A PUNCHING BAG THINGIE AND
RAN IN CIRCLES ON THE FLOOR-ALA-HOMER.

8.22.2005
I HATE BEARS.
GAVE BEN HIS SHIRT I GOT FOR HIM FROM SDCC. HAVEN'T SEEN HIM SINCE HIS BIRTHDAY. IT WAS NICE CATCHING UP... EVEN IF THE TIME WAS SHORT.
HUNG OUT WITH DOOX AND JAMESTOWN AT SILVER DOLLAR... THEN MATADOR... THEN MARATHON.
THE MOON IS CLOSER TO THE SUN THAN I AM TO ANYONE...

8.23.2009
GOSSIP GIRL...
I WAS SO INCREDIBLY HUNGOVER... HAVEN'T BEEN LIKE THIS SINCE MY BIRTHDAY. ACTUALLY MADE A HAM AND CHEESE SANDWICH... I DON'T EVEN LIKE SANDWICHES THAT MUCH. MISSED SKETCH GROUP AND STAYED IN BED UNTIL I HAD TO GO TO DINNER WITH THE TOPSHELF FOLKS AT 5:30.
BRYAN'S BOWL. BEANS, CHIX, RICE, GUAC, YUM.
TORTILLAS (FLOUR)
GOT FREE DIN AT PORQUE NO MEXICAN RESTAURANT. YUMMM! THANKS TOP SHELF!
BRETT WARNOCK
JEN VAUGHN
CHRIS ROSS
AFTER THE YUM YUM FOOD BRETT TREATED US TO SOME FANTASTIC COCKTAILS! THEY WERE SO DELISH I WISH HE'D HAVE PARTIES MORE OFTEN!... THAT I COULD COME TO!

8.24.200
SO WHAT IF I'M SHUT DOWN?
ZZZZZZ
SO TIRED
SLEEP W
BE
AWESON
TONIGH
!
I VERB YELLOWBALL
THIS RUBBER BRACELET WAS ON MY KEYBOARD WHEN I CAME INTO WORK... WTF IS "VERB YELLOWBALL"?!!
PEAS
CARROT
TORTILLA CHIPS
TONIGHT:
I HAD A SANDWICH FOR DIN. ITS WEIRD... BUT IT WAS REALLY YUMMY WITH HAM, CHEESE, AND AVOCA
TOMATOES

8.25.2009

SOME SAY THAT WHEN IT RAINS, PARTS OF YOUR BODY ACHES WHERE YOU HAD PREVIOUS INJURIES...
OR IS IT WHEN YOU BREAK A BONE?
WHATEVER. MY SCAR HURTS.
I EAT
Yoplait
Light
YOGURT...

THINKIN... MAYBE I SHOULD AT LEAST TRY...

BACK AT SEA:

THESE ONES JUST JUMPED IN!

THOSE DO NOT INTEREST ME...

THINKING OF APPLYING FOR THE XERIC GRANT... IF YOU GET IT, THEY HELP PAY THE COST TO SELF-PUBLISH YOUR COMIC... APPLICATIONS ARE DUE SEPT. 30... I'M GONNA NEED HELP ON THE NUMBERS! ACK! NUMBERS...

LETS JUST FLOAT FOR WHILE...

8.26.2009
DON'T ASSAULT OR RAPE ME, PLEASE.
ALL OVER THE LOCAL NEWS IS A STORY ABOUT A GUY WHO HAS BEEN ASSAULTING GIRLS AND ATTEMPTING TO RAPE THEM IN THE NORTHWEST PORTLAND AREA! MY NEIGHBORHOOD! THE FEAR... I HOPE THEY CATCH HIM BY THIS WEEKEND...
I CARE ABOUT PEACE OF MIND... I CARRY A KNIFE... BUT REALLY... I DOUBT IN THE MOMENT IT WOULD DO ANY GOOD... I SHOULD INVEST IN SOME PEPPERSPRAY FOR JAMESTOWN AND I.
GIGGLE...
THE FRIDAY AFTER NEXT, JAMESTOWN AND I ARE GONNA INFILTRATE THE AGENCY... I'VE BEEN WANTING TO DO THIS AND PEOPLE WATCH... ITS GOING TO BE SO FUNNY... OMG. I HOPE THERE ARE GUYS IN BUTTON DOWN COLLARED SHIRTS... *DROOL* AND TIE? *DOUBLE DROOL* MAYBE NOT...
ME? GO TO UFC?
I'M-A-GOIN TO A UFC FIGHT ON SATURDAY AT THE ROSE GARDEN... I'VE ONLY BEEN THERE FOR GRADUATION AND TONY HAWK.
ROSE GARDE
NOT BOXING
BUT I'M SURE I'LL GET WAY INTO IT!

T.O.S. INSPECTION

8.27.2009

WHERE IS THE LABEL MAKER?!
PUT AWAY THOSE BOXES...

SO EVERYONE WAS SCRAMBLING AROUND BECAUSE THERE WAS GOING TO BE A TOS INSPECTION. I HAD NO CLUE WHAT THAT WAS AND FEARED IF I WAS INVOLVED IN IT. WHICH I WAS... BUT IT DIDN'T SEEM LIKE **THAT** BIG OF A DEAL. A CO-WORKER FROM UPSTAIRS DID THIS QUICK SEEMING GLANCE AT EVERYTHING AND SCRIBBLE ON HIS CLIPBOARD... MEH... I STILL DID GOOD I THINK.

I AM FINE, OK

4!

8.28.2009

HELPED MY FRIEND CAT BY DOING KID VOICES FOR AN EDUCATIONAL ANIMATION... "HOW MANY?"

"FOUR!"

GOT KICK-ASS ART FROM MY SKETCH GROUP BUDS ANGIE WANG AND NATALIE (TALLY) NOURIGAT!! ♡

THE BEST PART?

THEY BOTH DREW THEIR VERSIONS OF OCEAN GIRL!

AFTER MEDICINE FRIDAY WITH CAT, RON, AND TALLY, I RAN INTO DANNY AT THE MATADOR. HE WAS GOING TO SOME BAR CALLED DEPARTURE AT THE NINES HOTEL DOWNTOWN. I HAPPILY WENT WITH HOPES OF SEEING DRESSED UP GUYS.

HELLOOO NURSE!!!
MY WEAKNESS... IT CANNOT BE HELPED.

8.29.2009
BLOOD!
I WAS TOLD THERE WOULD BE BLOOD AT THE UFC FIGHT... IF THERE WAS I MISSED IT...
THEREPROBABLY WAS....
DRUNK SCOOTER CRASH
PAIN... PRIDE HURT...
ENDED UP AT THE ITALIAN FESTIVAL WHERE IN SEEMING SECONDS I LOSE MY PHONE. LOOKED FOR AN HOUR AND FINALLY A LADY I HAD SPOKEN TO MULTIPLE TIMES PULLED IT OUT OF HER PURSE! SHE HAD IT THE WHOLE TIME! AN HOUR WASTED! PFFT...
LOST
M
LOST MY KEYS AGAIN
MY FOOL PROOF ANTI-LOSE STAR CLIP FAILED ME!
(I KNOW SHE HAD IT THE WHOLE TIME CAUSE SHE CALLED MY PARENTS AT 11pm...WELL...SHE HAD IT FOR HALF OF THE HOUR I SPENT LOOKIN')
DANG IT

8.30.2009

I MEAN IT WAS GOOD AND FUN BUT THAT WASN'T QUITE PART OF THE PLAN... DANG IT.

CALL ROSE GARDEN FOR KEYS. CLOSED UNTIL MONDAY!!

AURGH!

HAD A YUMMY CROISSANT AND HAM SAMMICH THING AT A PLACE I DON'T KNOW...

BUT IT WAS YUM!

I TELL JAMESTOWN MY ADVENTURE. SHE RIGHTLY DISAPPROVES. I'M SO LUCKY TO HAVE A FRIEND LIKE HER TO TELL ME WHATS WHAT, BE IT GOOD OR BAD.

8.31.2009

HMMPH.
I AM NOT A COMPLETELY UNREASONABLE PERSON... I'M NOT SORRY FOR MY FEELINGS BECAUSE IT IS HOW I FEEL. I SIMPLY DO NOT HAVE THE ABILITY TO HOLD IN THINGS THAT BOTHER ME...
BUT... I AM STUBBORN
AND I'M NOT SAYING I'M PROUD OF THAT... BUT I DO TRY TO SEE BOTH SIDES TO EVERYTHING...
I AM CONVINCED I MESSED UP MY CHERRY TOMATOES... THEY HAVE PRODUCED ME NOTHING! THEY ARE SUCH A HASSLE TO WATER TWICE A DAY AND THEY GIVE BACK NO LOVE!! BOO!
KEYS FOUND
MISS ME?
YES!

SEPTEMBER 2009

9/1 "IT'S A WONDERFUL LIFE"
-SPARKLEHORSE
9/26 "DRESS ME LIKE A CLOWN"
-MARGOT & THE NUCLEAR SO & SO'S

9.1.2009
OKAY...
I KNOW BANDAIDS ARE SUPPOSED TO KEEP INJURIES FROM GETTING INFECTED...BUT ISN'T IT GOOD TO NOT HAVE ONE SO THAT IT COULD SCAB OVER? THE BODY'S NATURAL BANDAID? WITH A BANDAID ON, IT JUST STAYS MOIST (EW...THE WORD "MOIST") AND CAN'T SCAB OVER... I'VE THOUGHT ABOUT THIS BEFORE...
MY INJURY FROM DRUNK SCOOTER FALL. NICELY SCABBED OVER. AND SHINY!
IT IS TIME, SOLDIER TO CHANGE UP THE STRAGETY
I'M A BOG WITH POISON FROGS

9.02.200

THIS MORNING WHEN I GOT TO MY CAR THERE WAS A NAPKIN UNDER MY WINDSHIELD WIPER THAT SOMEONE WROTE "I'M SORRY..." WHO LEFT IT? WHY ARE THEY SORRY? WAS IT MISTAKENLY PUT ON MY CAR?

ON THE MYSTERY.

I'M SORRY...

YIKES! I HOPE THESE BRUISES ARE GONE BY FRIDAY. I WAS GONNA WEAR A SLEEVELESS DRESS FOR JAMESTOWN/EMITOWN'S NIGHT OF FUN! I DON'T WANT TO LOOK LIKE A DOMESTIC ABUSE VICTIM!

I MISS U...

I HATE TO ADMIT IT... BUT WAKE UP... COME BACK... I NEED YOU..... I'M NOT ME WITHOUT YOU... WE ARE BEST AS A TEAM TOGETHER

ITS HARD TO BE BLACKHEARTED ALL THE TIME... I CAN'T DO IT... IT JUST AIN'T ME...

SAW ON TWITTER

THAT FLOATING WORLD COMICS RECIEVED COPIES OF JAMES JEAN'S

PROCESS RECESS 3

OH GOD... MUST HAVE!!

9.3.2009
MISSING
PENTEL POCKET BRUSH PEN... PLEASE CALL!!
HOW DID I LET THIS HAPPEN?!!
I SOMEHOW LOST MY BELOVED PENTEL POCKET BRUSH PEN...
IT WAS AN INCREDIBLY SAD MOMENT WHEN I SAW ITS ABSENCE
IN MY PEN CASE. I FEEL LIKE I'M MISSING A LIMB...
DO NOT KNOCK IT UNTIL YOU'VE TRIED IT
VOODOO DONUT'S BACON MAPLE BAR! YUM!!
LATELY, I'VE BEEN WAKING UP IN A TIGHTLY WRAPPED BLANKET BURRITO. I TURN INTO AN EMI BURRITO IN MY SLEEP

EMITOWN AND JAMESTOWN'S NIGHT OF FUN!

9.4.2009

WE START AT MY PLACE WHERE WE EACH HAVE 2 VODKA DRINKS. SAT ON THE FIRE ESCAPE AND CHIT CHATTED!

DID GO TO THE AGENCY BUT IT WAS PRETTY DARN LAME... WE **DID** HAVE SOME GOOD LAUGHS THERE THOUGH...

THEN WE TOOK SOMEONE'S ADVICE AND WENT TO A PLACE CALLED CANDY...

SOME PARTY PEEPS GAVE US A RIDE IN A LIMO DOWNTOWN! WE GOT TWO FREE SESSION BEERS! GOOD JOB!

AT CANDY, THERE WAS SOME SERIOUS D-BAG ACTION. ONE TOLD ME HE WAS A LAWYER LIKE THAT WAS SUPPOSED TO MAKE ME SWOON. IT WAS FUN... WE (JAMESTOWN AND I) DANCED AND SUCH...

OH YEAH... THERE WAS VIDEO POKER AT THE MARATHON **PARTY!**

ENDED THE NIGHT AT DEPARTURE BUT GOT THERE TOO LATE. IT WAS STILL NICE TO SIT AND GO OVER OUR EVENING.

WENT TO THE STEPPING STONE WITH JAMESTOWN FOR BREAKFAST
I HAD A DELISH BELGIAN WAFFLE WITH FRESH STRAWBERRIES ON TOP!

HUNG OUT AT JAMESTOWN'S
AND WATCHED AN EPISODE OF HOUSE...
I THOUGHT IT WAS THE PSP... IT WASN'T...
IT WAS THE SAND...

I STARTED GETTING REALLY STRANGE TEXTS FROM AN EX... HE MUST OF BEEN DRUNK... IT WAS NOT PLEASANT... AT ONE POINT, I THOUGHT SOMEONE IS PLAYING A MEAN TRICK...

let it go

WENT TO GET COFFEE WHICH LATER TURNED INTO BEERS WHEN IT STARTED TO RAIN BIGGIE TIME. DIDN'T WANT TO WALK IN THE RAIN SO WE WAITED IT OUT AT A BAR. DRINKING AT NOON? THATS NORMAL! NO, WAIT! IT WAS JUST ONE! WHATEVER...

GOT A CALL FROM THE OL' EX ABOUT LAST NIGHT. HE APOLOGIZED FOR THE DRUNK TEXTS AND FOR HOW OUR RELATIONSHIP HAD ENDED. I REALLY APPRECIATE THAT... ITS BEEN SEVEN MONTHS BUT AGAIN, STILL APPRECIATED... BUT THINGS WILL NEVER BE THE SAME. SORRY.

MYSTERY SOLVED!

-OH! AND HE WAS THE ONE THAT LEFT THE "I'M SORRY" NOTE ON MY CAR!

BEST THING: WATCHING A MOVIE ON YOUR LAPTOP WHILE TAKING A HOT BATH ON A RAINY DAY! ♡

FALL IS HERE I FEAR

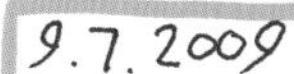
9.7.2009

DEATH HOWL
SNIP!
FINALLY TRIMMED HENRY'S NAILS... HE HATES IT SO MUCH... HE BARKS, WHINES, AND HOWLS... IT SOUNDS LIKE I'M MURDERING MY OWN DOG... JEEZ. MY BROTHER HAD TO HELP HOLD HIM STILL...
WENT TO PARENTS FOR LABOR DAY FAMILY LUNCH.
HOMEMADE SUSHI!
BBQ CHICKEN!

UNCE UNCE UNCE
HA
HA
HA
HA
HA
IT WAS THEIR SOCCER BALL TOO BTW...
AT SILVER DOLLAR A CAR BLASTING SOME RAVE TECHNO WAS WAITING AT A RED LIGHT... THERE WAS FOUR BALDING TRENDY MIDDLE AGED GUYS INSIDE AND ONE SUDDENLY JUMPED OUT AND KICKED A SOCCER BALL IN THE STREET AND JUMPED BACK IN. I FELT LIKE I WAS IN EUROPE OR SOMETHING.

LAUNDRY
COMPLETED
GO ME!

9.8.2009
$409.00
- 200.00 RENT
- 75.00 CC
$134.00
- 35.00 PGE
$99.00
WENT TO THE PARTS RETURN SECTION OF THE BUILDING AT WORK CAUSE THATS WHERE THE VENDING MACHINES ARE AND THE DUDES THERE LET ME HAVE COFFEE... EVEN SUPPLIED ME WITH A MUG! THEY EVEN BAKE FRESH BREAD THERE!! SHIT... I WANNA WORK IN THAT AREA!
MONEY IS KICKING MY ASS LATELY..
Yum!
WHEN LIFE GIVES YOU LEMONS, MAKE LEMONADE! OR LEMON SQUARES! THERE ARE TONS OF BUMPS IN LIFE... WITHOUT THE HARD WORK GETTING OVER THEM, YOU WOULDN'T GET ANYWHERE! I SINCERELY HAVE NO DOUBT THAT EVERY THING WILL BE
A-OKAY!
CAN WE JUST TAKE A MOMENT AND SHAKE OUR FISTS TO THE SELFISH JERKS IN THE WORLD? DON'T MESS WITH THE ONES I
LOVE.

9.9.2009

ERMM..

AARGH... NOTHING EXCITING HAPPENED TODAY... I WILL NOT DRAW ABOUT BURRITOS...OR FOOD... OR... BEER...

AND I'M GETTING IRED OF THE LAY-UT... I NEED TO FIGURE OUT A WAY TO AMP THIS UP SO I'M NOT BORED

TOMORROW I'LL GET A BREAK-FAST BURRITO!

9.10.2009
FINALLY DID THE DISHES. THE SMELL WAS TOXIC.
BUT I DID IT!
GOING TO THE MARATHON TO SAY HI TO BRIT AND THE GANG... FEELS LIKE FOREVER SINCE I'VE HUNG OUT WITH THEM! I MISS THEM!
I'm starting to feel like me again and it feels refreshing...

NOTICE!!
SO BIG
PICK UP!
ITS LIKE THE FEATHER TO THE MOTHERSHIP CROW...
YES... MY PA DID TEACH ME NOT PICK UP FEATHERS BECAUSE OF DISEASE...
BUT I AM PART NATIVE AMERICAN... I AM A GATHERER BY BLOOD...
I ALSO PICK UP SHINY THINGS UP FROM THE GROUND AND STARTED A
JAR WHERE I PUT EVERYTHING I FIND INTO. A JAR OF TREASURE.
MUST REMEMBER TO URN IN WONDER WOMAN PIECE TODAY
TO DO...
• POPGUN COMIC
• SWEET TOOTH ART
• DESIGN E.T.
-PROMOCARDS #2
-BOOKMARKS
-BUTTONS -B12 CARDS
-POSTCARDS
• RESEARCH PRINTERS
• PERU INTERVIEW
• TOP SHELF WIKIPEDIA
• JAMIE'S PRESENT
• E.T CARDBOARD CUT OUTS
GOT SWEET TOOTH BY JEFF LEMIRE... JAMIE RICH BOUGHT IT FOR ME SINCE I'M A FOOL WHO DOESN'T CARRY DOLLARS... THNX!
SWEET TOOTH
#1
OUR WEAKNESS IS THE SAME, WE NEED POISON SOMETIMES, SO COME HAVE A DRINK WITH ME...
MEDICINE FRIDAY... START!

9.12.2009

HEY! WHAT TIME IS IT?
ITS 9:15...

IT WAS A RHETORICAL QUESTION!

THERE WERE ALL THESE COSTUMED PEOPLE WANDERING ABOUT AND WHEN ASKED WHY, THIS GROUP WAS VERY RUDE... THEY ASKED WHAT TIME IT WAS AND WHEN WE RESPONDED THEY SNORTED " IT WAS A RHETORICAL QUESTION!" THEN LAUGHED AND LEFT.

....

WE FINALLY FIND OUT FROM NICE PEOPLE THAT THEY ARE TIME TRAVELERS. SO THE NEXT GROUP OF THESE "TRAVELER THAT CAME BY. I ASKED THEM WHAT TIME IT WAS.

I AM THE WINNER!
ONLY BY TEN POINTS...
2ND
HMMPH

PLAYED A CARD GAME CALLED WIZARD WITH JAMESTOWN, DOOX, AND DANNY... ITS LIKE HEARTS BUT WITH... WIZARDS... WE GET VERY COMPETATIVE

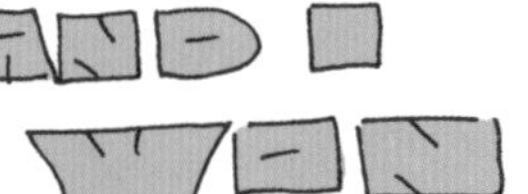
AND I

WON!

ITS BEEN AWHILE SINCE I'VE WON... AND YES, I REALLY DID STAND ON THE TABLE TO GLOAT TO THE MAXIMUM CAPACITY...

9.13.2009
ZZ
ZZ
I SLEPT SO MUCH TODAY... DON'T KNOW WHY... I DIDN'T EVEN GET THAT DRUNK AT ALL... ONLY THREE BEERS ALL NIGHT... MUST HAVE BEEN EXHAUSTED FROM THE WEEK...
JUST DON'T FEEL LIKE DRAWIN'!
BECAUSE I DIDN'T FEEL LIKE DRINKIN MY BEER AND POURED IT INTO JAMESTOWN'S GLASS, I ACCIDENTALLY GOT HER DRUNK!
Pour

9.14.200

BROUGHT A LUNCH TODAY AND EVEN THOUGH I TRIED NOT TO GET A BREAKFAST BURRITO... I WENT TO GET A BAGEL!!... I STILL GOT ONE...

CURSES

ONE A WEEK... I CAN DO IT!!

OK... YOU TWO COME WITH ME TO HELP SCOUT OUT THE SITUATION...

WAIT...

LETS GET READY TO RUMBLE

9.15.2009
AT PETSMART I SAW THE CUTEST CAT... ITS CHART THING SAID:
"MY OWNER PASSED AWAY AND I'M CONFUSED WHY I AM HERE"
DARN IT PETSMART!
I TEARED UP A LITTLE... A LITTLE!
EW PEW
PEW PEW PEW!
TO RELEASE SOME COFFEE ENERGY, I TWIRLED IN MY CHAIR MAKING LAZER NOISES AS I SHOT WITH MY "HAND GUNS" WHEN NO ONE IS WATCHING OF COURSE... DON'T WANT PEOPLE TO THINK I'M WEIRD...
EMI L.
THERE WAS JETS GOING WHAT LOOKED LIKE STRAIGHT UP IN THE SKY. IT LOOKED LIKE ROCKET LAUNCHES LIKE IN GATTACA...
"IF YOU WANT TO LOOK LIKE YOU DON'T CARE, DON'T LOOK UP"

ROCKS!
9.16.2
MY DESK BUDDY BROUGHT IN ALL THESE ROCKS SHE FOUND IN IDAHO... I WANNA GO ROCK HUNTING SO BAD!
WHAT WAS THAT?
IT JUST CAME RIGHT UP...
WEIRD...
DON'T NET IT.. JUST KEEP AN EYE ON IT... SEE WHAT IT DOES. IF ANYTHING...

9.17.2009
MY TOOTH HURTS... MORE OVER, MY WISDOM TOOTH HURTS! I KNOW I NEED TO GET THEM REMOVED... I HAVEN'T MADE THE APP. YET...
I'M MEAN
MISTER TOOTH!
TGUK CONCERT
AFTER CHECKIN THE OL' FUNDS, I LEARN I SIMPLY CAN NOT GO TO THE GET UP KIDS SHOW ON SATURDAY... OH WELL...
DID U KNOW...
OCEANGIRL CAN'T SWIM? STRANGE, HUH. EMITOWN IS THAT WAY...

TODAY, MY METHOD TO RELEASE COFFEE ENERGY (BESIDES ABUSING TWITTER) WAS TO AIR JAM.

9.18.2009

"SATISFACTION GUARANTEED OR YOUR MONEY BACK"? I WANT MY MONEY BACK!!

HAD A CLOGGED BATHROOM SINK. FINALLY BOUGHT SOME DRAIN-O AND AFTER THE FIRST HALF OF THE BOTTLE IT WAS STILL CLOGGED... **BUT** AFTER THE SECOND HALF, IT WAS UNCLOGGED!! IT WAS AMAZING! I WAS SO IMPRESSED THAT I DID MY HAPPY DANCE.

WATCHED THE MAYWEATHER VS. MARQUEZ FIGHT... LIKE A CAT PLAYING WITH A DEAD MOUSE... WHY DIDN'T HE JUST KNOCK HIM OUT IN THE LAST ROUND?!

WATCHED TEEN WITCH WITH THE GANG THEN BED BY 12:30AM.

IT WAS A NICE NIGHT.

LAUGHTER + FUN FUN TIMES

WATCHED SUNDAY FOOTBALL WITH JAMESTOWN... I LEARNED SOME STUFF... THIS WAS QUITE A SPORTY WEEKEND... THATS STRANGE FOR ME...

MY WONDER WOMAN PIECE WAS CHOSEN TO BE IN THE GALLERY FOR FIRST THURSDAY! I'VE NEVER BEEN IN A GALLERY BEFORE! THE OPENING SHOULD BE FUN!

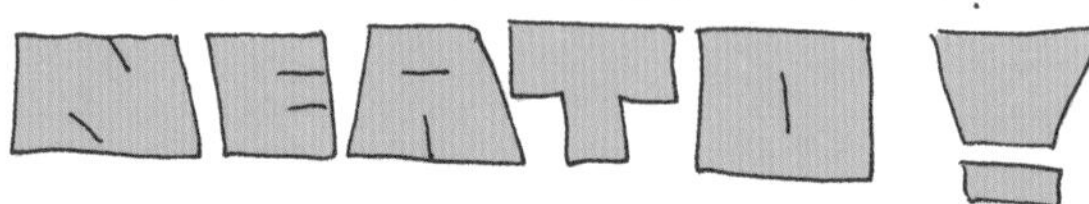

WALKED HENRY TO VISTA BRIDGE (SUICIDE BRIDGE) THEN THROUGH WASHINGTON PARK

ME!

9.21.2009
SHOPPING BUG HAS HIT AND NO MONEY TO CURE THE ITCH! BOOO!
I JUST DON'T GET IT... HOW WILL I GET ANY WHERE?
SO STUPID!!
SO WHY DO I KEEP PLAYING?
I DO NOT LIKE CONFUSION MUCH...
WAT ABOUT MEEEEE!
ON THE PACKWALKS WITH JAMESTOWN, I JUST DON'T FEEL LIKE BEER ANYMORE!

9.22.2009
GIVE ME A DAMN BREAK 90° WEATHER BE FALL NOW!!!
TOMORROW I MOVE IN THE OL' DRAFTING TABLE! ITS HUGE AND ITS GOING TO EAT UP SPACE IN MY APARTMENT BUT I REALLY NEED A DRAWING TABLE AND WORK SPACE!
SIGH...

9.23.2009
CHEESE BAGELS TOASTED WITH CREAM CHEESE HAVE BECOME MY NEW BREAKFAST ENEMY...
PRINCESS PEACH AGAIN)
2 NATIVE AMERICAN
3 GHOST!
WHAT TO BE FOR HALLOWEEN ?!

9.24.2009

DO YOU EVER FEEL STAGNANT IN LIFE? LIKE A LEAF ON A LAKE WITH NO CURRENT... WHICH CAN'T BE GOOD CAUSE THEN THE LAKE GETS ALL SICK AND GREEN AND GROSS... I NEED TO CHANGE THINGS UP!

I'M EVEN GETTING BORED OF MY ART... SOMETHING NEEDS TO CHANGE... I'M HOPING THE DRAFTING TABLE WILL HELP... I'M ALREADY TRYING TO DRAW PAGES AGAIN... STARTING WITH A NEW/OLD PERFECTING LONELINESS COMIC... I CAN! I HAVE TO GET OVER THIS HUMP!!

I LUB BEARS AND BEARS LUB ME...

LAST WEEK:

THE RIGHT SIDE WISDOM TOOTH HURTS!

THIS WEEK:

NOW THE LEFT SIDE HURTS INSTEAD!

MY WISDOM TEETH LIKE TO TAKE TURNS GIVING ME PAIN...

NOT!

SHOP!
9.25.2009
PILOT PRECISE V5 EXTRA FINE PENS ♥
POCKET BRUSH PEN CARTRIDGES
COMIC BOOK PAGE LAYOUT PAD!
COOL SQUARE SKETCH BOOK
HEELS FOR DRESS!
NEW FABLES TRADE
FABLES
UPTIGHT #3
I OWE HIM A DOLLAR!
STOPPED BY FLOATING WORLD TO SAY HI TO JAMIE RICH ON THE WAY TO MEDICINE FRIDAY. WHEN I GOT THERE, FOUND I FORGOT MY ID AND DEBIT CARD!
CHESTNUTS ARE FALLING FROM THE TREES! I GATHER ONE TO PUT IN MY COLLECTION JAR.
DALEETED!
LESSON LEARNED!
WISDOM: +1
WTF?!
EVER HAVE ONE OF THOSE DAYS WHERE YOU ARE REMINDED THAT PEOPLE EXIST WHO ARE MEAN AND CRUEL TO OTHERS AND YET FEEL NO REMORSE OR ERROR? FREAKS ME OUT!
THOUGH IT REMINDS TO ALWAYS TRY TO PUT MY BEST FOOT FORWARD AND SPREAD KINDNESS AND COMPASSION INSTEAD OF DARKNESS AND HURT.
IT'S NOT ALWAYS EASY BUT I TRY. DON'T WANT TO CONTRIBUTE TO WHAT MAKES THE WORLD A SHITTY PLACE. RATHER BE A PART OF WHAT MAKES IT WONDERFUL. ♥

9.26.2009
YOU ARE AN ASS
A SNAKE IN THE GRASS
VANITY SEEPS FROM OUT
YOUR PORES. AND MAYBE
ITS TIME TO PAY FOR
MY CRIME...
I DRAW COMIC
PAGE! ♡
WENT TO THE TEEN WITCH PARTY
WHERE I WAS CASTED AS KIKI.
DRESSED AS SUCH AND HAD A GOSH
DARN GOOD TIME
I LIKE
BOYS!

9.27.2009
THE LAZY DAY.
SNOOZE
....
NOTHING ACCOMPLISHED

9.28.20
DON'T HAVE MY ID OR MY DEBIT CARD. I DROVE ILLEGALLY!
ON THE EDGE, BABY, YEAH
NO COFFEE OR BURRITO TODAY...
OREGON

STORM A' BREWIN?

FEELS LIKE IT BUT NO RAIN... COME ON ALREADY!

9.29.2009
E
F
JAMESTOWN REQUESTS I PICK HER UP FROM THE AIR-PORT AT 5:10PM... PEAK TRAFFIC HOURS! HOPING I DON'T NEED TO GET GAS! HOPING TO HAVE ENOUGH UNTIL THURSDAY!
LET'S BE FRIENDS
I SAVE ZELDA
DAMMIT, GANON!
HOGWART'S OR BUST!

9. 30. 2009
I'M ACTUALLY ATTENDING A FIRST THURSDAY TOMORROW! I'LL ACTUALLY SEE MY DRAWING FRAMED IN A GALLERY! IT'S EXCITING TO ME! I'M GOING ON A WORK NIGHT... HAVE TO BE SURE TO GO EASY ON THE WINE...

OCTOBER 2009

10/5 "FLINT (FOR THE UNEMPLOYED AND UNDERPAID)"
-SUFJAN STEVENS
10/12 "BIG CASINO"
-JIMMY EAT WORLD
10/21 "ON MY WAY TO HELL"
-OLIVER

10.1.2009

PIDER ON MY DRAFTING TABLE!

GRAB NEAREST TISSUE-ESQUE ITEM!

SMASH!

ESTERDAY, A SPIDER (WORST) RAWLED/SKITTERED ACROSS MY RAFTING TABLE. I GRABBED PINK AJAMA (ONE OF MY MOST CHERISHED ITEMS) AND USED IT TO SQUISH HE SPIDER. I PANIC AND FRANTICALLY SHAKE PINK AND LUCKILY THE PIDER CARCASS FALLS OUT. OH PINK... I SORRY... I LUB U. WITH OR ITHOUT SPIDER RESIDUE.

BEEN CHILLY IN THE MORNINGS. TODAY, I NOTICED I COULD SEE MY BREATH AND LAST NIGHT WAS THE FIRST TIME I CLOSED MY WINDOWS WHEN I WENT TO BED.

24 HOUR COMIC CHALLENGE I LEARNED IS SATURDAY... DARE I MESS UP MY SLEEPING SCHEDULE AND DO IT? ALWAYS WANTED TO... HO HUM...

10.02.2009

MORE, PLZ?

DID YOU DRIVE? ...

WONDER WOMAN GALLERY OPENING WAS PRETTY FUN. TONS OF PEOPLE SHOWED UP! THANKS, FRIENDS! ♥

PAPER! WHAT KIND? HOW BIG?!

BRUSH, PEN!

RULER

INK?

INK

COMFORT ITEM

WHAT TO BRING TOMORROW FOR 24 HOUR COMIC DAY? I JUST DON'T WANT TO FORGET ANYTHING...

10.03.2009
ME
ANGIE WANG
Z
24 HR COMIC DAY
I ATE:
10AM BREAKFAST BURRITO... NOT AS GOOD AS THE KIND I GET AT WORK...
5PM GROSS VEGAN AVACADO WRAP
1PM NACHOS
1AM VOODOO DONUTS VODOO DONUT
I FINISHED THE COMIC AT 4AM. THATS 18 HOURS OF COMICKING!
I DID IT!
BUT WILL I DO IT AGAIN NEXT YEAR? I THINK NOT... BUT THEN AGAIN, I MAY!

10.04.2005
I WAS STILL TIRED WHEN I WOKE UP, I SCANNED THE COMIC IN BED... POSTED THEN SLEPT SOME MORE. HOUSE CHORES HAVE BEEN SORELY NEGLECTED.
TOO LAZY TO REALLY COOK (WHICH WOULD ALSO INVOLVE DOING THE DISHES) I MADE SOUP AND ATE WITH BREAD. THATS CANNED SOUP...
THE PAIN
IT WAS FUN AT FIRST...BUT BESIDES FATIGUE... WHY WOULD I EVER WANT TO TORTURE MY HAND AGAIN? POOR HAND... I CAN'T EVER LOSE YOU!

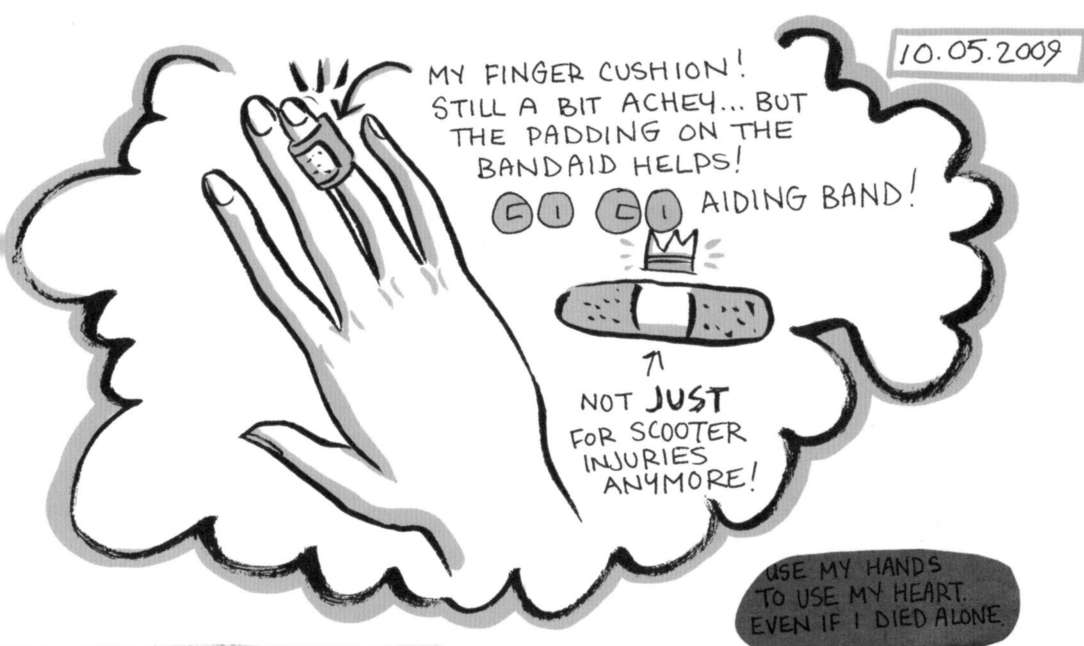

10.05.2009
MY FINGER CUSHION! STILL A BIT ACHEY... BUT THE PADDING ON THE BANDAID HELPS!
AIDING BAND!
NOT JUST FOR SCOOTER INJURIES ANYMORE!

I DUG UP AN OLD COMIC IDEA → FROM 2002 THAT I THOUGHT I'D WORK ON... BUT SOME ELEMENTS OF IT ARE SIMILAR TO A COMIC THAT JUST RECENTLY CAME OUT. DRAT! I'LL HAVE TO RETHINK CERTAIN ASPECTS... I WANT TO WORK ON THIS AND MY SUPERHERO STORY AS MY BIG PROJECTS... I CAN DO IT!!

USE MY HANDS TO USE MY HEART. EVEN IF I DIED ALONE.

SO I WAS LISTENING TO THE 'OL IPOD AT WORK WHEN A CERTAIN SONG TRIGGERED A MONTAGE OF MEMORIES. I REALIZED HOW MUCH TIME HAS PASSED AND HOW MUCH HAS CHANGED. HOW NOTHING WILL EVER BE LIKE HOW IT WAS... IT BROUGHT ME TO TEARS AT WORK. STUPID, I KNOW... ODD TOO... THEN I REALIZED. OH. I'M ON MY PERIOD... THAT EXPLAINS THIS... SHIT... I HATE BEING A GIRL SOMETIMES...

10.7.2009

EMI
CALL IN NOW

YESTERDAY, THERE WAS A LIVE PSYCHIC ON THE RADIO WHEN I DROVE HOME FROM WORK. YOU COULD CALL IN AND ASK A QUESTION... I THOUGHT ABOUT WHAT I'D ASK. BUT STUFF LIKE CAREER, LOVE, ETC SEEMED WAS ULTIMATELY UP TO ME ANYWAY... I WOULD HAVE TO ASK SOMETHING OUT OF MY CONTROL TO MAKE BEST USE OF MY ONE QUESTION... LIKE:

1. HOW WILL I DIE?
2. WHEN/HOW WILL THE WORLD END?
3. WILL I EVER SEE A GHOST OR ALIEN IN MY LIFETIME?

OH BOY
TODAY I GET INDESIGN! SO EXCITED!

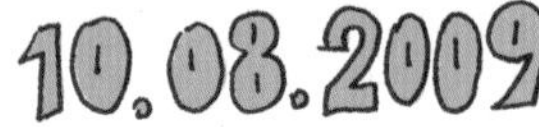

I THINK I NEED GLASSES... MY EYES GET SO BOTHERED LOOKING AT THE COMPUTER SCREEN... BUT ITS NOT WITH MY LAPTOP... IS IT JUST WORK OR IS IT MY EYES?! I SHOULD GET THEM CHECKED ANYWAY. ITS BEEN AWHILE... SINCE I WAS 12 OR SOMETHING.

I THINK I'D ONLY NEED THEM FOR THE COMPUTER. THEY WOULD BE ME 'PUTER GLASSES

WENT ON A DATE WHERE VIDEO GAMES, NATIVE AMERICAN GHOSTS, BIGFOOT, AND UFOs WERE DISCUSSED... IT WAS PRETTY FUN.

BIIIIIG FOOOOOOOT!!!

OH, SWEET POOP STICKS... THIS HURTS

10.08.08 ↓ 01.09.09

TODAY I HAVE BEEN DRAWING EMITOW

FOR 1 YEAR!

SO I READ THE FIRST BOOK I COMPLETED AND IT WAS A LITTLE PAINFUL... IT WAS MORE PERSONAL (WHY ITS NOT ONLINE!) AND THE DRAWINGS SHITTIER... I STILL THINK I'D PRINT IT OUT TO SELL SPECIALLY AT CONS... IN ONE YEAR I'VE COMPLETED 3 AND A HALF SKETCHBOOKS.

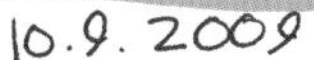

WENT TO KAIZER TO PICK UP MY MAGIC PILLS AND DID MY REGULAR TARGET EARRING CLEARANCE SECTION PILLAGE. SO FUN... SO GIRLY

BEEN RE-WATCHING DEXTER SEASON 2
OH MAN, DEXTER IS AWESOME!
AND I'M MISSING SEASON THREE!!

MED. FRIDAY:

ON MEDICINE FRIDAY, JAMESTOWN JOINED CAT, RON, AND I... ALSO VICKI. SHE VOLUNTEERED TO ROLL THE BALLS FOR STRIP BINGO. MY SHOUT OUTS WERE NOT TAKEN LIGHTLY BY THE STRIPPER. OOOPSIE.

TAKE IT OFF JAMESTOWN!!

DRUNK

TIGER BAR STRIP BINGO

10.10.2009

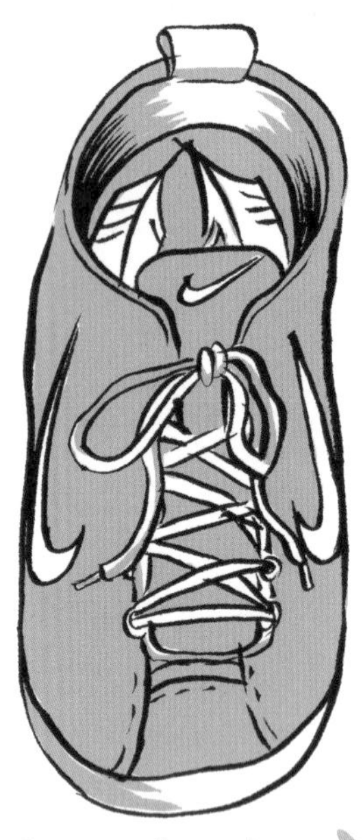

WENT TO MY PARENTS TO VOTE TRIBAL STUFF FOR MY UNCLE AND I LEARN NATIVE AMERICANS HAVE SPECIAL FEET? AND WE HAVE SPECIALLY MADE NIKE SNEAKERS WE COULD GET FOR FREE?! WHAAAAAAT?! I WISH NATIVE AMERICANS NEEDED SPECIAL CARS... AND I COULD HAVE ONE FOR FREE...

I TOLD MY MOM THERE WERE CHESTNUT TREES BY MY APT. DOWNTOWN AND SHE FREAKED OUT AND TOLD ME TO PICK THEM FOR HER... I SAID I DON'T WANT TO LOOK SAD PICKING UP NUTS FROM THE GUTTER BY MACDONALDS... SHE SAYS "ASIANS LOVE CHESTNUTS! YOU'RE ASIAN! IT WILL LOOK NORMAL!"

MAMA... I PICK FOR YOU...

"JAMESTOWN
EMITOWN
NIGHT ON THE TOWN
NIGHT!!!"
HEY, HEY, HEEEY!

WE WENT TO RINGLERS, HENRY'S, AND BLITZ... THIS WAS MY THIRD TIME TO BLITZ AND EVERYTIME FOR SOME REASON, THERE IS ALWAYS A GIRL PUKING IN THE BATHROOM

10.11.2009
I ALMOST POISONED MAMA!!!!!
I LEARNED TODAY THAT THE CHESTNUTS I PICKED ARE
POISONOUS!
OMG... IF SOMEONE HADN'T TOLD ME AND I DIDN'T RESEARCH, I MAY HAVE POISONED MY MOM!!
CRISIS AVERTED
phew!
WENT TO THE PORTLAND ART MUSEUM WHERE I DIDN'T "GET" HALF THE SCULPTURES OR ABSTRACT PAINTINGS... DID GET TO SEE AN ALPHONSE MUCHA PIECE IN PERSON... THAT WAS COOL AND A BOUGUEREAU PIECE!!!
?
BOTH MY ARMS HURT TODAY AS IF I HAD EXERCISED LAST NIGHT... BUT I DIDN'T...
BIFF!
MAYBE I'M A CRIME FIGHTER AT NIGHT AND KICKED SOME SERIOUS ASS AND DON'T REMEMBER. MULTIPLE PERSONALITIES!

10.12.2009

YIPE

STUB

WHENEVER I CROSS THE STREET AT WORK FOR MY BREAKFAST BURRITO AND COFFEE, I NOTICE THIS HUGE IRON NAIL THING IN THE GROUND... WHY ITS THERE? NO IDEA BUT I ALWAYS KNEW I'D TRIP ON IT SOMEDAY... TODAY WAS THE DAY. NO WORRIES, I DIDN'T FALL. I'M GOOD AT CATCHING MYSELF. BURRITO AND COFFEE SAFE! OH... AND ME TOO.

ROCK ON, YOUNG SAVIOR. DON'T GIVE UP YOUR HOPES.

HAND STILL HURTS A LITTLE FROM 24HR COMIC DAY. RECOVER HAND! RECOVER!

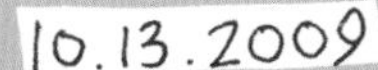
10.13.2009

NOT A BUNCH HAPPENED TODAY.
I DID GET LOCKED IN MY APT
BUILDING. FOR THE FIRST TIME EVER,
I LEFT THROUGH THE BASEMENT.
WE DON'T ALWAYS HAVE TO PRETEND WE ARE TOUGH.

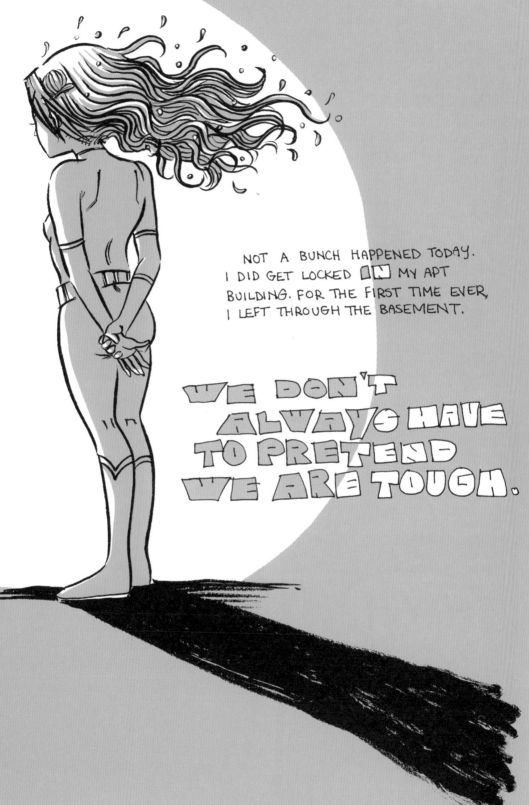

10.14.2009

SAD PETSMART KITTIE UPDATE!

THAT BLACK KITTY WITH THE INCREDIBLE HUGE GREEN EYES WHOSE OWNER PASSED AWAY IS STILL THERE! (REFER 9/15) AWW... NOT LOOKING SO CONFUSED NOW... SORTA LOOKS PISSED... I WOULD BE TOO...

COFF

MY SON HAS THE SWINE FLU...

COUGH

WORKING ON THE ECCC MONSTERS AND DAMES DRAWING

MONSTER = BEAR!!

10.15.2009
FINISHED A SPREADSHEET WITH 13,000 VINS. NICE! FEELS GOOD EVEN IF IT IS TRUCKS AND STUFF...
LATELY, THE GAME CUBE BECKONS...
PLAAAAY ME!! HOW IS YOUR TOWN,* BURRITOA DOIN? BET IT NEEDS TO BE WEEDED!
*ANIMAL CROSSING

10.16.2009
I'M NOT READYYYYY!
2010!
OH NO... THE HOLIDAYS ARE CLOSING IN! I'M NOT READY... BEFORE I KNOW IT IT WILL BE NEXT YEAR... 2010... ITS LIKE THE FUTURE WITH BOTS AND METAL CLOTHES... HUH?
• LEMIRE DRAWING
• MONSTERS/DAMES DRAWING (COLOR)
• PERFECTING LONELINESS (POPGUN)(COLOR)
• PROMO CARD #2 LAYOUT
• BUSINESS CARD
I WAS LATE TO DATE CAUSE I GOT LOST AND STOPPED TO PET TWO KITTIES...
HAAAY!!
!!
AT THE BAR ON MY WAY TO THE LADIE'S ROOM, SOME DOUCHE BAG STUCK HIS BUTT OUT AS I WALKED BY SO I WOULD BUMP INTO IT... I DIDN'T KNOW UNTIL I TURNED AROUND AND SAW HIS DUMB SMILEY FACE THAT IT WAS ALL INTENTIONAL...
DOUCHE!

10.17.2009
AT ELEVEN IN THE MORNING, IT WAS SUPER DARK OUTSIDE AND POURING RAIN...
GROSS.
11:15
STRUGGLE
LET JAMESTOWN USE MY OLD EMAC SO SHE TYPE HER STORIES AT HOME. THAT COMPUTER IS
HEAVY.
TO CELEBRATE HAVING MOVED IT UNHARMED TO HER APT, I GOT A BURGER. YUM
BIGGEST MOCHA
PARTLY EATEN GINGER COOKIE!
I DRANK A HUGE MOCHA WHICH I MANAGED TO STILL GET FROM COFFEEHOUSE NW TEN MINUTES AFTER CLOSE... WANTED TO GET A LOT DONE FOR MY ECCC MONSTERS & DAMES CONTRIBUTION!
THEN DREW AND HUNG OUT AT BRITTNEY'S UNTIL
4AM.
I GOT A LOT DONE!

10.18.2009

HUNG OUT AT BRITTNEY'S A LOT... SHE WORKED ON HER PAINTINGS AND I ON THE OL' MONSTERS AND DAMES PIECE... I ALSO SCORED A PIECE OF HER LASAGNA WHICH WAS DELISH!!

I FEEL LIKE I ACCOMPLISHED A LOT!
-MONSTERS/DAMES
-STARTED SWEETTOOTH DRAWING
-TURNED IN INTERVIEW
-SHOWERED
-EMITOWN
-DISHES

10.19.2009

THIS MORNING I HAD A "FAKE-OUT WAKE UP"... WHERE YOU DREAM YOU WOKE UP AND ARE GETTING READY FOR WORK. THAT SUCKS! IT'S LIKE GETTING READY FOR WORK TWICE!

HAI

FLU

FLU BUG CAME TO VISIT... I SLEPT ALL DAY AND MISSED WORK. BOO FEST.

OH, DEAR GOD

BARF

OH, MY

I TOOK HENRY OUT TO POTTY AND THIS OLD GUY'S FACE WAS ALL RED IN FRONT OF A BAR... THEN HE BARFED! RIGHT IN FRONT OF ME! I WAS NOT HIT BUT I SHUFFLED THE FASTEST SHUFFLE BACK TO MY APT... HE PUKED SO MUCH... IT WAS MOSTLY BEER.

DUDE! IT'S NOON ON A MONDAY!

10.20.200

TODAY IS MAMA'S
BIRTHDAY!

HAPPY
BIRTHDAY

THE WONDER WOMAN AUCTION IS UP! AT LEAST ONE PERSON BID ON MY PIECE! PHEW! I WAS SCARED NO ONE WOULD....

EMITOWN

WORKED ON EMITOWN PROMO CARD NUMBER

2

I NEED TO START MAKIN' STUFF FOR NEXT YEAR.

TODAY, I TOTALLY KICKED THE FLU'S ASS! I'M PRETTY MUCH ALL BETTER! NO FLU SHOT EVEN! MY IMMUNE SYSTEM RULES!

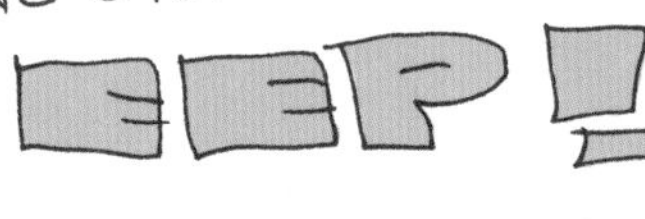
EEP!

FLU

KNOCK ON WOOD!

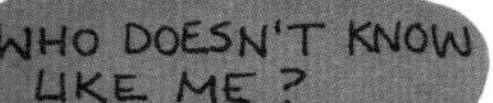

10.21.2009

SHIT...THAT DOES NOT LOOK GOOD.

POOR JAMESTOWN'S DOG, MARGOT, GOT SICK AND HER POO DID NOT LOOK GOOD...

CENSORED

10.22.2009

COOL WESTERN STAR
COFFEE TRAVEL MUG!
I DROPPED AND LOST $15.
THAT REALLY SUCKS!!
WHIRRRRR

WENT TO A SUSHI RESTAURANT CALLED MASU WHERE THEY HAD THESE WEIRD HAND DRYING MACHINES THAT I HAVE NEVER SEEN BEFORE... IT SCARED THE BA-JEEBUS OUT OF ME... I STUCK MY HANDS IN THINKING IT WOULD WARM LIKE A TOASTER. INSTEAD AIR (VERY LOUDLY) STARTED BLOWING AND I SCREAMED...

10.23.2009
IT COSTS WAY TOO MANY QUARTERS TO DRY CLOTHES IN THIS BUILDING!!!
KICK
OH GAWD!
ONE OF MY DEAR FRIENDS, DOOX, GOT ENGAGED LAST NIGHT!! I GOT TO TRY ON THE RING AND I HAD TO IMMEDIATELY TAKE IT OFF CAUSE IT FREAKED ME OUT TOO MUCH TO HAVE AN ENGAGEMENT RING ON THAT FINGER... HAD NO IDEA I'D REACT THAT WAY.
CELEBRATORY PIZZA DINNER!
RING!

10.24.2009

WHEN WILL IT BE SCARY?
Z

WENT AND SAW PARANORMAL ACTIVITY... I WAS A BIT DISAPPOINTED... IT WASN'T THAT SCARY AT ALL! IT DOESN'T HELP WHEN YOU KNOW IT ISN'T REAL... THE ENDING BLEW TOO...

CAN'T WAIT TO SEE 2012

APOCALYPTIC MOVIES AR

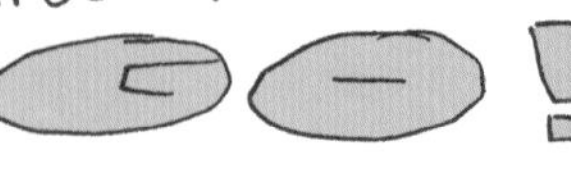

WENT TO FLOATING WORLD... GOT BARN'S BOOK THAT I'VE BEEN MEANING TO GET FOR LIKE, 2 YEARS...

ALSO WENT TO

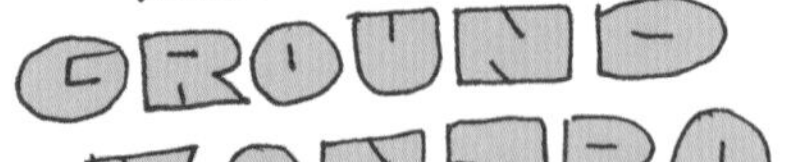
GROUND
KONTROL

IT WAS A GOOD DAY...

SIXTEEN MILES TO MERRICKS

ZOMBIES DON'T MOVE THAT FAST!!

THERE WERE ZOMBIES ALL OVER PORTLAND DROPPING BLOOD... THEY WERE QUICK... MUST BE THE RAGE VIRUS...

10.25.2009

HAI

DAVID HAHN →

WENT TO PERISCOPE STUDIO TO SCAN MY MONSTERS & DAMES PIC AND TO SAY HARRO TO THE THREE PEOPLE THERE ON A SUNDAY...

HAD A 2HR BRUNCH AT MORNING STAR WITH CAT & RON. WAITING = LAME! WAITING WITH AWESOME PEEPS = NOT LAME!

BOOTZ →

BOUGHT CHEAP BOOTS FOR MY "OFF THE REZ NATIVE AMERICAN" COSTUME. WIN!!

STARTING TO GET A COUGH... BUT I'M NOT SICK... 10.26.200

So... TIRED... BODY... ACHES... I... AM... SICK... AGAIN. 10.27.2009
I REFUSE TO MISS WORK!

10.28.2009
HEYYY! I'M ALREADY BETTER!!!
OH MAN, I RECOVER SO QUICKLY!
HALOOOO NURSE!
SO...
ON MY WAY HOME FROM WORK I SAW A HAWK ON A LIGHT POLE AND IT WAS HUGE! AND FOR SOME REASON I SAID "HELLO NURSE!" CAUSE I WAS HAPPY... IT WAS WEIRD... THIS IS NOT WHAT THAT PHRASE IS INTENDED FOR... AND THEN I SAID IT TO A CAR... I HATE MYSELF...

10.29.2009
GOT HIT IN THE HEAD BY A PURSE IN FRONT OF THE ELEVATOR
WHEN I TOOK HENRY OUT TO POTTY I STOPPED SHORT ONE STEP OUT OF THE BUILDING. IT LOOKED REALLY WEIRD OUTSIDE... LIKE THERE WAS A REDNESS TO EVERYTHING... THEN HENRY STARTED ACTING STRANGE AND SCARED... IT FREAKED ME OUT LIKE ARMAGEDDON...

10.30.2009
HOW FAST CAN THIS GO? CAN IT TAKE CORNERS FAST? IS THAT A MINI FRIDGE? WHAT'S THAT--
AT WORK FOR THE HALLOWEEN PARTY, THEY WERE GIVING KIDS TRUCK RIDES... I GOT ONE! I GOT A RIDE IN A FREIGHTLINER... IT WAS PRETTY COOL... NOW I WANT TO DRIVE ONE...
AND
THERE WAS A PIG... AND PEOPLE KISSED IT
FOR MEDICINE FRIDAY TALLY WAS HERE (YAY!) AND WE WENT TO A NICE MARTINI PLACE WHERE I GOT A DISAPPOINTING DRINK... EVERYONE ELSE'S WAS LIKE A FLAVOR PARTY... BOO... NEXT TIME I WON'T FAIL...

10.31.2009

WENT TO COFFEETIME FOR SKETCH GROUP WITH ANGIE & TALLY! VERY FUN! I MISS SKETCH GROUPS....

WATCHED THE DUCKS GAME WITH CORN, LINDS, DREW, AND JOHN AT THE MARATHON

MINI PITCHER

THEN HALLOWEEN PARTY AT PAUL GUINAN'S
GOOD PEEPS
GOOD FUN.

NOVEMBER 2009

11/2 "I AM A ROCK"
-SIMON & GARFUNKEL
11/3 "INSIDE OF LOVE"
-NADA SURF
11/8 "FARMER CHORDS"
-BEN GIBBARD & ANDREW KENNY
11/9 "A SUNDAY"
-JIMMY EAT WORLD
11/10 "BROADRIPPLE IS BURNING"
-MARGOT & THE NUCLEAR SO & SO'S
11/12 "THE FUNERAL"
-BAND OF HORSES
11/14 "FARMER CHORDS"
-BEN GIBBARD & ANDREW KENNY
11/15 "YOUR HEART IS AN EMPTY ROOM"
-DEATHCAB FOR CUTIE
11/16 "MARCHING BANDS OF MANHATTAN"
-DEATHCAB FOR CUTIE
11/19 "CLARITY"
-JIMMY EAT WORLD
"LOVERS WHO HAVE LOST THEIR CAUSE"
11/23 "DIZZY"
-JIMMY EAT WORLD
11/28 "CHASE THIS LIGHT"
-JIMMY EAT WORLD

11.01.2009

Zzz

I LEFT MY CELL PHONE IN MY FRIEND'S CAR WHEN HE DESIGNATED DROVE MY DRUNK ASS HOME. I HAD TWO DRUNK DREAMS THAT I HAD GOTTEN IT BACK. I HAD TO USE INTERNET TO TALK TO HIM AND GET MY PHONE BACK... FACEBOOK HELPED ME GET MY PHONE BACK!

DID THE DISHES
AND TOOK OUT
DA TRASH

I PICKED AT MY EAR AND IT STARTED BLEEDING! TURNS OUT THERE WAS A SCAB ON MY LOBE FROM WHEN I TOUCHED IT ACCIDENTALLY WITH MY HAIR IRON... I DIDN'T REALIZE IT HURT MY EAR AS BAD...
MAKES SENSE THO...
IT IS A HOT HAIR IRON... OF COURSE IT WOULD HAVE LEFT A MARK...
EW

11.02.2009
THINGS TO DO:
NEED TO DO:
• MONSTERS & DAMES (COLOR)
• SWEET TOOTH ART
• POPGUN COMIC
• OTHER COMIC
• PRINT COMICS
• DESIGN COVERS
• EMITOWN
WANT TO DO:
• WORK ON P.L.
• WORK ON COMIC ("BENEATH)
• WORK ON ESSENTIALS COMIC
• PAINTING FOR JAMESTOWN
• PAINTING FOR FUN
• DRAW IN MOLESKIN SKETCHBOOK
MAN, IT FREAKS ME OUT THAT THE YEAR IS ALMOST OVER. I THINK I ACCOMPUSHED A LOT SO FAR THIS YEAR... LEARNED A LOT TOO... AND YET THERE IS NEVER
ENOUGH TIME.
I AM SHIELDED IN MY ARMOR. HIDING IN MY ROOM, SAFE WITHIN MY WOMB. I TOUCH NO ONE AND NO ONE TOUCHES ME
I DON'T UNDERSTAND
GOOGLE WAVE...
DELL

11.03.2009
HAHA
DOH
DANG IT... I FEAR YOU MAY HAVE MISREPRESENTED YOURSELF...
ONLY WHEN WE GET TO SEE THE AERIAL VIEW, WILL THE PATTERNS SHOW. WE'LL KNOW WHAT TO DO.
WATCHING TERRIBLE T.V. IT KILLS ALL THOUGHT. GETTING SPACIER THAN AN ASTRONAUT...
I KNOW THE LAST PAGE SO WELL, I CAN'T READ THE FIRST. SO I JUST DON'T START. IT'S GETTING WORSE

11.04.2009
LAST NIGHT:
I STARTED TO MISS MY CAT AN INSANE AMOUNT... COME NOV. 13, IT WILL BE ONE YEAR SINCE I PUT HIM TO SLEEP... MAYBE IT WAS CAUSE I WAS TIRED... OR CAUSE I'M ON MY PERIOD... THAT I CRIED...
WEENIE'S ASHES
I DON'T CARE IF IT'S STUPID... HE WAS MY FIRST PET AND I LOVED THE SHIT OUT OF HIM! AND PUTTING HIM TO SLEEP WAS NO EASY TASK...
!?
BEEN WORKIN ON THE EMITOWN MINI COMIX... I CAN DO IT!
EMITOWN MARCH 2009
EMITOWN APRIL 2009
EMITOWN MAY 2009
SLIGHT SQUISH
AT WORK I HALF-STEPPED ON A DEAD BIRD. ACCIDENTALLY OF COURSE. I SCREAMED MY SPIDER SCREAM... THEN FELT SAD THE POOR DEAD BIRD WAS ON CONCRETE...

DRANK MORE THAN I DREW AT THE TRANQUILITY BASE DRINK & DRAW...
11.05.2009
ON MY WAY TO THE MARATHON I WAS CONFUSED WHY MY IPOD DIDN'T WORK... TURNS OUT THE "LOCK" WAS ON... DUH...
DRUNK COMIC SHOPPING!
NEW BRIGHTON ARCHEOLOGICAL SOCIETY
PAUL HORNSCHEMEIER'S ALLANDSUNDRY
ALLANDSUNDRY
WE ARE LIVING DEAD WHY ARE YOU SO SAD?

11.06.2009

Z

WAS PRETTY HUNGOVER FROM THE DRINK AND DRAW BUT HAD TO DRIVE TO KAIZER TO GET MY MAGIC PILLS! IT'S LIKE A 45MIN DRIVE! I FELT SO ILL, I ENDED UP SLEEPING IN THE CHEMOW PARKING LOT FOR TWO HOURS!

PLUS: A FELLOW NATIVE THERE READS EMITOWN! NEAT!!

ON OUR PACK WALK JAMIE SHOOK HER HEAD ABOUT MY DRINKING LIQUOR WITHOUT HER AROUND LAST NIGHT. I BROKE THE RULES... ALSO, AT THE LUCKY LAB A QUEER (AS IN STRANGE!) OLD MAN KEPT SAYING WEIRD THINGS TO US. HE SEEMED LIKE A HUGE WOMAN HATER...AND OIL CAN HENRY'S...

HE MADE IT VERY UNCOMFORTABLE... HE DIDN'T REALLY LIKE OUR DOGS TOO... THEN GO AWAY!

YOU NEED A MAN'S VOICE TO CONTROL A DOG...

WTF

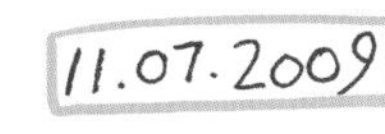

IT RAINED ALL DAY... **POURING** RAIN... THE STREETS OF DOWNTOWN PORTLAND WERE FLOODED! I DID GET TO SEE PEOPLE GET SOAKED ON THE SIDEWALK BY CARS DRIVING BY.

!!!!

HAD A BAD DREAM
HAT FEATURED A
GIANT
PIDER. I WAS VERY
CARED... EVEN THO
OR SOME REASON
WAS WEARING A
ATMAN CAPE...

A FRIEND FROM UTAH WAS IN TOWN. HUNG OUT WITH HER AND SOME OF THE GANG AT EASTBURN...

DANIELLE!!

PBR

THEN I WAS SHOWN A SOUTH PARK EPISODE: WHALE WHORES

11.08.2009

I CAN'T BEGIN TO COMPETE WITH YOU. AND EVERYONE KNOWS, I KNOW YOU KNOW IT TOO. IT'S A COMPLICATED FEAR THAT GROWS WITH EVERY YEAR AND IT'S WALKING ON IT'S OWN FINALLY.

MONTHLY MOVIE DAY!!

JAMESTOWN AND I TREATED OURSELVES TO OUR FAVORITE BURGER:

CPTN NEON BURGER!

TODAY SAW 500 DAYS OF SUMMER WITH JAMESTOWN AT THE MISSION. IT WAS AN ENJOYABLE MOVIE BUT BOTH OF US ARE SO CYNICAL AT THE IDEA OF FATED LOVE, THAT THERE IS ONLY ONE PERSON OUT THERE FOR EVERYONE... SOUL MATES... PFFT... AGAIN... WE DID ENJOY THE MOVIE!

PFFFT

11.9.2009
TURNS OUT, MONSTERS AND DAMES IS DUE THE 20 AND NOT THE 10!
PHEW!
YOU KNOW... I REALIZE THAT IT OREGON... BUT I'M SICK OF ALL THIS RAIN...
BOO!
ON A SUNDAY GO ONCE AROUND, CAUSE WHEN THE RIDE'S DONE, THE HOPES THAT YOU HAVE CARRIED, THEY FALL OUT FROM YOUR HANDS BACK TO THE GROUND

11.10.2009
BEEN FEELING REALLY BLAH ABOUT DRAWING... MAYBE CAUSE I LOOKED AT OLD SKETCHBOOKS AND I FEEL SAD... IT SEEMED LIKE I WAS A LOT MORE CREATIVE...
We got a lot Don't ever forget that.
HO HUM POOO..
2003
HE LOOKS MAD BUT HE LIKES IT... I THINK.
We got a lot don't you dare forget that.
GOT HENRY
A NEW COLLAR! RED NYLON LIKE WHEN HE WAS A PUPPY... KINDA BRINGS ME BACK A LITTLE...
SIGH...

11.11.2009
COFFEE HAS BEEN REALLY KICKING MY ASS THIS WEEK... I FEEL LIKE I'M HOOKED ON THE DRUG... TO FEEL BETTER IS TO DRINK MORE!
NOO!
•START X-MAS SHOPPING
•GET OIL CHANGE
•ART MORE
•ECCC ART
•LEMIRE ART
•PACQUIO VS COTTO
2012
I LISTENED TO SOME EXPERT TALK ABOUT 2012 ON THE RADIO TODAY AND IT REALLY FREAKED ME OUT... HE TALKED ABOUT THE MAYANS, EGYPTIANS, NATIVE-AMERICANS ETC... RELIGIONS... ALL THESE CULTURAL BELIEFS THAT ARE SIMILAR... AND SCIENTIFIC BELIEFS... THAT REALLY FREAKED ME OUT!!!

11.12.2009
!!!
OH NO! I'M ALL OUT OF RICE!
WHAT IS A HALF ASIAN TO DO?!
HAD WEIRD THING PHO
FOR THE FIRST TIME
AT THIS PLACE ON
21ST
I'M COMING UP ONLY TO HOLD YOU UNDER. I'M COMING UP ONLY TO SHOW YOU WRONG. TO KNOW YOU IS HARD AND WE WONDER. TO KNOW YOU ALL WRONG WE WERE
TO KNOW ME AS HARDLY GOLDEN IS TO KNOW ME ALL WRONG, THEY WERE.

11.13.2009
ON MY WAY HOME FROM WORK, THIS CUTE NEIGHBORHOOD KITTIE WALKED WITH ME FOR ALMOST AN ENTIRE TWO BLOCKS UNTIL IT REACHED WHAT SEEMED LIKE AN INVISIBLE BARRIER... DON'T BLAME IT... BURNSIDE ST. IS A SCARY PLACE... IT DID MAKE ME FEEL SAD SINCE IT IS OFFICIAL WEENIE DEATH DAY.
PHO AGAIN
I JUST CAN'T SEEM TO GET ENOUGH!
WENT TO THE GALAXY FOR ERIC'S BIRTHDAY. GOOD TIMES SHARED BY ALL! EVEN SAW BEN WHOM I HAVEN'T SEEN IN THREE MONTHS! YAY!
LIFE IS A MYSTERY

11.14.2009

FROM MY LONELY ARMS OUTSTRETCHED JUST BEYOND YOUR REACH...

WENT TO THE SATURDAY MARKET FOR THE FIRST TIME IN AROUND THREE OR FOUR YEARS! SAW A KITTIE BOOTH WITH PHOTOS OF CATS ENJOYING THE PRODUCTS... MY HEART YEARNS FOR ONE SO BAD IT'S BEYOND PATHETIC.

MADE IT IN TIME TO WATCH THE LAST HALF OF THE PACQUIAO VS COTTO FIGHT! IS MAYWEATHER NEXT?! THAT WOULD BE EPIC!!

FOR THE MOST PART IT WAS A PRETTY GOOD DAY. FORGOT TO MENTION THE INSANE AMOUNT OF CHICKEN I GOT WITH MY CHICKEN AND WAFFLES AT GREEN DOOR

THREE CHICKEN STORIES HIGH!!!

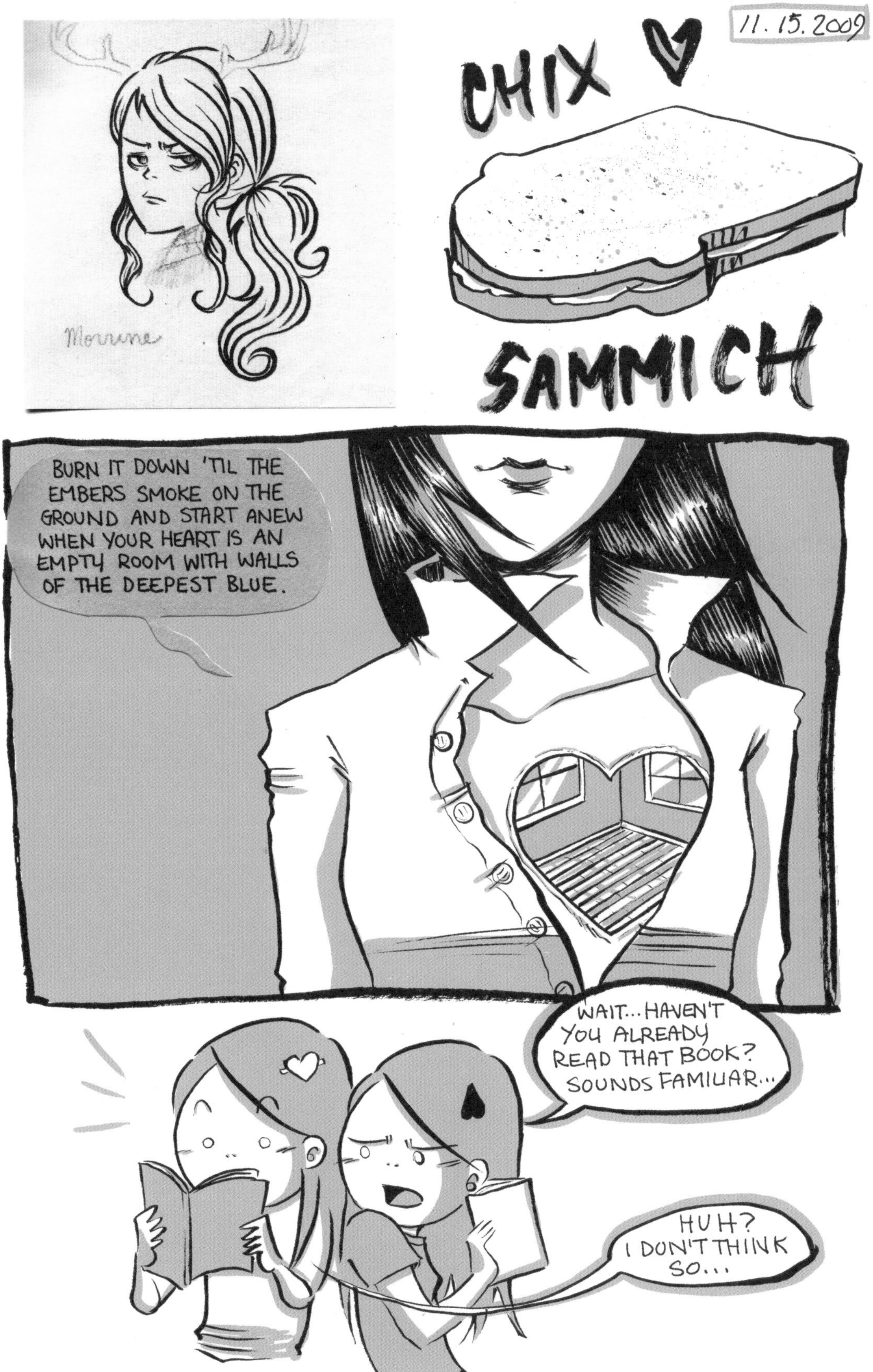

BURN IT DOWN 'TIL THE EMBERS SMOKE ON THE GROUND AND START ANEW WHEN YOUR HEART IS AN EMPTY ROOM WITH WALLS OF THE DEEPEST BLUE.

WAIT... HAVEN'T YOU ALREADY READ THAT BOOK? SOUNDS FAMILIAR...

HUH? I DON'T THINK SO...

11.16.2009
STOP IT!!
BOTH Y'ALL!
YOU'RE DRIVING ME BANANA SAND-WICH! IT IS WHAT IT IS!!!
URK
WHINE
WHATEVER
OH, WHAT A BEAUTIFUL VIEW IF YOU WERE NEVER AWARE OF WHAT'S AROUND YOU

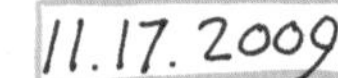
11.17.2009

PSHAW... YOU'LL BE BACK... JUST WATCH
GAVE UP COFFEE TODAY... PROBABLY JUST FOR TODAY... SOMETIMES IT JUST MAKES ME FEEL PLAIN-OL-SHITTY!

WHY FRET OR WORRY ABOUT THINGS YOU HAVE NO CONTROL OVER? IT REALLY IS JUST A WASTE OF TIME... BUT SOMETIMES I CAN'T HELP IT... GRR! NOOOOOOOOO OOOOOOOOOO
OH WELL
IT'S OK!
WORRY!
WHATEVS

DON'T BE AFRAID
WACOM FROM 2001
MORE COLORING FOR MONSTERS AND DAMES... GOT FAR BUT STUPID ME FLATTENED IT AND MESSED WITH THE LEVELS AND SAVED IT AS A SEPARATE FILE BUT DIDN'T SAVE BEFORE SO LOST SOME WORK. DUMB.

11.18.2009

YESTERDAY SAW A CUSTOM LICENSE PLATE THAT SAID "SERUM"... HUH? WHY? WHAT? DO THEY MAKE SERUM? LIKE TRUTH SERUM? THE SERUM IN COMICS THAT WILL GIVE SUPER POWERS? SUPERPOWER SERUM? IT BOGGLED MY MIND.

OO WAT
I KNOW, I KNOW, I KNOW
AND RIGHT NOW, I DON'T CARE.
I'M PREPARED FOR ANYTHING!
THIS YEAR HAS TAUGHT ME A LOT.
TAKE THAT, 2009!! MUAHA.

FINALLY GOT AN IDEA FOR MY ENTRY FOR POPGUN 5... I'M RUNNIN WITH IT AND AIN'T TURNIN BACK! DREW THE THUMBS FOR THE NINE PAGES! I'M A TAD CONCERNED ABOUT THE STORY... I LIKE IT... IS THAT ENOUGH?

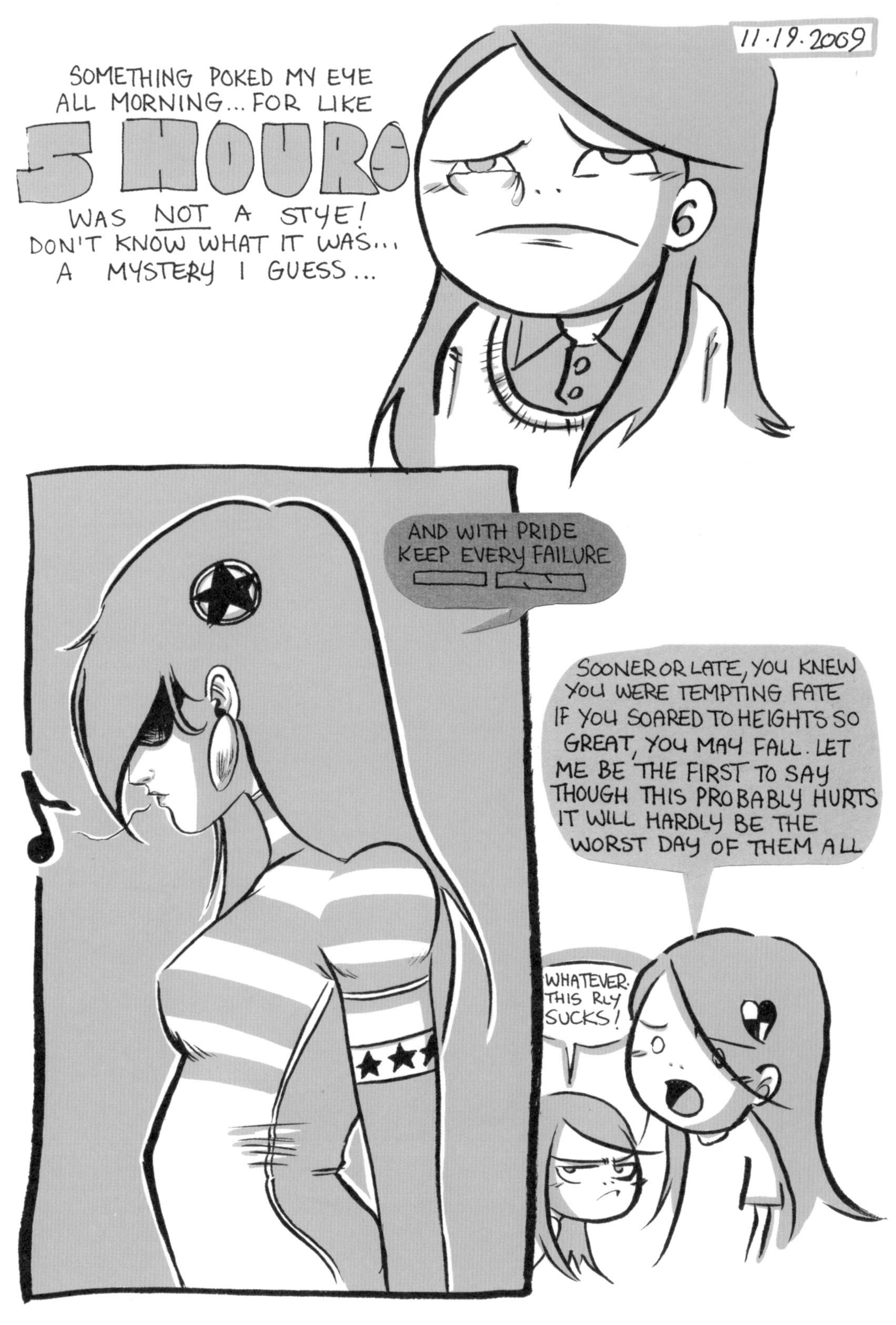
11·19·2009
SOMETHING POKED MY EYE ALL MORNING... FOR LIKE
5 HOURS
WAS NOT A STYE! DON'T KNOW WHAT IT WAS... A MYSTERY I GUESS...
AND WITH PRIDE KEEP EVERY FAILURE
SOONER OR LATE, YOU KNEW YOU WERE TEMPTING FATE IF YOU SOARED TO HEIGHTS SO GREAT, YOU MAY FALL. LET ME BE THE FIRST TO SAY THOUGH THIS PROBABLY HURTS IT WILL HARDLY BE THE WORST DAY OF THEM ALL
WHATEVER. THIS RLY SUCKS!
11·19·2009

11.20.2009

AT THE MATADOR WITH ANGIE, I OVERHEAR INTERESTING THINGS THAT ENDED UP NOT BEING SO INTERESTING...

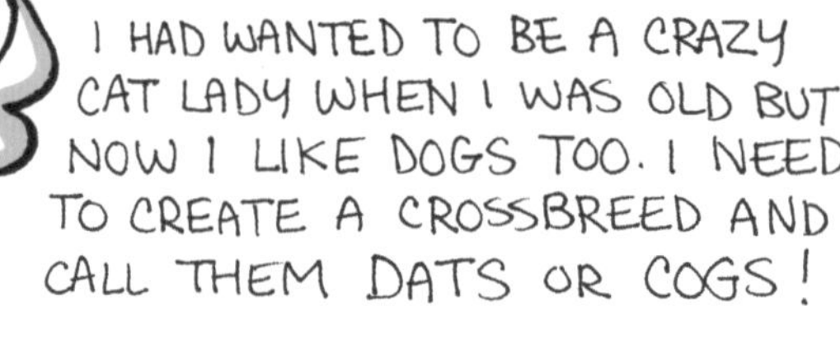

I HAD WANTED TO BE A CRAZY CAT LADY WHEN I WAS OLD BUT NOW I LIKE DOGS TOO. I NEED TO CREATE A CROSSBREED AND CALL THEM DATS OR COGS!

← PLAYED DR. MARIO AT GROUND KONTROL GOT A WUSSY HIGH SCORE...

LEFT CONCERT BEFOR IT STARTED CAUSE I WAS SO TIRED AND FELT ICKY...

A VISIT TO ART MEDIA
11. 21. 2009
MOLESKINE WATERCOLOR BOOK
SKETCHBOOK
INK CARTRIDGES
WAAAA!
STOP COMPLAINING
COMIX
WENT TO FLOATING WORLD COMICS WHERE I BUGGED JAMIE RICH FOR LIKE AN HOUR.
JOINED SOME PALS TO WATCH THE UofO GAME AGAINST ARIZONA... AND IT WAS INTENSE. I DON'T WATCH FOOTBALL OFTEN BUT ONCE I GOT WHAT WAS GOING ON, I WAS REALLY INTO IT. SO STRESSFUL! LOTS OF CLAPPIN AND SCREAMING...
OMIGOD OMIGOD...
I EVEN WORE TEAM COLORS... UNINTENTIONALLY. I FELT LIKE PART OF THE FAMILY.

11.22.2009

READ 12 REASONS WHY I LOVE HER IN BED AND FELT A LITTLE SAD... I LIKED THE BOOK A LOT BUT THE SUBJECT IS OH SO TENDER...

MARGOT! NO!!!

!!

YAP

WENT TO SILVERDOLLAR PIZZA TO HANG WITH JAMESTOWN. MARGOT BARKS AT WHEELCHAIRS, PEOPLE, BIKES, AND OTHER DOGS... EACH TIME GIVES ME A NEAR HEART ATTACK.

DREW IN BED UNTIL MIDNIGHT...
YIKES! ON A WORK NIGHT!

11.23.2009

I FEEL A BUMP ON MY FACE... IS THERE STILL GLASS IN THERE? I HAD GLASS REMOVED IN AROUND 2001 FROM WHEN I FELL THROUGH A GLASS DOOR IN THE MID NINTIES... HOPE NOT....

WHEN I HAVE PENT UP EMOTION I DRAW. I THINK MOST OF MY WORK IS EMOTIONALLY DRIVEN. I CAN'T HELP IT... I WHIPPED UP A 12 PAGE STORY/COMIC CAUSE OF IT... AT LEAST I ACCOMPLISH SOMETHING WITH IT! I HOPE I DON'T COME ACROSS AS SAD... IN LIFE I'M TOLD I HAVE A HAPPY ENERGY. AH, CONTRADICTIONS!

TIME NEVER HAD A CHANCE TO HEAL YOUR HEART. JUST A NUMBER ALWAYS COUNTING DOWN TO A NEW START. IF YOU ALWAYS KNEW THE TRUTH THEN THE WORLD WOULD SPIN AROUND YOU.

WHY OPEN THE DOOR IF YOU WON'T GO. DON'T ASK TWICE IF YOU DON'T WANT TO KNOW.

11.24.2009
SPLENDA
SPLENDA
RUINED MY COFFEE... THEY RAN OUT OF SUGAR SO I USED SPLENDA... IT'S SO GROSS
HAI
URK
I SQUEALED AT WORK NO THANKS TO A BLOODY SPIDER LOWERING ITSELF INCHES FROM MY FACE... THIS IS A MASSIVE BUILDING TO YOU SPIDER... REALLY? REALLY?! THIS IS WHERE YOU CHOSE TO DESCEND?! UGH TO YOU!
TODAY I HAVE BEEN CORRECTING ADDRESSES IN THE SYSTEM FROM RETURNED RECALL LETTERS. I RAN INTO ONE THAT SAID DECEASED
POOR EDGAR. I HOPE THE RV SERVED HIM WELL... AND THAT THE POWER STEERING FILTERS PLAYED NO ROLE IN HIS DEATH...

11.25.2009
FOR SOME REASON GOING TO A JUNKYARD AND CLIMBING ON BEAT UP CARS SOUNDED REALLY FUN TODAY AT WORK... TOO BAD I DIDN'T... MAYBE SOMEDAY I WILL... I'M SURE I'D FIND ALL SORTS OF COOL SHINY THINGS THERE TOO!
ビーフカレー
ビーフカレー
GOT A PACKAGE FROM MY PAL MATT WITH INSTANT CURRY FROM JAPAN! PLUS I GOT AN R2D2 PEN AND AN INDIANA JONES LEGO KEYCHAIN! THANKS! SO NICE!! ♥

HUNG OUT WITH LAURA, JAMES-TOWN... IN THE COLD... AT THE PIZZA PLACE...

11.26.2009
HAPPY TURKEY DAY!
TURKEY
GRAVY
MASHED TATERS
APPLE PIE
PUMPKIN PIE
PEAS
SQUASH
WENT TO THE PARENTS FOR EATS AND TORRENTED TONS OF STUFF! DID LAUNDRY...DRANK WINE.... IT WAS QUITE PLEASANT!
YUM
RICE
CARRIED SO MUCH STUFF TO MY APT TO MY CAR IN ONE TRIP. SHOULDERS AND ARMS ACHED FOR TWO DAYS AFTER. UGH
I AM THANKFUL FOR ALL MY FRIENDS AND FAMILY... ALL THE AWESOME THINGS THAT HAPPENED...AND EVEN THE BAD. I HAVE LEARNED A LOT THIS YEAR WHICH WILL HOPEFULLY HELP ME MAKE WISER CHOICES.

11.27.2009
SPENT WAY TOO MUCH FOR THIS JAMES JEAN SWEATSHIRT... BUT IT'S JAMES JEAN
I DO LOVE IT! SO I GUESS IT'S WORTH IT!
SOB
GAP
20% OFF
SAW SANTA INTERACT WITH EXCITED HAPPY CHILDREN... SO TOUCHING...
DECORATE THE APT FOR X-MAS DAY!
WENT TO CAT'S NEW PAD FOR A GATHERING OF SORTS... BROUGHT HER A "FORK" PLANT AND WINE ♥ IT WAS PRETTY FUN... AND HER PAD IS SO SWANK!!

11.28.2009
AIM:
ECOLI HAS BEEN FOUND IN THE WATER, EMI! DON'T DRINK THE WATER UNLESS YOU BOIL IT!!
WATER
DELL
I WAS SO BORED I LITERALLY WOULD MOAN OUT LOUD IN MY APT... I DON'T REMEMBER BEING THIS BORED SINCE I WAS LITTLE WHINING TO MY DAD...
SOOOOO BORED!!
THE BEAUTY IS IN WHAT ISN'T SAID, I'M RISING TO MY FEET.
BECAUSE TONIGHT THE WORLD TURNED IN ME. BECAUSE RIGHT NOW I DON'T DARE TO BREATHE. I KNOW IT'S ALIVE AND SOMEWHERE FOR US TO FIND.
TONIGHT CHASE THIS LIGHT WITH ME.
DROVE TO HOOD RIVER AND ON THE WAY ON HWY 84 THERE ARE THESE LIGHTS ON TOP OF A CLIFF THAT, IN THE DARK, LOOK LIKE A UFO JUST SITTING THERE! WATCHING... WAITING... OBSERVING...

11.29.2009
ONA
THE WATER IS NOW SAFE TO DRINK! NO NEED TO BOIL IT ANYMORE!!
JAMESTOWN TOOK ME TO LUNCH! MOST PLACES WERE CLOSED IN THE DAY DUE TO THE WHOLE CONTAMINATED WATER FIASCO... SO WE HAD BURRITOS AND CORONAS.
WATER
DELL
WAIT-A-MIN... WHAT GAME ARE YOU PLAYING?!
HUH? WHA-
YOU'RE PLAYING THE WRONG GAME!!
OH YEAH...WTF
YOU HATE THAT GAME!! WHAT'S WRONG WITH YOU?!

11. 30. 2009

PEOPLE SAY TO LISTEN TO YOUR GUT... BUT WHAT THE HELL DO YOU DO WHEN FEAR/HOPE IS THOROUGHLY MIXED IN TALKING AT THE SAME TIME YOUR GUT IS? IT'S LIKE A PUREE. I CAN'T TELL WHAT'S WHAT OR WHO IS SPEAKING!!

MAMA CALLS AT WORK AND LEAVES ME A MESSAGE TELLING ME NOT TO DRINK THE WATER... A LITTLE LATE BUT THANKS! NOT THAT IT WOULD HAVE STOPPED ME!

DECEMBER 2009

12/1 "TITLE AND REGISTRATION"
-DEATHCAB FOR CUTIE
12/2 "WEIGHTY GHOST"
-WINTERSLEEP
12/8 "DEAD LETTER AND THE INFINATE YES"
-WINTERSLEEP
12/22 "HOW IT ENDS"
-DEVOTCHKA
12/30 "COLD, KIND, AND LEMON EYES"
-MARGOT & THE NUCLEAR SO & SO'S

12.01.2009
OH...THIS BOOK IS LIKE THE LAST BOOK... BUT NOT AS BAD...
OH JEEZ!! AND SNAP OUT OF THAT MIND SET!
WENT TO CHEMOWA FOR THE OL' YEARLY PAP... IT WAS NOT FUN. BOOBIE EXAM PROVED FUN AS I WAS SO TICKLISH AND KEPT LAUGHING
THE INDIANS HAD A HELICOPTER CARRYING THEIR X·MAS TREES TO GATHER FOR SALE... COOL.
HERE I REST WHERE DISAPPOINTMENT AND REGRET COLLIDE. LYING AWAKE AT NIGHT
keep your Pride INSIDE...

12.02.2009
I GOT OUT OF BED TODAY SWEAR TO GOD I COULDN'T SEE MY FACE. I GOT OUT OF BED TODAY STARING AT A GHOST
WHO FORGOT TO FLOAT AWAY, DIDN'T HAVE ALL THAT MUCH TO SAY. WOULDN'T EVEN TELL ME HIS OWN NAME
WHERE'D MY BODY GO ?
WHERE OH WHERE'D MY BODY GO? AFRICA OR MEXICO ?
WHERE OH WHERE'D MY BODY GO ?
WHERE'D MY BODY GO ?
HAVE YOU SEEN MY GHOST? STARING AT THE GROUND? HAVE YOU SEEN MY GHOST? SICK OF THOSE GODDAMN CLOUDS
ARE YOU SOME KIND OF MEDICINE MAN CUT THE DEMONS OUT OF MY HEAD. YOU CAN'T KILL SOMETHING THAT'S ALREADY DEAD. JUST LEAVE MY SOUL ALONE.
I DON'T NEED NO SURGERY. TAKE THOSE KNIVES AWAY FROM ME. JUST WANNA DIE IN MY OWN BODY
A GHOST JUST NEEDS A HOME

12.03.2009

THINKING ABOUT CHANGING THE COLORS ON EMITOWN WHEN THE NEW YEAR HITS. I LOVE THE BLUE BUT HOW MUCH BLUE CAN YOU TAKE?! I DIG THE WEEZER IDEA...2009 IS MY BLUE ALBUM...NEXT PINK FOR PINKERTON...SOUNDS COOL EXCEPT THAT IN MY OPINION WEEZER WENT DOWNHILL AFTER PINKERTON!

I LOST MY POOR RAZOR PHONE FINALLY TO A SLOW DEATH BY WATER DAMAGE

NOKIA

NOW I HAVE A NOKIA MUSIC PHONE OR OTHER. NOT EVEN A FLIP PHONE! IT'S OK I GUESS. I LIKE THE WAY THE BUTTONS FEEL...

DEAD ALIVE

YOU KNOW...ACTUALLY... THIS BOOK ISN'T REALLY THE SAME AS THE LAST ONE AT ALL. LETS READ THIS ONE...SOME MORE. MIGHT BE A GOOD ONE FOR NOW...

12.04.2009
WEEZER IS GEEK ROCK!
WTF DOES THAT EVEN MEAN?!
MEDICINE FRIDAY! STARTED AT THE SHANGHAI TUNNEL... WHICH WAS FUN! AND HAD THEIR SPECIAL PULLED PORK CHEESE FRIES! THAT WAS SOME TASTY FRIES! THEN WE WENT TO THE TUBE. HAVEN'T BEEN THERE IN TWO YEARS... I THOUGHT IT SMELLED LIKE B.O. AND PISS... STRONG DRINKS THO!
THEN TOOK A MINI TRIP TO HOOD RIVER.... AGAIN... I LOVE NIGHT COUNTRY DRIVES. IT'S MY OWN CONCERT...
SUZY

12.05.2009

BEFORE LEAVING HOOD RIVER WENT TO McDONALD'S AND GOT A CHIX WRAP, MOCHA, AND A VITAMIN WATER.

THE DRIVE HOME WAS PLEASANT BEFORE I FACE A VERY BUSY DAY.

THEN

AS SOON AS I GET BACK TO PORTLAND, I MEET UP W/ MY OLD PAL JOE KEATINGE WHO WAS IN TOWN FOR THE ONE MODEL NATION COMIC RELEASE PARTY. WENT TO POWELL'S, ROXY, COUNTER MEDIA, READING FRENZY, AND GROUND KONTROL...

THEN

THE COMIC RELEASE PARTY AT FLOATING WORLD! MET MIKE ALLRED, CRAIG THOMPSON STOPPED BY, JAMIE RICH GRUMPED AROUND, AND TONS MORE. IT WAS AN AWESOME TIME... THEN WENT TO MY FRIEND'S GOING AWAY PARTY THEN HOME AT MIDNIGHT WHERE I PASSED THE EFF OUT...

12.06.2009
MET UP WITH MY OL' ART TEACHER FROM HIGH SCHOOL! HAVEN'T SEEN HER IN ABOUT SIX YEARS
ALSO RAN INTO BRETT FROM TOPSHELF IN BEAVERTON...
RANDOM!
THEN
MET W/ CAT AT PIONEER PLACE WHERE I HELPED HER FIND A DRESS FOR HER WORK HOLIDAY PARTY
THEN
BRRR!
WALKED JAMESTOWN HOME FROM WORK AND THEN SAT WITH HER OUTSIDE AT SILVERDOLLAR... (SHE SMOKES!) IN THE FREEZING COLD!
brrrrr
WHEN I WALKED HOME, MY FOOT WAS ASLEEP SO I WALKED REALLY SLOWLY AT FIRST... IT SUCKED! IT WAS SO COLD!!!!

12.07.2009
NOBODY THROWS ME MY OWN GUNS AND SAYS, "RUN". NOBODY
WHY CAN EVERYONE ELSE SEE MY WORTH AND POTENTIAL BUT I CAN'T REALLY? IT MAKES ME SAD AND ASHAMED A LITTLE.
I AM VERY GRATEFUL TO HAVE FRIENDS WHO REMIND ME ♥

12.08.2009
SO
COLD...
TODAY I WAS REALLY LOVIN THE WORLD AND EVERYONE I KNOW... SOMETIMES COFFEE MAKES ME SO EMOTIONAL. TODAY, IN A GOOD WAY!
I THINK IT'S REAL INSIGNIFICANT. I THINK I THINK A LITTLE TOO OFTEN

12.09.2009

ROCK YOU LIKE A HURRICANE!

BAJA FRESH AT WORK.
FREE FOOD = HAPPY TIMES.
PLUS I MADE SOMEONE THINK
I SING A THEME SONG BEFORE
I EAT. BWA HA.

- ECCC
- WONDERCON
- STUMPTOWN
- SDCC
- APE

SO MANY CONS TO GO TO! NEVER BEEN TO APE... OR WONDERCON... FREE PASSES, A PLACE TO STAY, FRIENDS, AND RETURNING TO S.F?!

DON'T MIND IF I DO!

OPENED MY ETSY STORE TO SELL SOME ORIGINALS PEOPLE BOUGHT THEM! WOWZERS! I SHOULD DRAW MORE... I COULD USE THE EXTRA MONIES...

12.10.2009
WORK HAS BEEN A REAL BLASTY BLAST... HA HA HA!
OH BOY
SAMMICH & BREWSKI ♥
BEFORE I GO TO SKETCH GROUP, I WENT TO THE MATADOR FOR A MUCH NEEDED BEER AND BLT... ON THE T.V.'S THERE WAS SOME SCI-FI MOVIE WITH A SWEATY ICKY GUY WHOSE EYES WERE POPPING OUT OF HIS HEAD...
[SCREAMS IN PAIN]
OMG EW...

12.11.2009
GOT A MUCH NEEDED HAIRCUT...
I FEEL SO FRESH AND SO CLEAN! CLEAN!
SNIP
SNIP
THEN I GO MEET UP WITH MY MEDICINE FRIDAY PALS AT
WENT TO MARTINI BAR AND HAD A REALLY TASTY DRINK CALLED THE JOYFUL GIRL! IT WAS REALLY REALLY GOOD! I ALSO HAD A LEMON DROP! THEN WE WENT TO SUSHI-LAND THEN BLITZ WHERE WE PLAYED SHUFFLE BOARD AND DARTS...
MISO
DARTS!
SUSHI
Z
YOU CAN'T SLEEP AT THE BAR, EMI...
THEN HUNG OUT W/ JOHN, JAKE, AND DREW AT SHANGHAI TUNNEL... AT THIS POINT I WAS WIPED OUT. WEIRD TO END THE NIGHT THERE... USUALLY START THERE...

12.12 2009
TODAY WAS DOOX'S ENGAGEMENT PARTY. SPENT A LOT OF THE DAY HELPING JAMESTOWN PREPARE.
GOT COFFEE
STOPPED BY THE $1 TREE FOR GAME STUFF
PICKED UP THE CUPCAKES

TOOK TAXI TO TANASBOURNE AND GOT DRINKS AND JAMESTOWN PREPARED HER GAME AT MAC. GRILL

(THEY HAVE AN AWESOME HAPPY HOUR!)

WENT TO THE PARTY WHICH WAS VERY FUN. EVEN WHEN SOMEONE TOLD JAMESTOWN AND I THAT WE AREN'T "SPRING CHICKENS" ANYMORE AND WE NEED TO "SETTLE"

I DON'T HAVE TO SETTLE

AFTER THE ENGAGEMENT PARTY, WE WENT TO THE MATADOR BUT JAMESTOWN AND I WERE SOOO TIRED. DRANK WATER AND HIT THE HAY VERY SHORTLY AFTER ARRIVING. SORRY, DOOXIE! ♥

12.13.2009

EXCUSE ME!!! EXCUSE ME!! YOU DROPPED YOUR BEER!

BEER

BEEN READING "BLACK HOLE" BY CHARLES BURNS... ABOUT A LITTLE OVER HALF-WAY THROUGH... I HOPE WHEN I'M DONE IT'S NOT A "WTF?" BUT A "OH WOAH" OR EVEN A "OH, I SEEEEE." OR...OR...MAYBE A "HOLY CRAP!"

I WENT GROCERY SHOPPIN AT FRED MEYER AND A LADY DROPPED HER CASE OF BEER FROM HER CART... IT WAS FUN SAYING "YOU DROPPED YOUR BEEEER!!" EHEH...

OH GOD

IT'S ALMOST X·MAS AND I'VE DONE NO SHOPPING...

12.14.2009
WHEN THINGS/FACTORS AT WORK AFFECT ME TO THE POINT WHERE I COULDN'T EAT ALL OF MY BREAKFAST BURRITO. SOMETHING HAD TO BE DONE. I COULDN'T TAKE IT ANYMORE!!
SO... I FINALLY ADDRESSED IT... AND FEEL SO MUCH BETTER! YAY, ME!
GOT A FOURTH MOVIE FROM NETFLIX EVEN THOUGH MY PLAN IS ONLY FOR THREE... COOL I SUPPOSE... BUT ALL THE MOVIES I HAVE ARE DEPRESSING AND I'M NEVER IN THE MOOD TO WATCH THEM... I NEED TINY TOON ADVENTURES...
?
NETFLIX
BUSTER
BABS!

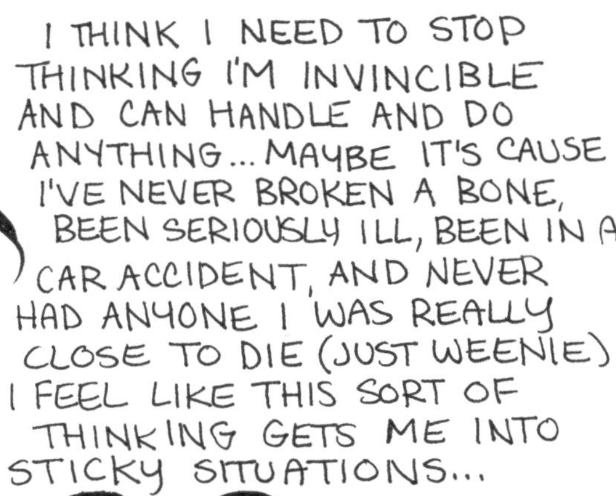
12.15.2009
I THINK I NEED TO STOP THINKING I'M INVINCIBLE AND CAN HANDLE AND DO ANYTHING... MAYBE IT'S CAUSE I'VE NEVER BROKEN A BONE, BEEN SERIOUSLY ILL, BEEN IN A CAR ACCIDENT, AND NEVER HAD ANYONE I WAS REALLY CLOSE TO DIE (JUST WEENIE) I FEEL LIKE THIS SORT OF THINKING GETS ME INTO STICKY SITUATIONS...

I'M NOT A SUPER HERO...

12.16.2009

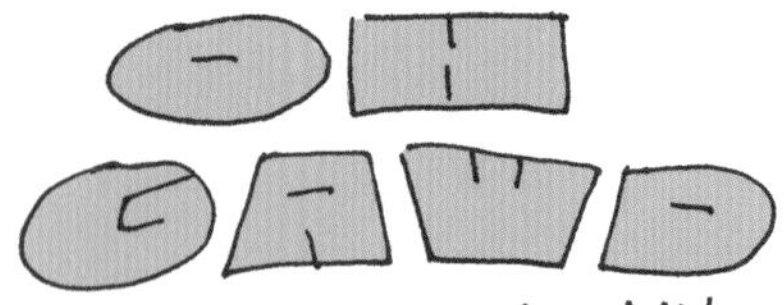

I HAVEN'T DONE MY

IN SO LONG.

I WISH I HAD A DISHWASHER...

- POPGUN COMIC
- DOOX CARD
- X-MAS CARDS
- POSTOFFICE
- EMITOWN COVERS
- X-MAS SHOPPING
- JAMESTOWN PAINTING
- BIZNISS CARDS
- OIL CHANGE
-

JUST

CAN'T CLIMB!

BE..

12.17.2009
DEFEND!
MY DOG STINKS BUT I LOVE HIM ANYWAY. ♥
WELL, AIN'T IT THE LIFE
AND YET ANOTHER JOURNAL COMIC. YIKES I NEED TO STOP THE MADNESS.
I AM SO READY FOR 2010

12.18.2009
WUMP!
GOT A KEY TO PERISCOPE STUDIO WHERE I CAN COME IN WHEN I NEED TO WORK ON MY COMICS AT ANY EMPTY DESK! I AM SO DOING THIS DURING MY TWO WEEKS OFF TO WORK ON MY POPGUN ENTRY.
RON GAVE ME A COOL SAKURA KEYCHAIN TOO!
♥ THANKS PERISCOPE!
TODAY'S MEDICINE FRIDAY FEATURED RON RANDALL'S DAUGHTER, LISA! SHE IS COOL AS SHIT.
WENT TO SHANGHAI, TUBE, BLITZ, AND THE FEZ WHERE WE DANCED AND DANCED AND DANCED

12.19.2009

AT PIONEER PLACE THEY HAVE A SNOW MACHINE THAT THEY TURN ON EVERY HOUR OR SO FROM THE TOP FLOOR. WATCHING THE FAMILIES GET EXCITED ON THE BOTTOM FLOOR TOUCHED MY HEART. DAMMIT, I TOLD MYSELF I WOULDN'T CRY!

AFTER MALL MAYHEM AND DESPITE MY LOW FUNDS, I TREATED MYSELF TO

SUSHI LAND!

Merry Christmas Mug

WENT TO JOHN'S ANNUAL XMAS PARTY. IT WAS SUPER FUN! GOT TO SEE TONS OF WONDERFUL PEOPLE AND SOME I DON'T SEE OFTEN (LIKE BEN & DANIELLE!)

HAD HOT COCOA W/ PEPPERMINT SCHNAPPS

SO DELISH

12.20.2009

DUMBLEDORE, NOOOO!!

GOT A BURGER TO·GO FROM THE MATADOR AND RENTED THE NEW HARRY POTTER. I HAD CLUE WHAT WAS GOING ON... MY DAD HAD TO EXPLAIN SOME OF IT TO ME!

12.21.2009

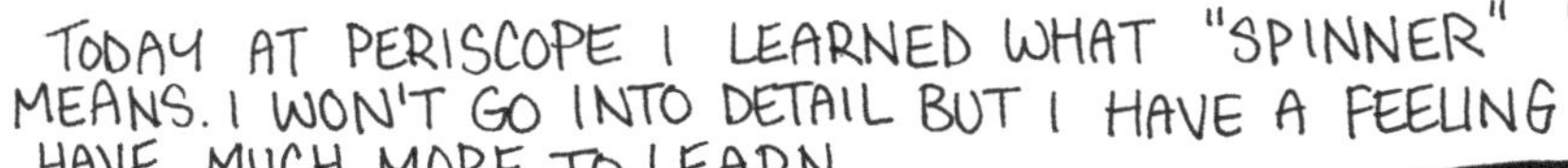

TODAY AT PERISCOPE I LEARNED WHAT "SPINNER" MEANS. I WON'T GO INTO DETAIL BUT I HAVE A FEELING I HAVE MUCH MORE TO LEARN.

WALKED JAMESTOWN HOME (SHE WORKS A COUPLE BLOCKS FROM THE STUDIO) AND HAD A BEER W/ HER AT SILVER DOLLAR. THERE, I HELPED OPEN A HARMONICA CASE FOR A BUM AND HE GAVE US SIX PEANUT BUTTER CUPS... I DID NOT TAKE.

SAW TOM AT AUSTIN'S B-DAY CELE AND I FINALLY GOT MY FLASK BACK!!!

HUNG OUT WITH MY DAD AND GOT PHO AND WENT TO FRY'S WHERE I FINISHED MY CHRISTMAS SHOPPING! HOORAY! GO ME!!!

YOU ALREADY KNOW HOW THIS WILL END.

NO, WE DON'T. SOME THINK THEY KNOW. BUT NOBODY DOES.

12.23.2009

GOT CAT'S OLD COUCH! I HAVE A COMFY COUCH TO REST MY BUM ON AND IT'S SO NICE! THANKS TO THOSE WHO MOVED IT IN MY APT! TIGHT SQUEEZE FROM THE HALL IN! I CAN'T MOVE OUT NOW! THE COUCH IS STUCK IN HERE.

12.24.2009
OMIGOD
SLEPT ON MY LEG/HIP WRONG AND IT HURTS LIKE A MOFO TO STAND. I WRITE THIS AT 9:15PM AND IT STILL HURTS! WAAAAH!
PAIN
MY X·MAS EVE DINNER!!
BACON CHICKEN RANCH
CAME IN TO PERISCOPE AND IT WAS ALMOST EMPTY SAVE JEFF PARKER. STAYED PRETTY LATE DRAWIN AND WATCHING "INTERNET TV"
P.S. I NEVER WEAR MY HAT BACKWARDS BUT I HAD NO HAIR CLIP TO HOLD MY BANGS BACK! FEEL LIKE I SHOULD BUST-A-MOVE! EHEH.

12 25. 2009

LAST MINUTE LENOX WRAPPING PRESENTS RIGHT BEFORE GOING TO THE PARENT'S HOUSE FOR CHRISTMAS.

I MADE MY FAMILY WATCH UP AND THEY MISSED THE FIRST 15MIN OF IT SO WHEN WE FINISHED, I REPLAYED THE BEGINING AND IT MADE MY MAMA CRY! SEEING HER CRY MADE ME CRY! IT WAS A CRY FEST.

PRIME RIB
WINE!
MASHED TATERS
I ATE GOOD. BY THAT I MEAN I TOOK SMALL PORTIONS AND I FINISHED MY PLATE!
AND HENRY PEED ON MY PARENT'S RUG TWICE
ASPERAGUS
A? UGH!
SQUASH
OH SHIT

12.26.2009
WHEN I GROW UP (I'M NOT GROWN UP!) I CAN BE ANYTHING! A SUPERHERO, A NINJA, A BANKER, A ZOOKEEPER... I THINK I WILL BE A CARTOONIST THOUGH....
THATS AS COOL AS A NINJA, RITE?
I HAVE'TA PEEEEE!
YOU CAN PEE ON THE SPRUCE GOOSE, DANIELLE
YEAH! BUT IT'S INSIDE THE HANGAR. I'LL PEE ON THAT ONE!
NO PEEING
I'LL PEE ON THAT PLANE!!
ME TOO!

ON A WHIM MY FRIENDS DECIDE TO TAKE A TRIP TO SPIRIT MOUNTAIN CASINO. I LOST $14 BUCKS AND GAVE A DJ FIVE DOLLARS TO PLAY THE JACKSON FIVE SONG "ABC 123" AND HE DIDN'T EVEN PLAY THE WHOLE THING. PFFT. IT WAS A FUN TRIP. GOT HOME AROUND 4 AM AND PASSED OUT LIKE NOBODY'S BUSINESS!

AFTER WATCHING THE ENTIRE FOURTH SEASON OF DEXTER, I HAD A BRAINSTORMING SESSION AT TALLY'S BDAY CELEBRATION... IF ☐ WAS A SERIAL KILLER...

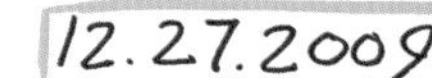

I WOULD POKE THEM W/ A NEEDLE LIKE DEXTER...

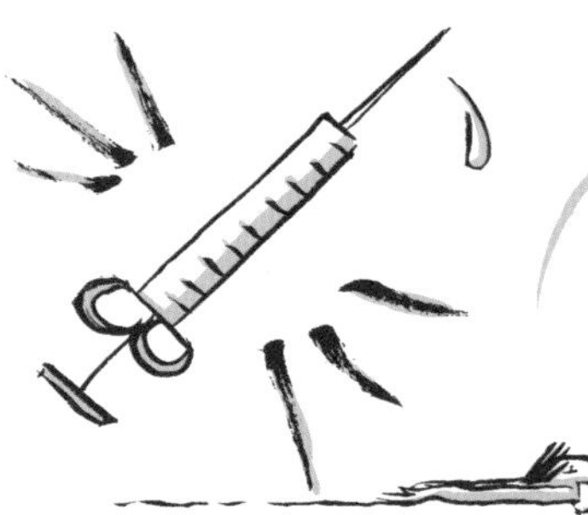

BUT MY VICTIMS HAVE TO BE SMALL SO I COULD MOVE THEM...

SO MY PATTERN VICTIMS WILL BE VEGAN HIPSTERS...

LIKE 100lbs!

MY SIGNATURE WOULD BE TO LEAVE WEENIE ASHES LIKE ON DEXTER... AS A HOMAGE TO MY FAVORITE SHOW.

I WOULD KEEP STRANDS OF THEIR HAIR AS MY TROPHIES.

"CAT ASH? WHY?!" THEY WOULD ASK

AND DUMP THE CUT UP BODIES (LEGS AND ARMS) INTO THE COLUMBIA TO BE WASHED TO THE PACIFIC.
SLICE OF LIFE

12.28.2009

HAD A DREAM WHERE I WAS PULLING OUT ENDLESS AMOUNTS OF LEECHES FROM MY WRIST. IT WAS GROSS AND SCARY.

I AM WAITING FOR SOMETHING TO GO WRONG...

JEREMY IS IN TOWN FROM INDIANA FOR THE HOLIDAYS. HUNG OUT WITH HIM AND LAURA AT NEW OLD LOMPOQUE... WAIT IT'S LOMPOC WHATEVS...

REMEMBER THOSE CAMPING TRIPS AND WHEN MATTY JUMPED INTO THE RIVER?

YEAH~ LIKE, NAKED IN WINTER!

I TOOK A DUECE AND WHEN I CAME OUT OF THE BATHROOM I SAW THAT IT WAS SNOWING! I JUMPED UP AND DOWN AND SCREAMED. RAN UP TO THE WINDOW AND ALMOST CRIED. SNOW IS A BIG DEAL TO ME!!

I WALKED DOWN-TOWN AND I COULDN'T STOP SMILING CUZ OF THE SNOW... BUT THEN I REALIZED EVERYONE WAS SMILING! AT LEAST EVERYONE WHO WAS NOT IN A CAR...

SNOW!

HAD SUSHI WITH RON, CAT, AND TALLY AND HAD PEPPERMINT PATTIES AT THE LOWBROW AND TALKED ABOUT DATING NIGHTMARES.

HA HA HA

SO I SAID "I HAVETA GO,,.NOW"

HA

HA

12.30.2009
PLEASE DON'T DROP BOMBS ON ME. I BEG OF THEE JUST LEAVE ME IN PEACE

12.31.2009

2009 WAS A GOOD YEAR. CONSIDERING WHO/WHERE I WAS A YEAR AGO, I'D GIVE IT A THUMBS UP. COMICS WISE, I'VE COME A LONG WAY! TRYING TO MAKE A CAREER WITH MY COMICS WAS NOT A THOUGHT ON MY MIND. A YEAR LATER IT'S ALL THAT IS ON MY MIND!

I INTERNED AT BOTH:

BRETT

LEIGH

TOP SHELF AND PERISCOPE

ENTERED THE DATING FIELD AND LEARNED A LOT ABOUT MY HEART AND WHAT I WANT IN THAT DEPT. 2009 WAS PROBABLY THE WORST BUT I HAVE HIGH HOPES FOR 2010!

MADE A TON OF AWESOME NEW FRIENDS! ♥ I HAVE COMIC FRIENDS! I REMEMBER DRAWING ABOUT HOW I DIDN'T HAVE ANY!

IN A LOT OF WAYS 2009 TREATED ME WELL... IN OTHER WAYS IT WAS TOUGH. BUT I KNOW

IS GONNA BE SO AWESOME! I KNOW IT! IT'S GONNA BE ALL AROUND EFFING FANTASTIC! LOTS OF HARD WORK AHEAD BUT I KNOW I CAN DO IT!

JANUARY 2010

1/10 "KILL"
-JIMMY EAT WORLD
1/11 "DIZZY"
-JIMMY EAT WORLD
1/13 "WHY DO YOU LET ME STAY HERE?"
-SHE AND HIM
1/20 "HALLELUJAH"
-A LA RUFUS WAINWRIGHT
1/21 "CHASE THIS LIGHT"
-JIMMY EAT WORLD
2010
POO

1.1.2010
LAST NIGHT HUNG OUT AT THE LOMPOC WITH JAMES-TOWN, JEREMY AND LAURA. THEN WE CABBED OVER TO STEVE & SARA'S PARTY WHERE I LOST MY MIND. LETS JUST SAY I TRIED ABSINTHE FOR THE FIRST. I DON'T THINK THAT I AM A FAN...
AT THE LOMPOC WE WENT OVER THE "BEST AND WORST OF'S" OF 2009
CLINK!
DOING THE "WORST OF'S" WAS THE BEST. SAYING IT OUT LOUD AND DUMPING IT BEHIND IN '09. WE WOULD SAY "EFF ______" THEN CHEERS!
WORE SOME NEW HEELS THAT MURDERED MY FEET! BUT HEY, AT LEAST FOR ONE NIGHT I WAS A LITTLE BIT TALLER... NOT QUITE A BALLER...
Le Pain
CHATTED WITH ERIKA (DAR) WHO TOLD ME ABOUT SOME OF THE UPS AND DOWNS SHE WENT THROUGH WITH AUTO-BIO COMICS. IT WAS ALL VERY INSIGHTFUL I REALLY NEED TO CHAT WITH HER SOMETIME WITHOUT BEING UNDER THE INFLUENCE!
WENT TO TONY'S... SAW BEN...
GOT HOME AROUND 3AM. I WAS THOROUGHLY PARTIED OUT
AND TODAY...
UGH
I PAID THE TOLL HAPPY NEW YEAR!

1.2.2010

PLUCK

CRACKED WINE GLASS FINALLY BROKE

BUH BYE CHRISTMAS... I LUB U...

FOR BEING SO USELESS YESTERDAY, I DID TONS OF CHORES TODAY. PUT AWAY THE CHRISTMAS STUFF, DID THE DISHES, VACCUMED, AND PAINTED AN OLD SKATEDECK I FOUND ON THE STREET WITH ARMY KITTIES. FEELS LIKE SUNDAY BUT THANK GOODNESS IT'S ONLY SATURDAY!

EMITOWN

2010

emi lenox

PAINTED THIS OLD SKATE DECK I FOUND IN THE STREET LIKE, 6 YEARS AGO! I KNEW EVENTUALLY I'D KNOW WHAT TO PAINT ON IT! MAYBE I'LL SELL IT ON ETSY...

WE GOTTA WAIT IT OUT!!

2009 HAS CLAIMED TOO MANY CASUALTIES... SO MANY IT'S LEAKING INTO 2010! BACK INTO THE BUNKER!

PICKED UP MY DAD'S MEDS FOR HIM. HE HAS SO MANY MEDS. WHAT DO THEY ALL DO?! WILL I NEED TONS OF MEDS WHEN I'M OLDER? I HOPE NOT. I SUCK AT SWALLOWIN PILLS.

MET SOMEONE THAT JAMESTOWN KNEW WHO WE RAN INTO ON THE STREET. SHE GIVES A MEAN HANDSHAKE! I THINK SOME BONES SPLINTERED IN MY HAND. I THOUGHT "DOES SHE HATE?! IS THIS A WARNING?" TURNS OUT SHE JUST HAS A POWERFUL HANDSHAKE...

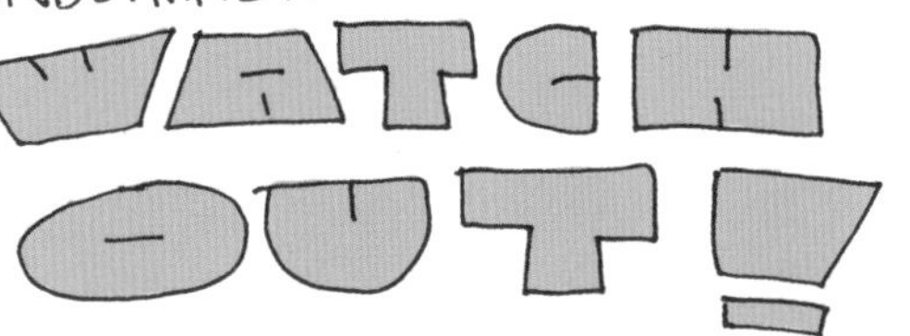

WATCH OUT!

WOULD YOU LIKE TO PET ONE?
WENT TO PETSMART WHERE A LADY ASKED IF I WANTED TO PET THE KITTIES. WHEN I SAID I REALLY WANTED TO BUT CAN'T BUY ONE AT THE MOMENT, SHE BLEW ME OFF! I DIDN'T GET TO PET THE KITTIES...
?

1.4.2010

TODAY I CHANGE BUILDINGS FOR WORK. I NO LONGER WILL BE ABLE TO GET MY BREAKFAST BURRITOS... I HAD MY LAST ONE TODAY BEFORE MOVING MY STUFF ACROSS THE RIVER TO MONTGOMERY PARK.

BYE

THE NEW BUILDING USED TO BE A MONTGOMERY WARD BUT NOW IT'S AN OFFICE BUILDING... OH-MY-GOD THEY HAVE A **PIANO** PLAYER THAT PLAYS EVERY DAY IN THE LUNCH AREA FROM 11:30 ~ 1:00

WAAAAT?!

THEY ALSO HAVE A NEAT FOUNTAIN IN THE FRONT... AND ORIENTAL VASES ON EACH FLOOR (THERE ARE 9 FLOORS) BY THE REALLY NICE ELEVATOR

THERE IS A GIFT SHOP HERE TOO! IT SELLS THOSE TWIRLY BAMBOO PLANTS, SODA, AND GREETING CARDS!

I ALSO SAW SOME SUITS! ♥

I THINK I'M GONNA LIKE IT HERE...

ON A SIDE NOTE, I GOT A HIT ON MY SITE FROM THE ATLANTIC OCEAN.

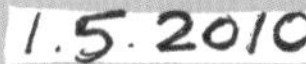
1.5.2010

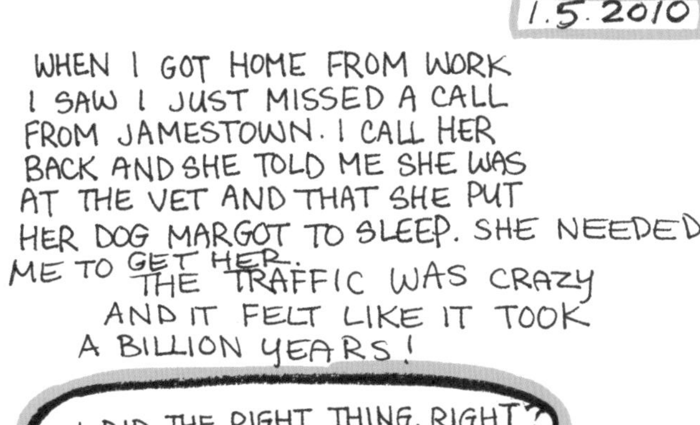
WHEN I GOT HOME FROM WORK I SAW I JUST MISSED A CALL FROM JAMESTOWN. I CALL HER BACK AND SHE TOLD ME SHE WAS AT THE VET AND THAT SHE PUT HER DOG MARGOT TO SLEEP. SHE NEEDED ME TO GET HER.
THE TRAFFIC WAS CRAZY AND IT FELT LIKE IT TOOK A BILLION YEARS!

WHAT?
I DID THE RIGHT THING, RIGHT? SHE DIDN'T KNOW, RIGHT?
I GUESS POOR MARGOT SUDDENLY WAS PARALYZED FROM THE WAIST DOWN DUE TO A RUPTURED DISC.
MARGOT
IT'S SO HARD TO SEE SOMEONE YOU LOVE SO SAD. AND YOU CAN'T FLICK A SWITCH AND MAKE EVERYTHING BETTER. JUST TRY AND BE STRONG FOR THEM AND BE THERE...
I WENT INTO HER APT FOR HER AND GATHERED ALL OF THE MARGOT STUFF AND PUT IT IN THE TRUNK OF MY CAR. WHICH IS KINDA FUNNY SINCE WEENIE'S STUFF IS STILL IN THERE TOO...
MARGOT HAD A GOOD LIFE... THOUGH IT WAS ONLY THREE YEARS, IT WAS THE BEST THREE YEARS ANY DOG COULD HAVE!
NOW, SHE'S CATCHING SQUIRRELS IN DOGGIE HEAVEN.

1.06.2010
I GOT MY JOB CAUSE THE PERSON I REPLACED WENT TO JAIL FOR MURDER. AND I WORKED ON THE SAME TEAM AS HIM AT OUR OLD JOB...
WHEN ASKED TO INTRODUCE MYSELF TO THE TEAM AT MONTGOMERY PARK I ENJOY TELLING THEM HOW I GOT MY JOB THERE IN THE FIRST PLACE.
I USE BOTH A CLOCK ALARM AND A CELL PHONE ALARM... I WAKE UP TO THE FINAL FANTASY OPENING SONG. DOOD, I'M SO COOL
CHEESE IT
Cheetoes
Lay
SHHHIT...
I... AM... TOM KINDA... NOT AS CRAZY...
ANNOYED AT THE MACHINE AT WORK... I WANT THE CHEESE-ITS... I SEE THE CHEESE ITS... BUT IT WON'T LET ME HAVE THE CHEESE ITS... "CHOOSE ANOTHER SELECTION" MY ASS. I CHOOSE CHEETOES AND AM NEVER HAPPY...

1.07.2010

JAY

LENO PUNCH!

WHAT IS THIS?! JAY LENO WANTS HIS SHOW BACK?! HEY IT'S NOT YOUR SHOW ANYMORE! IT'S CONAN'O!

2010

WTF.

WHATS WITH ALL THIS SHIT IN THE FIRST WEEK OF THE YEAR! THIS BETTER BE 2010 GETTING THE SHIT OUT OF THE WAY FIRST...

TO DO:

- EMITOWN COVERS
- MAIL
- REPLY E-MAILS
- POPGUN
- COMIXS
- PAINT

JUST DEW IT

AT THE NEW BUILDING I HAVE MOVED TO A FANCIER BREAKFAST REGULARITY: THE BREAKFAST PANINI! IT TOO IS NICELY CUT IN HALF AND IT CONSISTS OF CHEESE, BACON, AND EGG... A LITTLE PRICIER THAN THE BURRITO.

THE BURRITO WAS BETTER THOUGH... *SIGH*

IN MY NEW TEAM (I'M PART OF A TEAM!) I GET TO GO TO THE HUDDLES WITH EVERY ONE ELSE! IT'S SO AWESOME! I NEVER GOT TO GO AT THE OTHER BUILDING. IT FEELS NICE TO BE A PART OF SOMETHING

OWL TICKETS URGENT...cbFC... PROD... Q1...
YAY!
CONFERENCE SPACE

DUE TO MY LACK OF FUNDS, I STAYED IN ON A FRIDAY NIGHT. I DREW A BIT AND IT WAS PRETTY NICE.

FOR CAT'S BIRTHDAY, A GROUP OF US DID VOICEBOX KARAOKE. IT'S A PLACE WITH PRIVATE ROOMS SO THE ONLY PEOPLE YOU'LL BE A FOOL TO ARE YOUR FRIENDS. BECAUSE OF THIS, I ATTEMPTED A BUNCH OF SONGS I'D NEVER TRY AT A BAR.
1.09.2010
I TRIED:
"YOU GIVE LOVE A BAD NAME" BON JOVI
"SUNGLASSES AT NIGHT" COREY HART
"NEVER GET OVER YOU..." EXPOSE
"STARLIGHT" MUSE
"IRONIC" ALANIS
"BASKET CASE" GREEN DAY
"IN THE END" LINKIN PARK
"I SWEAR" ALL 4 1
HEE HEE!
HA HA!
AFTER
THE FESTIVITIES, MET UP WITH JAKE TO GET MY FREE
BOOTS
AT THE MATADOR.
THANX! I DRAW U PICTURE
DRAW ME VENOM?
POOR PERSON SHOPPING.
SALAD
BREAD
ORGANIC
TOMATOES
EGGS
CUZ IN THE END, IT DOESN'T EVEN MATTERRRRRR
ZZZZZZZZ
ASLEEP BEFORE MIDNIGHT ON A SATURDAY! YIKES...

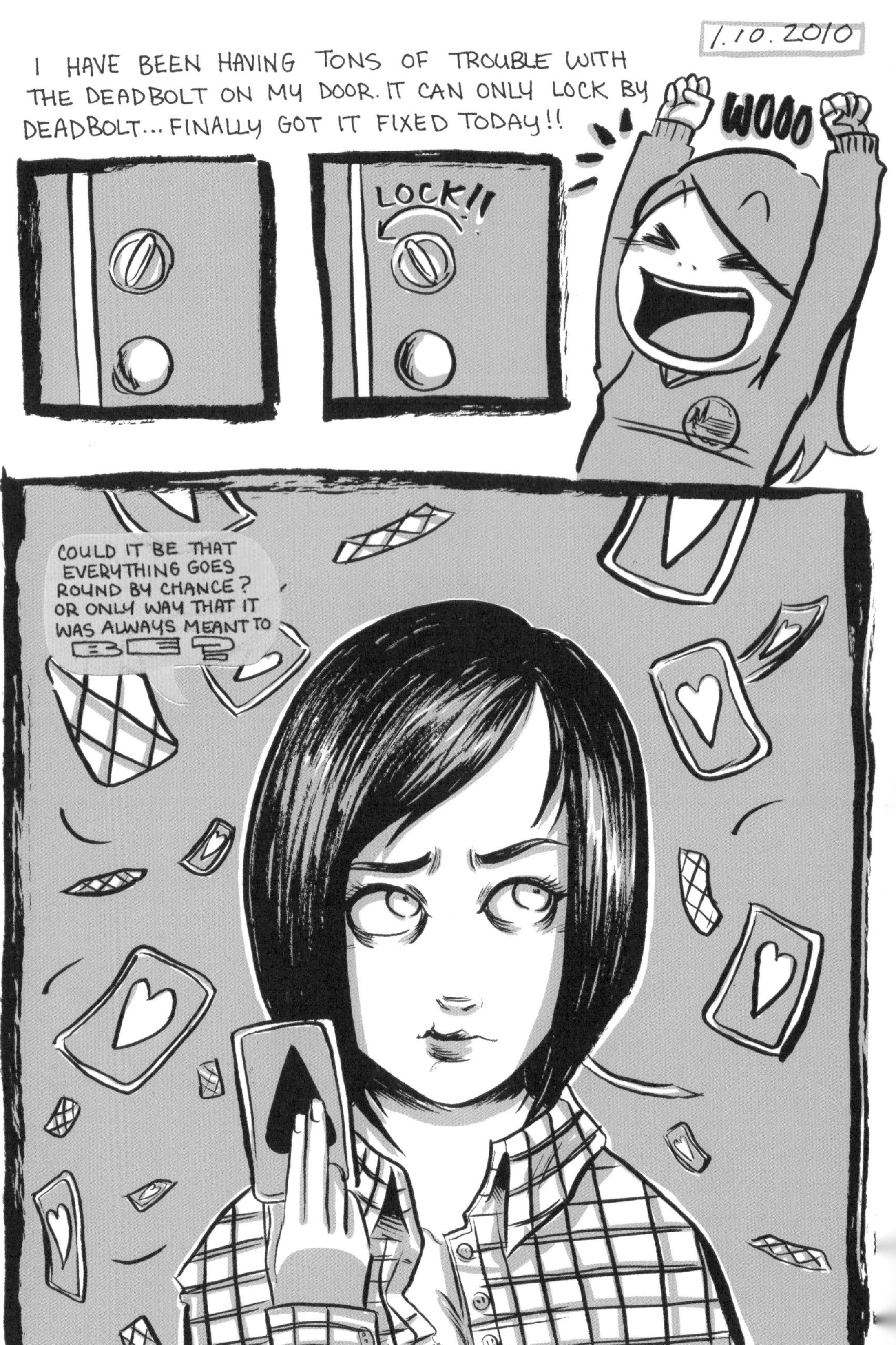
1.10.2010
I HAVE BEEN HAVING TONS OF TROUBLE WITH THE DEADBOLT ON MY DOOR. IT CAN ONLY LOCK BY DEADBOLT... FINALLY GOT IT FIXED TODAY!!
LOCK!!
WOOO
COULD IT BE THAT EVERYTHING GOES ROUND BY CHANCE? OR ONLY WAY THAT IT WAS ALWAYS MEANT TO BE?

1.11.2010
GAS
CHECKED MY BANK ACCOUNT AND SAW I HAVE $1.78... CHECKED MY CREDIT CARD AND SAW I HAVE $3.24 AVAILABLE CREDIT... THREE AND A HALF WEEKS OF NO PAY IS PROVING FRIGHTENING. THURSDAY IS PAYDAY... COME QUICK
BEEN PAYING FOR COFFEE WITH MY LAUNDRY QUARTERS...
8 QUARTERS
RESPECTFULLY, SOME HONESTY, I'M ASKING NOW. DO YOU HEAR THE CONVERSATION WE TALK ABOUT? I'LL BACK AWAY TO THE SAFETY OF A QUIET HOUSE. IF THERE'S HALF A CHANCE IN THIS MOMENT, WHEN YOUR EYES MEET MINE I SHOW IT ALL.
IF THERE'S SOMETHING LEFT TO LOSE THEN DON'T LET ME WEAR OUT MY SHOES. I'M STILL WALKING...

1.12.2010

TEAM COCO

TEAM COCO

LENO!? SERIOUSLY? CONAN IS THE BIGGER MAN FOR BACKING DOWN SO HE DOESN'T RAIN ON FALLON'S PARADE ... YOU CAN'T DO THE SAME FOR CONAN WHO WORKED HARD AND EARNED HIS SPOT?! PFFT. WHOTEVS.

POOR PERSON'S

BREAKFAST & LUNCH

BAR MIX

FREE FROM BREAK ROOM

COFFEE

$2 IN QUARTERS

COOKIE

SUPERVISOR GOT ME

PEANUTS

FREE FROM COMMUNITY BOWL IN A CUBICLE

WE COULD BREAK THE WINDOW WITH THE FIRE EXTINGUISHER...THEN CLIMB UP TO THE TOP SINCE THE FIRE ESCAPE IS MISSING THE BOTTOM...WAIT FOR THE COPS

WHAT IF THEY CHASE AFTER YOU?

SMOKE EM WITH THE EXTINGUISHER THEN HIT THEM ON THE HEAD WITH IT...

MY COWORKERS AND I DISCUSS WHAT WE'D DO IF SOMEONE WENT POSTAL AT THE OFFICE

1.13.2010
WHY DO YOU LET ME STAY HERE ALL BY MYSELF WHY DON'T YOU COME AND PLAY HERE? I'M JUST SITTING ON THE SHELF.
WHY DON'T YOU SIT RIGHT DOWN AND STAY AWHILE. WE LIKE THE SAME THINGS AND I LIKE YOUR STYLE.
IT'S NOT A SECRET WHY DO YOU KEEP IT? I'M JUST SITTING ON THE SHELF.
I GOTTA GET YOUR PRESENCE... LETS MAKE IT KNOWN. I THINK YOU ARE JUST SO PLEASANT. I WOULD LIKE YOU FOR MY OWN.
WHY DON'T YOU SIT RIGHT DOWN AND MAKE ME SMILE. YOU MAKE FEEL LIKE I'M JUST A CHILD. WHY DO YOU END IT? JUST GIVE ME CREDIT. I'M JUST SITTING ON THE SHELF...

I SAVE U! 1.14.2010
NOTHING IS GROWING...
OF COURSE NOT. IT'S JUST DIRT...
GO FIND A POT WITH A SEED IN IT!
?
FOUND A LADYBUG IN THE WORK BATHROOM. I TOOK IT OUT OF THERE BUT IT INSISTED ON FLYING AWAY INTO THE LOBBY...
JUST CUZ YOU CAN'T SEE IT, DOESN'T MEAN IT'S NOT THERE...
THERE'S ALWAYS A SEED. MAYBE IT'S JUST NOT THE RIGHT SEASON
HMMPH! IT'S NEVER THE RIGHT SEASON! GIVE UP!
GOT PAID TODAY!!
IT'S BEEN ALMOST FOUR WEEK
I FEEL SO RICH NOW! LIKE I COULD BUY A BOAT!!
MAI BOAT
WE ALL HAVE OUR MOMENTS OF COMPLETE TRANSPARENCY. SHIELDS DOWN UNEXPECTEDLY. OUR WEAK, PATHETIC, AND VULNERABLE CORE EXPOSED. IT'S NOTHING TO BE ASHAMED OF. EVERYONE HAS A HEART.
BUT DANG IT
I HATE IT WHEN ALL DEFENSES ARE DOWN!
I BLAME COFFEE.
IT IS ONE SOURCE THAT CAN SOMETIMES SHRED ALL PROTECTIVE ARMOR.
CURSE YOU

1.15.2010

TURNS OUT MY PLACE OF WORK HAS LADYBUGS EVERYWHERE! THEY COME OUT OF THE HEATING VENTS... THEY FALL!! AND DIE!

OH NO. WHERE I WORK IS A PLACE OF DEATH LADYBUG DEATH... I SAVE WHAT I CAN BUT I CAN'T SAVE ALL...

YOU STILL WATCHING THAT POT?! OMG... GIVE UP!!!

DUMB!

JAMESTOWN CAME HOME FROM CALIFORNIA AND SHE, DOOX, AND I WENT TO THE M BAR. IT WAS FUN AND PRETTY LOW KEY. AFTER THAT, JAMESTOWN WENT HOME AND DOOX AND I HUNG OUT AT THE MATADOR.

1.16.2010

THERE WAS A SOLAR ECLIPSE YESTERDAY... TOO BAD I COULDN'T SEE IT... WASN'T VISIBLE IN THE STATES. AN ECLIPSE IS A SYMBOL FOR CHANGE AND NEW BEGINNINGS...

LET THE NEW BEGININGS START!

OHH SHIIIT !!!!

PLAYED WIZARD (A TRUMP CARD GAME WHERE YOU NEED TO DO "TRICKS") WITH JAMESTOWN, AND DOOX. LIKE ALWAYS IT WAS VERY FUN. WE **NEVER** PLAY SAFE. WE MAKE SURE THE BIDS ARE NEVER EVEN ON EACH ROUND JUST SO IT MAKES IT MORE INTERESTING AND COMPETITIVE. WE SHOW NO **MERCY** WHEN WE PLAY. SOMETIMES OUTSIDERS WHO PLAY WITH US GET OFFENDED. HA HA. NEEDLESS TO SAY, I GOT LAST PLACE... BUT IT WAS REALLY NICE TO SEE JAMESTOWN LAUGH AND SMILE. SHE HAS BEEN OUT OF SORTS SINCE MARGOT PASSED...

DID THE DISHES AND VACUUMED WHILE HAVING A PRIVATE DANCE PARTY WITH MY IPOD! OH JOYS OF HOUSE CHORES!

WENT TO FIRE ON THE MOUNTAIN WHERE I HAD MY FIRST DEEP FRIED PICKLE. I WAS SCARED TO TRY IT... BUT WHEN I FINALLY DID... IT WASN'T SO BAD. PRETTY TASTY ACTUALLY. I DO LIKE MY PICKLES!

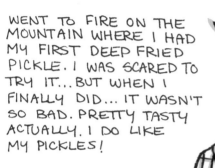

TRY IT!

eeerM...

JUMP KICK

WHIRLWIND!

JUMP KICK

TAPPA TAPPA TAPPA

WENT TO GROUND KONTROL WHERE WE PLAYED A RACING GAME (I SUCK) AND SOME PIN BALL AND FINALLY X·MEN I PLAYED STORM... AND DIED LIKE A TRILLION TIMES...

1.18.2010

POP!

EEP

DELL

11:01

FOR THE FIRST TIME LAST WEEK I HEARD A LOUD SNAPPING SOUND IN THE LIVING ROOM. SCARED BOTH HENRY AND I. I HAD NO IDEA WHAT IT WAS. THEN LAST NIGHT IT HAPPENED AGAIN! RIGHT BY MY BED. SOUNDED LIKE A LIGHTBULB BURSTING BUT SUPER LOUD. I CHECKED EVERYWHERE! IT DOESN'T MAKE SENSE! IT'S LIKE PARANORMAL ACTIVITY IS HAPPENING IN MY APT! OR IT'S JUST THE APT BUILDING ITSELF "BREATHING" AND "SETTLING"... HMMPH!

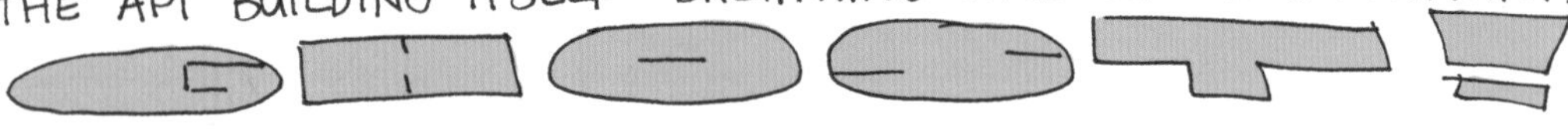

FINALLY HAVE CASH FOR THE ESTEEMED BURRITO CART AT MONTGOMERY PARK AND TURNS OUT... THEY OBSERVE MLK DAY... DARN! TOMORROW

HUNG OUT W/ SEAN FOR A LITTLE BIT BEFORE HE LEAVES TO BE A MOVIE STAR.

1.19.2010
BEANS AND RICE AND GUAC AND CHICKEN AND HOT SAUCE AND SOUR CREAM AND DELICIOUSNESS!
I DID IT
I FINALLY GOT THE BURRITO! IT WAS REALLY GOOD!
SCAR!!
BALLOON SCAR FROM LAST YEAR STILL THERE! SOME DEADLY BALLOON!!!
GOT SOME GOOD ADVICE FROM DEREK... HE SHOULD SET UP A COUNSELING BOOTH LIKE LUCY.
ADVICE 5¢
CAN NOT HEAR. HEADPHONES!
IDIOT
JAMIE
SHUT UP!!!

SOMETIMES THE END IS VISIBLE IN THE BEGINNING. YOU JUST NEED TO BE MORE AWARE. JUST JUMP BUT WITH YOUR EYES **OPEN.**

1.21.2010
CONFETTI RAINFALL AND THE QUIET STREET. THESE THINGS I'VE FOUND ARE SPECIAL NOW, THE KNOT IS IN MY REACH. BECAUSE TONIGHT, THE WORLD TURNED IN ME. BECAUSE RIGHT NOW I DON'T DARE TO BREATHE. OH BABE, I KNOW IT'S ALIVE AND SOMEWHERE FOR US TO FIND TONIGHT. CHASE THIS LIGHT WITH ME...
YAY
THE POLES ARE SHIFTING. I CAN FEEL IT! THINGS ARE GETTING BETTER!
GHOST ATTACK
SLICE
CUT
I SUDDENLY HAD A REALIZATION LAST NIGHT. IT HIT ME LIKE A FLASH OF LIGHTNING! IT WAS SO OBVIOUS! WHY DIDN'T I SEE IT BEFORE? WHY I HAVE BEEN THE WAY I AM... IT'S A TOXIC LINE OF THINKING SPAWNED BY UNFORTUNATE PAST EXPERIENCES. IT'S SO OBVIOUS BUT SOMETIMES IT CAN CLOUD YOUR MIND SO MUCH, IT'S HARD TO SEE IT. NOW THAT I CAN, I WILL NOT ALLOW IT TO HINDER OR POISON MY FUTURE EXPERIENCES!!!
TAKE THAT!
I AM GROWING UP!
CONFIDENCE = +10 EXP
GHOST ATTACK = LEVEL UP!

1.22.2010

GAB GAB GAB

GOT OUT OF WORK EARLY AND SO I DECIDED TO GO TO THE STUDIO (PERISCOPE) BUT INSTEAD OF DRAWING, I END UP BEING A CHATTY MC CHATTERSON... DYLAN DID TEACH ME HOW TO PAGINATE IN INDESIGN.

BLAH

I ♥ JORDAN

?

-IN BLITZ'S BATHROOM THERE IS A CHALK BOARD...

MEDICINE FRIDAY WAS AWESOME! TALLY WAS IN TOWN FOR THE WEEKEND! CAT, RON, TALLY, AND I WENT TO A MARTINI BAR WHERE WE SPOILED OURSELVES WITH FANCY MARTINIS! THEN TO BLITZ AND THEN SUSHILAND ♥♥ (WE HAD "NAUGHTY TALK") AND FINALLY TALLY AND I FINISHED THE NIGHT AT THE MARTHON WHERE WE DREW DRUNK! I LOVE HOW NERDY THAT IS! ♥♥♥

DRUNK SKETCH GROUP!

1.23.2010

TODAY DOOX AND I WENT WITH JAMESTOWN TO PICK UP MARGOT'S ASHES. IT WAS A VERY SAD MOMENT WHEN THE WOODEN BOX WAS HANDED OVER TO HER. I AM VERY GLAD WE COULD BE THERE FOR HER... ♥♥♥

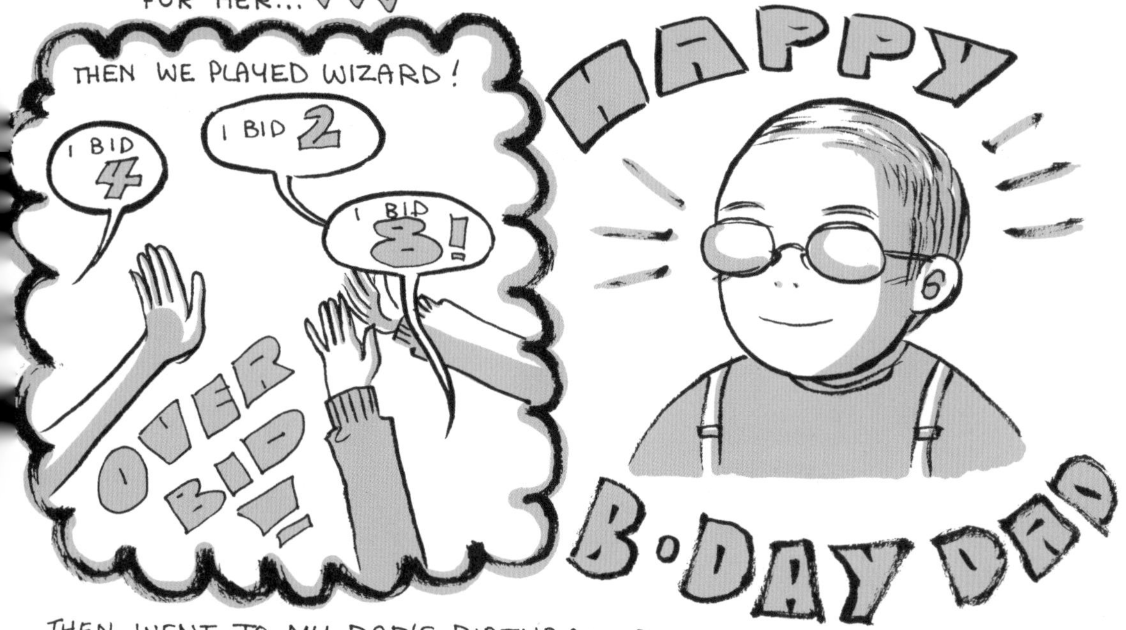

THEN WE PLAYED WIZARD!
I BID 4
I BID 2
I BID 8!
OVER BID!
HAPPY
B.DAY DAD

THEN WENT TO MY DAD'S BIRTHDAY DINNER. MY MOTHER TRIED TO EXPLAIN THE MOVIE AVATAR WHICH WENT AS FOLLOWS: "IT'S ABOUT SPIRIT... THEN (WAVES ARMS IN THE AIR) BIG EXPLOSION". REST OF THE FAMILY "..... WHAT?!"

THEN I HUNG OUT WITH THE CREW AT MY FATHER'S PLACE (A BAR) THEN WE WENT TO THE GALAXY FOR KARAOKE... EVERYONE WAS GOING TO PLAY LATE NIGHT B·BALL BUT ▭ WAS VERY TIRED... BUT BEFORE GOING HOME, BRITNEY AND STEPHAN INSISTED I TRY A KOI PORK TACO... KOI IS AN ASIAN FUSION TACO CART OFF BURNSIDE. I ADMIT THEY WERE TASTY!!

1.24.2010

HAD SKETCH GROUP WITH CAT AND TALLY AT PERISCOPE. DAVID HAHN WAS THERE TOO. IT WAS PRETTY QUIET BUT IT WAS STILL FUN!

ENERGY GIRL!

IF I WAS A SUPERHERO I WOULD BE ENERGY GIRL! POWERED BY SPAZ ATTACKS! MUAHAHAHA! I'LL HYPE MY ENEMIES TO DEATH!

YAY!

SPAZ ATTACK!

1.25.2010

♪ I GET TEN THOUSAND HUGS FROM TEN THOUSAND LIGHTNING BUGS ♫

HAD TO DO SOME WORK AT CORP VI (OLD BUILDING) WHICH IS AWESOME CAUSE I GET TO HAVE A BREAKFAST BURRITO!

I ALSO FIGURED OUT HOW TO USE THE RADIO ON MY PHONE. THERE ARE SOME SERIOUS LAME SONGS

WTF

ZZZZ

ENERGY GIRL'S WEAKNESS... THE COFFEE CRASH!

JAMESTOWN, DOOX, AND I WATCHED THE BACHELOR. JAMESTOWN USED TO HAVE PEOPLE OVER TO WATCH IT ALL THE TIME BACK IN THE DAY. I'M GLAD WE'RE DOING IT AGAIN! IT'S SO MUCH FUN!

1.26.2010

THIS WHOLE TIME I THOUGHT MY MONSTERS & DAMES FOR THE ECCC BOOK DIDN'T GET IN...

BUT TODAY

THEY PUT UP INFO ABOUT THE BOOK ON THE ECCC SITE WHICH INCLUDED THE NAMES OF THE ARTISTS IN IT... AND MY NAME WAS ON THE LIST! WHAT AN AWESOME SURPRISE. I'VE NEVER BEEN IN A BOOK BEFORE...

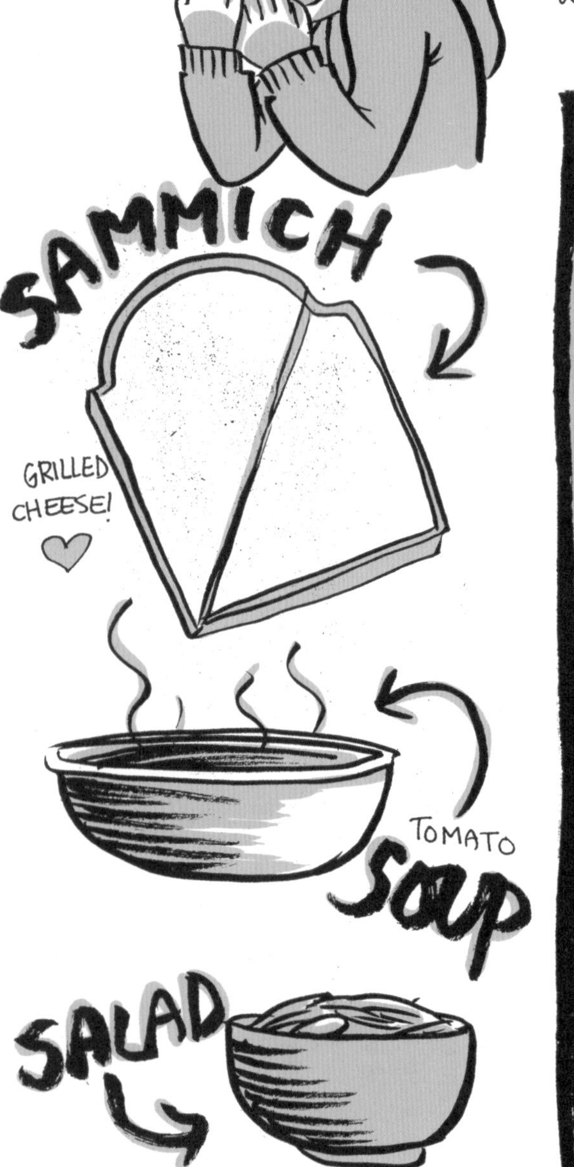

YAY!
SAMMICH
GRILLED CHEESE!
TOMATO SOUP
SALAD

I'M SO TIRED... WHAT'S THE POINT ANYWAY? IF I'M ALWAYS FIGHTING AND HIDING, I'D NEVER BE HAPPY... I SHOULDN'T ACT LIKE BAD THINGS WILL HAPPEN... OR EXPECT IT... I'M JUST SETTING MYSELF UP FOR DISASTER!!!
I'LL KEEP THE ARMY OF CATS ON THE DEFENSIVE THO... HEH...

1.27.2010

BEEN GETTING TIRED OF THE TUNES ON MY IPOD SO I STARTED TO LISTEN TO THE RADIO AT WORK. HIP HOP / R&B OR WHATEVER HAS SOME VERY SUGGESTIVE LYRICS. I DON'T EVEN KNOW WHAT HALF OF IT MEANS! THEY USE THE WORDS SWAGGER AND EGG WHITES... WTF DO THEY MEAN BY EGG WHITES?! I'LL TELL YOU WHAT THOUGH... THAT J.R. DERULO HAS SOME CATCHY SONGS!

MAKES ME WANNA

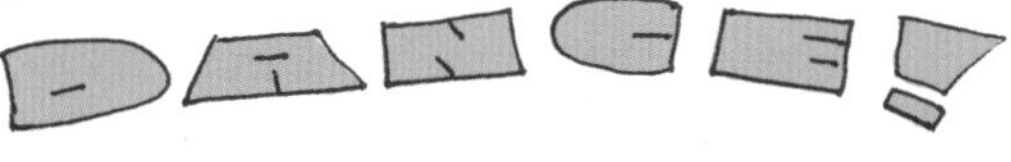

DANCE!

SO I HEAR THAT THE SUICIDE GIRLS WILL BE AT COMIC-CON THIS YEAR. YA GOIN TO SEE THEM?
....HUH
?!!

COWORKER ASKS ME IF I'M GOING TO SEE THE SUICIDE GIRLS AT COMIC-CON IN THE BREAK ROOM. I WAS SO THROWN OFF. I WASN'T SURE WHY HE WAS ASKING ME... WAS HE IMPLYING I'M DIRTY AND INTO TATTOOED LADIES? THEN I REALIZED HE HAD NO CLUE WHO THE SUICIDE GIRLS ARE. TALK ABOUT AWKWARD!!

1.28.2010

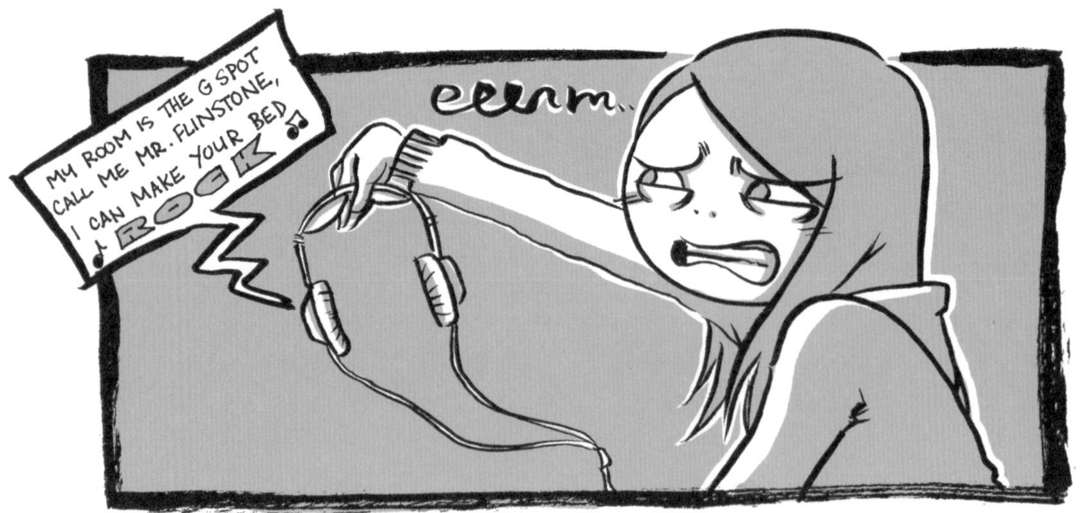

STILL LISTENING TO THE DIRTY SONGS. SOME OF THEM MAKE ME FEEL LIKE I COULD CONTRACT STD'S JUST FROM LISTENING TO THEM! LIKE I NEED TO CONDOM MY EARS! EWWWW!

FOCUS!

EMI! GET A BEER WITH ME! I DON'T WANNA GO HOME!

I'M SO TIRED OF FEELING SAD...

EMI! COME OVER PLEASE! SOMETHING BAD HAPPENED!

FOCUS!

I FEEL SO FOOLISH! I CAN'T BELIEVE IT...

I'LL DO WHATEVER I CAN FOR THE ONES I LOVE...

1.29.2010

WALKED INTO THE BREAK ROOM AND TONS OF PEOPLE WERE HANGIN OUT BY THE WATERCOOLER. I THOUGHT 'OH COOL! LIKE ON T.V.!' AND MADE A JOKE ONLY TO RECEIVE ABSOLUTELY NO REACTION

WENT TO MUU MUU'S WITH JAMESTOWN AND DOOX TO GET DRINKS, GRUB, AND PLAY **WIZARD!**

WHEN PEOPLE ASK, I FEEL SO NERDY... IT SOUNDS ALL D & D OR SOMETHING. HA HA

AFTER THAT I HOOKED UP W/ BRIT AND LINDS AT THE MATADOR

WAS TOLD THERE WILL BE A SCRABBLE

E

TOURNAMENT ON SUPER BOWL SUNDAY!

DARE I PARTICIPATE?!

WHAT DO THEY MEAN BY "EGG WHITES"?!

OH, EMI...

THEN STEPHAN PICKED US UP AND WE HUNG OUT AT MY FATHER'S PLACE... WHERE I DRANK TOO MUCH... I **HATE** WHEN THAT HAPPENS. I SUCK.

WAS A BIT HUNG OVER. THINK IT WAS DUE TO NOT EATING MUCH OF A DINNER LAST NIGHT. DRINKS DESTROYED ME! I TRY TO AVOID IT. SOMETIMES I FAIL!

1.30.2010
WAH

BOUGHT MY PA SOME WENDY'S AND TOLD HIM HOW I WANTED A CAT... BUT ONE LIKE WEENIE. WEENIE WAS PRETTY CALM AND MELLOW FOR A CAT... NEVER BIT OR SCRATCHED. NEVER MEAN. THIS IS WHAT MY DAD HAD TO SAY ABOUT THAT:

WEENIE WAS A RETARDED CAT. I HAD ONE WHEN I WAS YOUNG. DON'T THINK CATS LIKE WEENIE ARE A COMMON THING
YOU'RE SAYING I ALREADY HAD THE ONE RETARDED CAT IN MY LIFETIME? DARN.

EMITOWN
QUIT IT!

I FEEL UNSETTLED KNOWING GUYS I DATE COULD BE READING EMITOWN... I ASK THEM NOT TO. ALTHOUGH IT'S NOT MAJORLY REVEALING, IT'S ENOUGH. IT MAKES ME VULNERABLE! AND THEY WOULD KNOW MORE ABOUT ME THAN I DO OF THEM! NOT FAIR! PLUS I DON'T WANT TO BE JUDGED BY EMITOWN.

IT'S SO WEIRD. BUT I DO PUT IT OUT THERE... IF I'M DATING YOU AND YOU'RE READING THIS

STOP!

PLEASEE!!

BAAH! I'D NEVER KNOW. CURSE DIARY COMICS

1.31.2010

WENT ON A SUPER LONG WALK IN WASHINGTON PARK. IT WAS PRETTY FUN. HAD NO SPECIFIC ROUTE OTHER THAN TO JUST KEEP WALKIN. I FORGET HOW MUCH I ENJOY IT. I LOVE THE WOODS! LISTENING TO TUNES AND DANCE WALKING ADDS TO THE FUN TOO! ♥♥♥

.....
I LOVE HOW IN MY NEIGHBORHOOD EVERYONE SAYS HI TO ME! THE COFFEESHOP FOLKS BOTH BARS, THE OLD DUDES WHO HANG OUT SMOKING OUTSIDE THE BARS AND MY NEIGHBORS IN THE APT

FEBRUARY 2010

2/9 "ALWAYS LOVE" -NADA SURF
2/11 "DO IT AGAIN" -NADA SURF
2/12 "SENTIMENTAL HEART" -SHE & HIM
2/15 "TINY VESSELS" -DEATHCAB FOR CUTIE
"ALL THE RIGHT MOVES" -ONE REPUBLIC

2.01.2010
BEEEP BEEEP
OKAY SOHO THE CHOCOBO. LESSEE IF I CAN GET YOU SOME SYLKIS GREENS-- WHATS THAT NOISE?
THE FINAL FANTASY THEME SONG ALARM MIXED WITH MY REGULAR ALARM THIS MORNING...A TAD CONFUSING FOR ME IN MY TOTALLY RAD NERD DREAM...
THEN TONIGHT FOR THE FIRST TIME EVER HENRY POOPED IN MY APT LOBBY... AND THE MANAGER SAW...
YIPE
NOOOO!

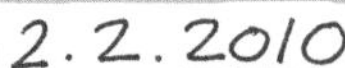
2.2.2010

OH NO! COFFEE ANXIETY IS AT A HIGH! MY HEART! UGH! DOES THIS HAPPEN TO MOST PEOPLE OR IS IT
JUST ME?
I'LL TELL YA WHAT. IT DOES MAKE FOR A CHALLENGING DAY...
ECCC PANIC!

SAMMICH POTLUCK!

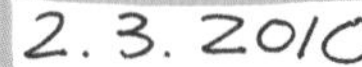

THE SANDWICH POTLUCK WAS THE COOLEST EVER! BUILD YOUR OWN SAMMICH IS ABSOLUTELY BRILLIANT! HAPPIEST PART OF THE DAY!

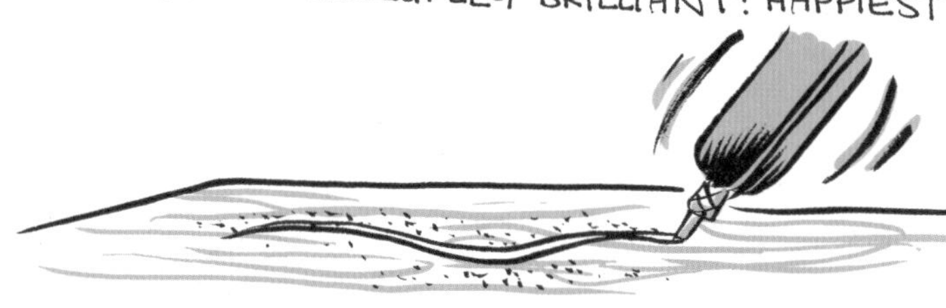

BRITTNEY SHOWED ME HER NEWLY AQUIRED DREMMEL THING. IT WAS PRETTY FUN CARVING INTO WOOD!

FINALLY WATCHED THE STAR TREK MOVIE AND IT MADE ME CRY WITHIN THE FIRST FIFTEEN MINUTES! IT BROUGHT ME BACK TO MY CHILDHOOD DAYS WHEN I WATCHED NEXT GENERATION ALL THE TIME. I EVEN MADE A STARSHIP ENTERPRISE MODEL THAT I HUNG OVER MY BED NEXT TO MY F-117 MODEL. THOSE WERE THE ONLY MODELS I HAVE EVER MADE.

I EVEN WORE MY HEADBAND OVER MY EYES SO I COULD PRETEND TO BE LIKE, GEORDI LAFORGE.

2.04.2010
ON MY WAY TO SEE JAMESTOWN I ALMOST GOT HIT BY A CAR LEGALLY CROSSING THE STREET. I MAY HAVE YELLED:
"NOOO! HOLY F*@!!# SHIT! I DON'T WANT TO DIE TODAY!!"
PLUS I DON'T HAVE INSURANCE SO I'D PREFER TO AVOID INJURY AT ALL COSTS...OR BLEED IN THE GUTTER.
NOOOOO!
M·BAR
HAPPY HOUR W/ JAMESTOWN
I SAW ON T.V. THAT THESE EXPERTS ARE 100% CERTAIN THERE WILL BE ANOTHER TERRORIST ATTACK IN 2010
DEADLY BOMBS!?
JAMESTOWN TOLD ME THAT THEY THINK IT MAY BE BY BOOB BOMBS!
WTF!

2.05.2010

FRIDAY AT WORK SUCKED BECAUSE A SUNNY AND DRY DAY IN PORTLAND IS MEANT TO BE TREASURED OUTSIDE... NOT INSIDE.

LENOX

W

MY PAL DOOX HAS BEEN LOSING WEIGHT WITH THIS NEW DIET PLAN WHERE YOU ONLY EAT ONE MASSIVE STEAK MEAL A DAY. I LOVE ME SOME STEAK... IF I COULD AFFORD IT, I WOULD TOTALLY BE ON THAT GRAVY TRAIN!!

PLAYED WIZARD AGAIN WITH JAMESTOWN AND DOOX! IT'S BECOME SUCH A REGULAR THING, IT'S LIKE WE ARE OUR OWN WIZARD CLUB! I SUGGEST WE MAKE CUSTOM WIZARD SHIRTS WITH OUR NAMES ON THE BACK, BASEBALL STYLE... WE ARE SO NERDY FOR THIS GAME!

2.6.2010

PLAYED WIZARD AGAIN WITH JAMESTOWN AND DOOX THEN MET UP WITH CORN AND MARCIE AT THE DOUG FIR FOR SOME BUFFALO BURGERS... IT WAS MY FIRST ONE EVER!! AND GOLLY GEE, IT WAS BOOFALICIOUS! ♥♥♥

BOOFALO!!!

2.7.2010

IT'S SUPER BOWL SUNDAY SUNDAY SUNDAY!

AND I GO TO MY NEIGHBORHOOD BAR FOR A SCRABBLE TOURNAMENT!!! IT WAS SO FUN.

ROUND ONE
SEVEN LETTER WORD!
PLAGUEY!
WIN!
ROUND TWO
STARTED OFF BEHIND... THEN WIN!
BWAHAHA
DRUNK AND HIGH
ROUND THREE
LOSE
THIS GAME IS SOOOO STUPID...

2.8.2010

HOW MUCH DO YOU CHARGE FOR COLOR PRINTING ON CARDSTOCK PAPER? B/W COPIES DOUBLE SIDED?

CALLED PLACES TODAY TO INQUIRE ABOUT COLOR PRINTING AND COPIES. I KNOW IT'S NOT COMPLEX BUT EFF IF I'M GONNA PAY MORE THAN I NEED TO.

MY FRIENDS SAY I'M CHEAP...AND THEY ARE RIGHT. I WONDER IF I'D STILL BE CHEAP IF I WAS RICH... PROBABLY... HAAAH.

Waves of change

CAN'T STOP!!

あっ…

OOOHKAY THEN... I SEE...

2.9.2010

I WAS WATCHING "HOW I MET YOUR MOTHER" AND I LOVED THIS!

HERE'S THE THING ABOUT MISTAKES. SOMETIMES YOU NEED TO MAKE THE MISTAKE TO KNOW FOR SURE IT'S A MISTAKE. OTHERWISE YOU'LL ALWAYS WONDER IF IT WAS A MISTAKE OR NOT."

TO MAKE A MOUNTAIN OF YOUR LIFE IS JUST A CHOICE. BUT I NEVER LEARNED ENOUGH TO LISTEN TO THE VOICE THAT TOLD ME:

Always Love HATE WILL GET YOU EVERYTIME

Always Love EVEN WHEN YOU OUTTA FIGHT

Always Love DON'T WAIT 'TILL THE FINISH LINE

ANY CARD YOU GET DELT *Always Love*

2.10.201
CLEARANCE SANDALS!
CLEARANCE SHORTS!
BATMAN SHIRT!
SKETCH BOOK
SKETCH BOOK!

THE SHOPPING BUG IS HITTING ME HARD RIGHT NOW. I ALREADY ONLINE SHOPPED FOR CLEARANCE CLOTHES... SO MANY SALES!! BUT I MUST SAVE FOR COMIC PRINTING, CONS, ETC!

MY HAIR IS GETTING
LONG
I WONDER IF I SHOULD GET A BOB AGAIN... OR MAYBE I'LL WAIT UNTIL SUMMER FOR THAT DECISION

BEST FRIEND SQUABBLES GET RESOLVED QUICKLY AND LOVINGLY

2.11.2010

LISTENED TO THE RADIO AT WORK NOT REALIZING IT WAS THE VALENTINE'S DAY FOR THE CCA FUNDRAISER (CHILDREN'S CANCER ASSOCIATION). THEY HAD FAMILIES COME IN TO TELL THEIR STORIES SOME WERE ABSOLUTELY HEART BREAKING. IT MADE ME CRY AT WORK. I PROBABLY SHOULDN'T HAVE KEPT LISTENING! BUT I DID. SUCH COURAGEOUS CHILDREN. *SOB*

MAYBE THIS WEIGHT WAS A GIFT. LIKE I HAD TO SEE WHAT I COULD LIFT.

- SHOES
- OIL CHANGE
- HAIR CUT
- CLOTHES (CLEARANCE!)

SPEND

2.12.2010

OLD HABITS DIE HARD WHEN YA GOT, WHEN YA GOT A SENTIMENTAL HEART.

CLOTHES CAME IN THE MAIL! MUST STOP ONLINE PURCHASING! I LUB THE CLOTHES THOUGH!

LOOKED UP AT THE TV IN TIME AT THE BAR TO SEE TEAM U.S.A WALK INTO THE ARENA FOR THE OPENING OLYMPIC CEREMONY.

I FELT A SLIGHT PANG OF TEARS.
GO U.S.A ♡ !!!

ATTENDED A BUDDY'S BIRTHDAY AT A TIKI BAR WHERE EVERYONE SHARED A VOLCANO DRINK! TASTED LIKE A FIRE JOLLY RANCHER!

02.13.2010

JAMESTOWN AND I HEAD OUT TO THE BURBS SO I CAN GET A NEW SKETCHBOOK. I LIKE GETTING THIS CERTAIN KIND FROM BARNES AND NOBLE. IN THESE, I DRAW THE EMITOWN ENTRIES THIS WILL BE MY SIXTH SKETCHBOOK! ANYWAY, JAMESTOWN AND I WERE PLANNING TO SHOP AFTER BUT MADE THE MISTAKE OF EATING FIRST! CUZ THEN WE FELT TOO TIRED TO SHOP.

OH NO!

THE SKETCHBOOK I BOUGHT HAS A GROSS HEART PATTERN INSIDE THE COVER. WHY ME?! SO STUPID! OH WELL, FIGURES.

AT BARNES & NOBLE I SHOWED JAMESTOWN MY NAME IN THE "ALEC: THE YEARS HAVE PANTS" CREDITS. I WAS EXCITED. NEVER HAD MY NAME IN A BOOK BEFORE! I HELPED LAY OUT ALL SIX HUNDRED AND SOME ODD PAGES WHEN I INTERNED FOR TOP SHELF. SO COOL!

LATER THAT DAY HOOKED UP WITH DOOX & JAMESTOWN'S FRIEND JILL FOR DRINKY DRINKS!

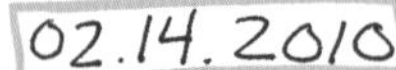

VALENTINE'S DAY IS JUST ANOTHER DAY FOR ME... I'M NOT AT ALL CYNICAL ABOUT IT AT ALL! SEEING COUPLES AND FLOWERS EVERYWHERE. PEOPLE DRESSED UP AND SHIT...

JAMESTOWN WANTED TO SEE THAT MOVIE VALENTINE'S DAY ON VALENTINE'S DAY. SO WE DID THAT. I DID **NOT** LIKE IT SO MUCH. DON'T GET ME WRONG, I LIKE ME A GOOD CHICK FLICK WITH AN ALL-STAR CAST BUT THIS ONE WAS

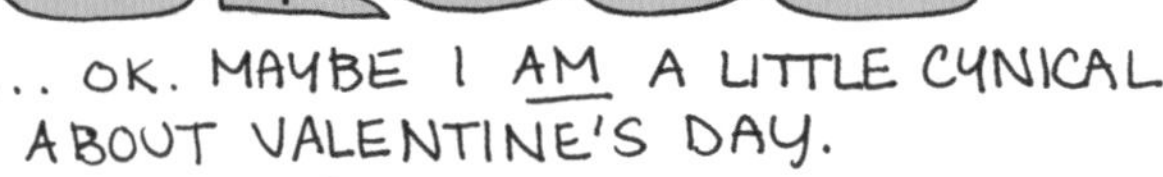

... OK. MAYBE I <u>AM</u> A LITTLE CYNICAL ABOUT VALENTINE'S DAY.

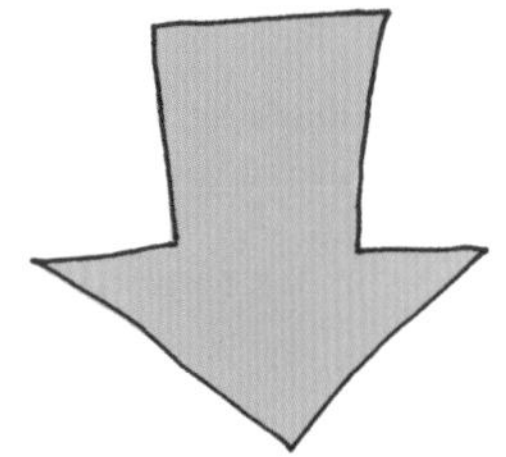

BUT THEN WE ALL WENT TO A WHISKEY BAR CALLED THE POPE HOUSE FOR DRINKS AND A GAME OF WIZARD. GOOD END TO VALENTINE'S DAY!

02.15.2010
SAW THE FIRST BLOOMED
DAFFODIL
IT WAS NICE. SPRING IS ALMOST HERE! ALTHOUGH, IT'S A LITTLE ODD SINCE IT'S ONLY MID FEB. AH WELL, THE SOONER THE BETTER!
YAY!
YOU ARE BEAUTIFUL BUT YOU DON'T MEAN A THING TO ME...
CLEARLY...
DO YOU THINK I'M SPECIAL, DO YOU THINK I'M NICE. AM I BRIGHT ENOUGH TO SHINE IN YOUR SPACES?
BETWEEN THE NOISE YOU HEAR AND THE SOUND YOU LIKE, ARE WE JUST DROWNING IN A SEA OF FACES...

02.16.2010

STUMPTOWN TABLE
CONFIRMED
HOORAY! LOAD OFF MY MIND!
(APR. 24-25)

BUT

ONLY ONE MONTH UNTIL ECCC!
YIKES SOOOO MUCH TO DO!

02/17/2010

TODAY I HAD MY FIRST P.C. CRASH SCARE. ALL OF A SUDDEN MY LAPTOP WOULD JUST SUDDENLY FREEZE. I CALLED DELL TECH SUPPORT AND THEY JUST SAID IT WAS A VIRUS AND I'D HAVE TO SEND IT IN. ALSO I'D HAVE TO PAY $400 - $500 SINCE MY WARRANTY WAS FOR HARDWARE AND NOT SOFTWARE. I WAS VERY UPSET. PLUS I HADN'T BACKED ANYTHING UP AND ALL MY COMIC STUFF WAS ON THERE! I BROUGHT IT TO PERISCOPE FOR RON TO LOOK AT AND THEN MY TECH BROTHER CAME. THREE OR FOUR HOURS LATER IT WAS FIXED!!!

A MESS...

RON

BRO

02/18/2010
PEOPLE WERE ASKING HOW THEY COULD DONATE TO HELP ME PRINT MY COMICS SO I SET UP A DONATE BUTTON ON THE SITE. I NEVER THOUGHT I'D GET THE RESPONSE I DID! I FELT SO TOUCHED AND EXCITED THAT I COULD PRINT THE MINI'S W/O HAVING TO GIVE UP EATING!
THANKS
OH MAN. I HOPE I DON'T LET PEOPLE DOWN
I WORK HARD!!!
I DO GOOD JOB!

02/19/2010

A LOT OF PEOPLE WERE BUSY EARLY FRIDAY EVE AND I WAS SUPER ANCY SINCE I WORK ALL WEEK AND DON'T REALLY GET OUT UNTIL THE WEEKEND. SO TO ENTERTAIN MYSELF, I POURED A GLASS OF WINE AND ALMOST PLAYED FFXII FROM THE BEGINING BUT THEN I THOUGHT SOLO KARAOKE ON THE PS2 WOULD BE MORE FUN...
WHY YA GOTTA GO AND MAKE THINGS COMP-LI-CATED?

MET UP WITH CORN AT MARATHON WHERE I SAW THE END OF THE BLAZER GAME AND THEN GOT THE BAR GUY TO CHANGE THE CHANNEL TO THE OLYMPICS. IT WAS COUPLES ICE SKATING WHICH I THOUGHT WAS HILARIOUS SINCE THE BAR WAS FILLED WITH GUYS... SOME ANGRY CAUSE OF PORTLAND'S LOSS IN THE BASKETBALL GAME.

WENT TO THE BAR MFP AND WENT POTTY... I DO NOT POO IN PUBLIC EXCEPT MY WORK I HAVE POO STAGE FRIGHT...
I DIDN'T MAKE THE POOP SMELL!
BUT IT SMELLED LIKE POO IN THE BATHROOM AND I FELT THE NEED TO MAKE IT KNOWN IT WASN'T ME...

02/20/2010

WHEN PLAYING PUTT-PUTT GOLF, I WAS TOLD YOU NEED TO HAVE A COOL CODE NAME. I HAD NO IDEA WHAT MINE WOULD BE ... I LOOKED AROUND AND SAID THE FIRST THING I SAW.

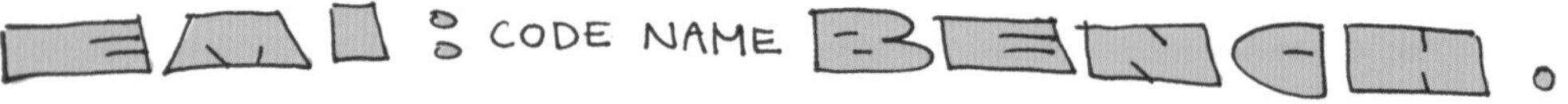

I'VE NEVER PRINTED MY STUFF BEFORE SO WHEN I SAW THE SAMPLE PRINT I COMPLETELY FREAKED OUT. THE GUY MUST HAVE THOUGHT I HAD NEVER SEEN A PRINTER BEFORE.

I AM SUPER EXCITED TO SEE THE FINISHED PRODUCT! THERE WILL BE:

- EMITOWN JUNE 2009
- EMITOWN JULY 2009
- EMITOWN AUGUST 2009
- PERFECTING LONELINESS 24 HR COMIC
- SUNLESS: THREE STORIES

02/21/2010

CREEPY ME

SAW THE MOST ADORABLE COUPLE ACROSS THE STREET IN THE STARBUCKS. THE DUDE WAS TOTALLY IN LOVE WITH HER! YOU COULD TELL BY THE WAY HE LOOKED AND TALKED TO HER. TOTAL ADORATION. SO HAPPY. I COULDN'T STOP SPYING... IT WAS LIKE SEEING A ROMANTIC MOVIE IN LIFE. IT WAS REASSURING THOUGH THAT IT DOES EXIST...

SIDE NOTE: MAN, I'M CREEPY

THEN...

GOT COFFEE WITH DOOX AND SAT IN THE SUN AND DRANK THEM BEFORE BEING COOPED UP INSIDE TO DO COMIC STUFF ALL DAY. IT WAS VERY RELAXING. THIS WEATHER IS SO NICE FOR PORTLAND IN FEB.!

02/22/2010
ACCIDENTALLY WROTE TUESDAY INSTEAD OF MONDAY.
THAT CAN'T BE GOOD.
BLEH.
GAIN ITEM
LONG ARM STAPLER

BRETT (TOP SHELF) LET ME BORROW HIS LONG ARM STAPLER SO I CAN STAPLE MY MINI COMIX. THANKS!

GOT TO GO TO LUNCH WITH ALL THE MANAGERS TODAY! PAID FOR ON THE COMPANY CARD. WE WENT TO MERRIWEATHER'S (SP?) AND IT WAS A LITTLE (A LOT) NICER THAN A BREAKFAST BURRITO. I GOT A CHICKEN SALAD SANDWICH WHICH WAS SUPER
I LOVE FOOD SO MUCH!!

HAVING SOME WOMANLY PAIN AND THE ONLY OPTION FOR RELIEF ARE THESE ADVILS THAT WERE 6 YEARS OLD!!
I THOUGHT ABOUT IT AND DECIDED TO TAKE THEM ANYWAY...
I SURVIVED.

I SAW THE BIGGEST PILE OF HORSE POO... IF I COULD GET FINED FOR NOT PICKING UP LITTLE DOG NUGS THEN THE PO-POS SHOULD PICK UP THEIR HORSE POO!
SERIOUSLY... THEM HORSE POLICE IS ALL FOR SHOW. DO THEY CATCH CRIMINALS ON HORSE-BACK?

SO I ASK: WHY IS IT THAT IN ORDER FOR WOMEN TO GET WHAT THEY BLAH BLAH BLOOP

02.24.2010

BORROWED JAMESTOWN'S SEX & THE CITY COLLECTION AND HAVE BEEN WATCHING IT A WHOLE BUNCH. I FEEL SO FEMINIME AND LIKE I HAVE A CARRIE BRADSHAW MONOLOGUE IN MY HEAD ALL THE TIME.

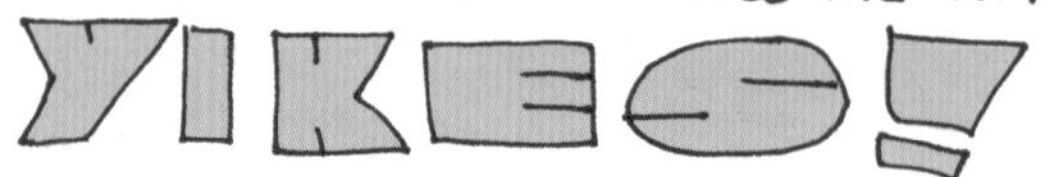

WHERE'S MY PRADA?! HA, HA!

NOT THE RIGHT SIZE

OH DRAT! WENT IN TO GET MY PRINT ORDER IN AND FIND OUT I DIDN'T SIZE THINGS RIGHT... THEY ACTUALLY FIXED MOST OF IT FOR ME THERE BUT THE STRESS WAS INSANE!!

SO NERVOUS

TO SEE HOW THEY TURN OUT TOMORROW...

02.25.2010

PICKED UP MY COMICS AND DIDN'T WANT TO CARRY SUCH A HEAVY BOX AND AS LUCK WOULD HAVE IT, A SHOPPING CART WAS ABANDONED ON A STREET CORNER FAR FROM IT'S HOME. I FELT LIKE A BUM BUT I HAD JUSTIFIED THAT I WAS TAKING THE CART HOME. THE STORE IT BELONGED TO WAS A BLOCK FROM MY APARTMENT. SCORE! RIGHTO!

ANOTHER LUNCH WITH THE MANAGERS! AND ANOTHER CHIX SAMMICH! I LOVE FOOD!

EMITOWN JUNE 2009

STAPLED AND FOLDED! FINALLY THE BOOKS ARE COMING TOGETHER! SO THRILLING!!!

02.26.2010

I GET HOLES IN THE HEELS OF MY SHOES ALL THE TIME...IT'S BECAUSE I DRAG MY FEET!! I WISH I WOULDN'T. MY SHOES WOULD LAST LONGER! SAVE MONEY! ALSO PREVENT TRIPPING ALL THE TIME.

JAMESTOWN'S FRIEND MATT WAS IN TOWN AND I HUNG OUT WITH THEM FOR AN HOUR OR SO AT M·BAR.

I TOOK A HALF DAY AT WORK SO I COULD PUT TOGETHER MY COMIC BOOKS. I STAPLED AND FOLDED FOR 9 HOURS! THE STAPLES WENT IN WONKY A LOT AND I KEPT HAVING TO TAKE THEM OUT. MY PALM HURT SO BAD BY THE END OF THE DAY. WHO KNEW STAPLING WAS SO HARD!

HAD A SESSION AND SOME GOOD CONVO. IT WAS NICE!!

02.27.2010

WENT AND BOUGHT SOME CHEAP SUNGLASSES. THE BRIGHT SUN CAN BE TOO MUCH FOR THESE EYES. ALSO BOUGHT A PLAID BUTTON UP. I HAVE SUCH A FOND LOVE FOR PLAID...AND BUTTON UP SHIRTS... IS IT THE SCOT IN ME? PROBABLY THE NORTHWEST IN ME.

AFTER COMPLAINING ABOUT MY STAPLE PAINS, MY FATHER BOUGHT ME A NEW SPRING POWERED LONG ARM STAPLER COMPLETE WITH A HANDLE AS AN EARLY BIRTHDAY PRESENT. IT'S AMAZING! I CAN STAPLE WITH ONE FINGER! I HAVE NEVER BEEN MORE EXCITED TO

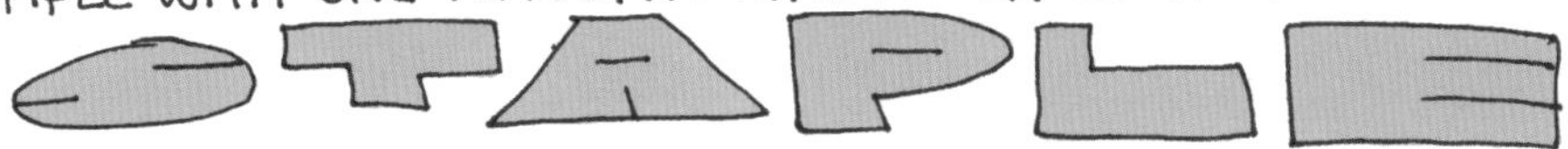

WENT TO PERISCOPE AND MADE MY PINS TO SELL AT THE CONVENTIONS! THERE ARE 40 DIFFERENT KINDS!

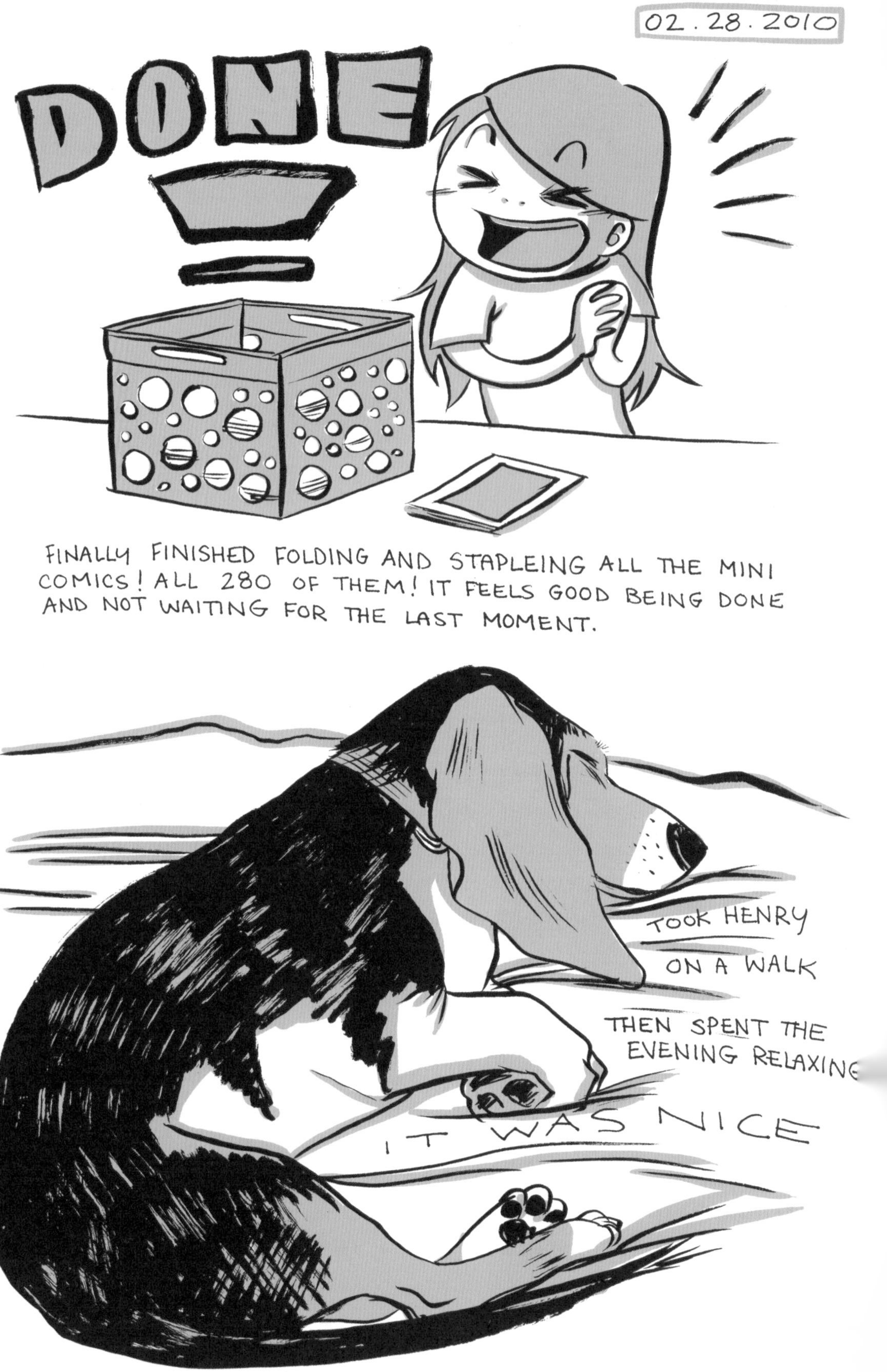

FINALLY FINISHED FOLDING AND STAPLEING ALL THE MINI COMICS! ALL 280 OF THEM! IT FEELS GOOD BEING DONE AND NOT WAITING FOR THE LAST MOMENT.

TOOK HENRY ON A WALK

THEN SPENT THE EVENING RELAXING

IT WAS NICE

MARCH 2010

3/23 "BABY"
-JUSTIN BEIBER
3/25 "IN OUR BEDROOM AFTER THE WAR"
-STARS

3. 01. 2010

URK

GOT A STRANGE ITCH IN MY THROAT... HOW THE HECK DO YOU RELIEVE AN ITCHY THROAT?! I SWALLOWED AND BURPED AND IT DID NOT HELP. BOO FEST.

HUNG OUT WITH JAMESTOWN AT THE SILVERDOLLAR AND THE BARTENDER MADE A NEW DRINK AND LET US NAME IT. I SUCK AT NAMING ALCOHOLIC BEVERAGES (NOT THAT I HAVE PREVIOUS EXPERIENCE) AND AM PRETTY SURE HE DID NOT USE MY LAME IDEA. PFFT. HIS LOSS!

WATCHED THE BACHELOR FINALE AT JAMESTOWN'S

HE WANTS THE INNOCENCE AND SWEETNESS OF TENLY AND THE SEX AND SPONTANEITY OF VIENNA!

HE NEEDS A MS. POTATOHEAD GIRLFRIEND!

3.02.2010
PBTTT
THE THROAT TICKLE AND THE SNIFFLES TURNED OUT TO BE THE START OF A COLD! TOOK A HALF DAY AT WORK AND SLEPT ALL DAY. THIS BLOWS. LITERALLY!!!

FELT BETTER AND WENT TO PLAY PUTT PUTT GOLF. IT WAS PRETTY FUN BUT THE BLACK-LIGHT LIT COURSE WAS PRETTY TRIPPY WHEN YOU'RE A LITTLE SICK AND LIGHT-HEADED. BUT DESPITE THIS, I STILL WON! YESSSS. I RULE... KINDA... I DON'T.

SO TIRED

3.03.2010

HAD A SICK DREAM THAT COMBINED STAR TREK AND STAR WARS. I ALSO TOOK COOL PICTURES ON MY OLD RAZR CELL PHONE OF THE GALAXY. YODA WAS THERE TOO... WAS THIS A FEVER DREAM? IF IT WAS, MAN THEY ARE AWESOME!

WENT IN FOR THE SECOND HALF OF WORK. GUESS I'M MORE SICK THAN I THOUGHT. THERE WAS A HOLI (FESTIVAL OF COLORS) POTLUCK AND A BALLOON STATICALLY CLUNG TO MY BUM. OR SOMEONE PUT IT THERE...

YA GOT SOMETHIN ON YA, EMI. HA, HA
HA, HA

SO TIRED!

03.04.2010

HOME SICK ALL DAY. GOOD TIME TO CATCH UP ON EMITOWN!

SNIFF

03.05.2010

WORKED A FULL DAY AT MY JOB. IT WAS SO EXHAUSTING SOMEHOW JUST SITTING ON MY BUM IN FRONT OF A COMPUTER. MY CO-WORKERS EVEN ENCOURAGED ME TO NAP AT MY DESK! AWE. WHEN I GOT HOME I FLOPPED AROUND AND WAS IN BED BY NINE.

TISSUE GHOST!

TISSUE GHOST!

HI!

!!

03.06.2010

HONK HONK

HAD TO DRIVE TO THE 'BURBS TO GET HENRY HIS SHOT. ON THE WAY ON THE HIGHWAY, SOME JERK CUT ME OFF AND BRAKED IN FRONT OF ME IN WHICH HAD I NOT BRAKED, I WOULD HAVE HIT HIM. THEN HE PROCEEDED TO DRIVE 45 IN FRONT OF ME FOR A MILE THEN SPED AWAY. WHAT-THE-HELL... I WAS ALREADY GOING 63 IN A 55 ZONE! HE WAS AN ASSHOLE CAUSE HE WANTED TO DO 70?! ACT LIKE I AM DOING SOMETHING WRONG?!

WHAT A DANGEROUS STUNT HE PULLED TO MAKE THE POINT HE IS A DUMBASS MOFO. AND HE HAD HIS WIFE AND KID IN THE CAR! HE SEEMED TO BE ON HIS WAY TO THE COAST SO I HOPE HE GETS STUCK BEHIND A BUNCH OF RV'S!!!! !!!!!

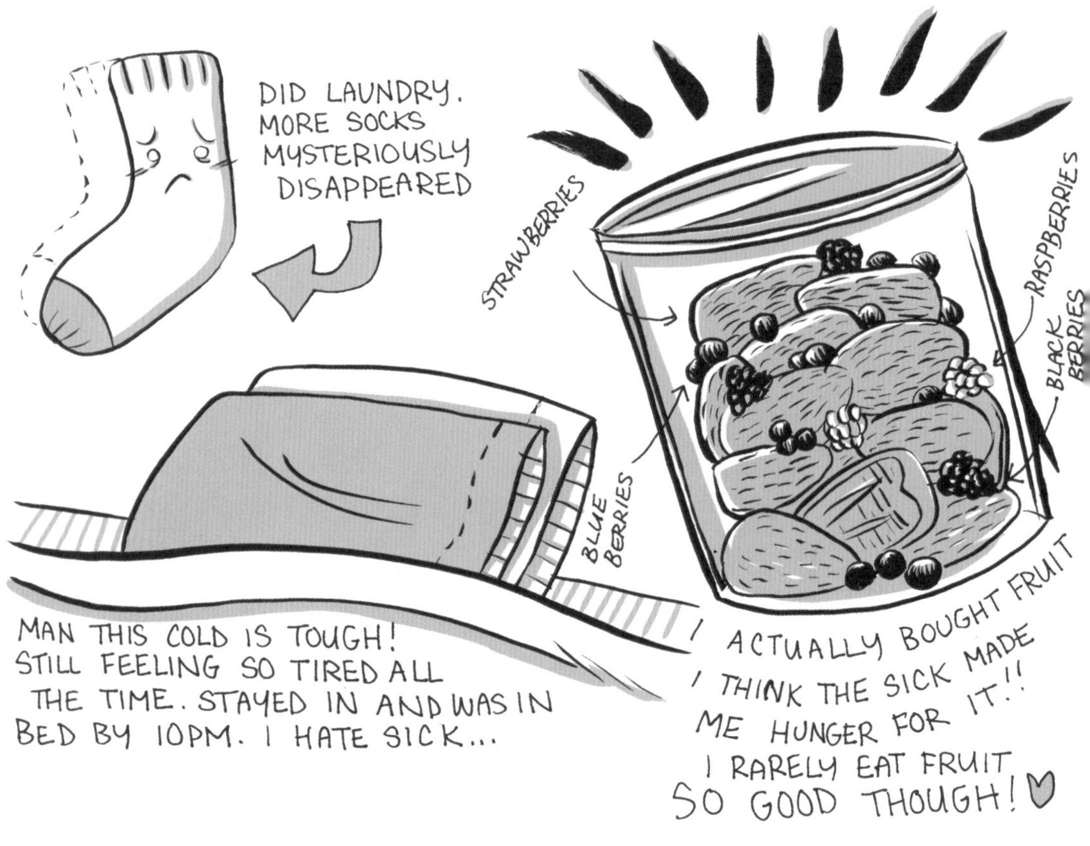

DID LAUNDRY. MORE SOCKS MYSTERIOUSLY DISAPPEARED
STRAWBERRIES
RASPBERRIES
BLACK BERRIES
BLUE BERRIES
MAN THIS COLD IS TOUGH! STILL FEELING SO TIRED ALL THE TIME. STAYED IN AND WAS IN BED BY 10PM. I HATE SICK...
I ACTUALLY BOUGHT FRUIT
I THINK THE SICK MADE ME HUNGER FOR IT!!
I RARELY EAT FRUIT
SO GOOD THOUGH!

03.07.2010

HAD TO SCAN A COMIC SO I DRAGGED MY SICK ASS DOWNTOWN TO PERISCOPE STUDIO. SUSAN AND RICH WERE THERE AND SINCE I RARELY SEE THEM, I HUNG OUT A BIT AND DREW. TOGETHER WE THOUGHT UP THE MOST BRILLIANT IDEA FOR A STRIP CLUB. I DARE NOT GIVE MORE INFO. I'M BOUND TO SECRECY. DOLLAS!!!

THEY RAN OUT OF DEVILED EGGS! BUMMER...

WENT TO THE POPE HOUSE WITH DOOX & JAMESTOWN AND HAD INTERESTING CONVOS. I'M CONCERNED BUT WHAT CAN YOU DO. PLUS I LEARN ONE OF THE DOWNSIDES OF DIARY COMICKING. ERIKA EVEN TOLD ME ABOUT THIS. WHY... A BIT FRUSTRATING...

BLACKBERRY BRAMBLES!

YUM YUM

SICK BE GONE!

03.08.2010

I'VE BEEN ITCHIN TO WORK ON MY FICTIONAL COMICS IN DUE TIME I SUPPOSE. I'M HOPING TO HAVE SOME FOR THE CONS NEXT YEAR.

WHAT IS UP WITH THE SUDDEN COLD?
DANG PORTLAND!!

SOMETIMES I THINK ABOUT WHAT IT WOULD BE LIKE IF I WAS IN HIGH SCHOOL BEING WHO I AM NOW. I... IT WOULD STILL SUCK... EXCEPT ART

03.09.2010

SDCC PLANE FARE WATCH BEGINS NOW! EVERY YEAR I CHECK KAYAK DAILY FOR AIR PRICES. LIKE A HAWK!!

PRO-REG OPENED TODAY TOO. NEED TO FIGURE THAT OUT. I HOPE I QUALIFY!! I'D FEEL SO GROWED UP IF I DID.

YAY

CLIPPED HENRY'S NAILS AND FOR THE FIRST TIME **EVER** HE DIDN'T WHINE OR STRUGGLE MUCH. SO AMAZING! IS MY BOY GROWING UP?! ♥

HAVE PRETTY MUCH ALL THE DEETS FOR MY S.F/WONDERCON TRIP FIGURED OUT! PLUS I'LL GET TO TOUR PIXAR!

SO EXCITED

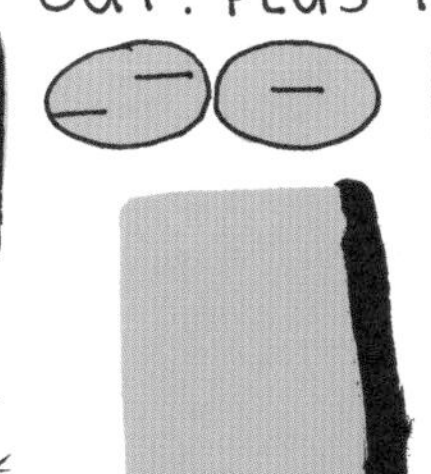

03.10.2010

GOT MY HAIRCUT SO I CAN LOOK SHARP FOR ECCC! THE GIRL THAT CUT MY HAIR WAS REALLY COOL. I RARELY ENJOY HAIR-CUTS BUT TODAY WAS NOT-TOO-SHABBY! HOORAY! ♡

MADE A LARGE CUT OUT CAT FOR THE CON USING CARDBOARD AND PAINT PLAN IS TO TIE A BALLOON TO IT'S PAW THAT CAN BE SEEN FROM AFAR!

I WAS THINKING ABOUT TRYING TO FLUSH MY OWN EARS USING A SPRAY BOTTLE ON LASER MODE. MY EARS FEEL SO CLOGGED! OR MAYBE IT'S MY COLD... I'M STILL GONNA TRY IT THOUGH! I'M EXCITED! I HOPE IT WON'T CAUSE DAMAGE...

03.11.2010

ECCC KICK OFF!

(EMERALD CITY COMIC CON)

HUNG OUT WITH JAMESTOWN & LAURA BEFORE A WEEKEND OF COMICS! LAURA GOT US ANKLETS OUT OF RED BEADS FROM HER TRIP TO HAWAII!

AFTER THAT, PICKED UP JAMIE RICH AND DROVE TO BRETT'S FOR THE TOP SHELF PRE-CON COCKTAIL PARTY!

MY FAVORITE PART (BESIDES HANGING WITH ALL THE AWESOME PEOPLE) WAS THE "STORY TIME W/ MIKE ALLRED." I TOLD HIM THAT I BELIEVED IN GHOSTS AND HE TOLD US A COUPLE TRUE GHOST STORIES. AND ONE UFO STORY.

SOME PEOPLE WHO WERE THERE INCLUDED BRETT, LEIGH AND JEFF LEMIRE, MATT KINDT, THE ALLREDS, MATT WAGNER, AND JAMIE RICH, COLLEEN COOVER AND PAUL TOBIN ♥

COLLEEN WAS TELLING ME ABOUT PUGS AND I SAID IF I HAD A PUG I'D NAME IT DUG! NOT DOUG... BUT DUG! BUT YEAH... I RAN THAT JOKE INTO THE GROUND. BLAME THE DRINK!

PUT!

GOT HOME LATE AROUND 1AM AND OF COURSE LAST MINUTE LENOX WAITS TO PACK UNTIL THE LAST MINUTE FOR THE CONVENTION!

TOMORROW: SEATTLE OR BUST!

03.12.2010

I DROVE TO SEATTLE FOR EMERALD CITY WITH TALLY AND ANGIE. IT WASN'T TOO BAD OF A DRIVE. NO COPS AND NO SCARY MEAN DRIVERS. AT ONE POINT BOTH TALLY AND ANGIE FELL ASLEEP. AWW. SLEEPY-BYE! I LOVE THAT FEELING OF A QUIET CAR WITH SOUND SLEEPERS AND I KEEP THEM SAFE BY DRIVING SMOOTH AND LAW-ABIDING! :)

OH-MY-GOODNESS. I FORGOT TO MENTION THAT LAST NIGHT I WAS TOLD THAT I GOT A GIG!!!
IT'S THE SECOND GIG I CAN'T EVEN SAY ANYTHING ABOUT. BUT OMIGAWD... I'M SO EXCITED AND SO NERVOUS FOR BOTH! I HOPE I DO GOOD.

SHARED A HOTEL ROOM WITH JAMIE RICH, JÖELLE JONES, MATT, AND TALLY. THE HOTEL WANTED

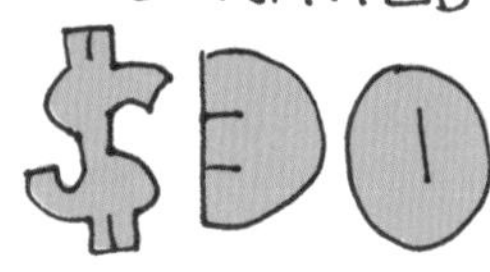

A NIGHT TO PARK THE CAR. WTF. NO. ALTERNATE PLANS WERE MADE. STRESS BE GONE.

WHO WOULD YOUR DREAM PUBLISHER BE?

COMIC NERD SLUMBER PARTY!!!!

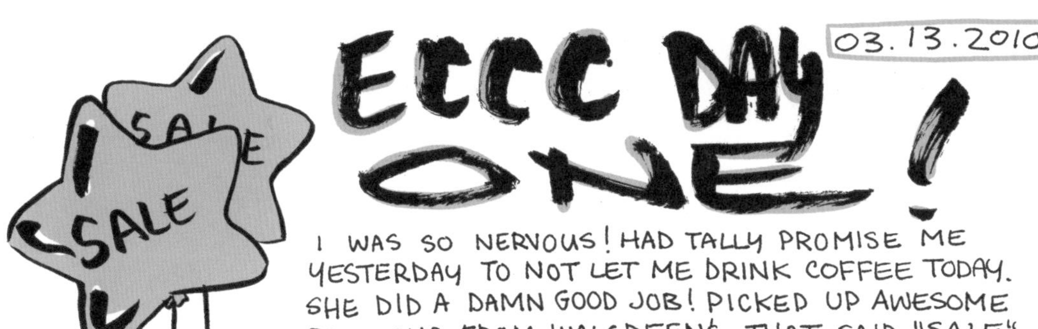

I WAS SO NERVOUS! HAD TALLY PROMISE ME YESTERDAY TO NOT LET ME DRINK COFFEE TODAY. SHE DID A DAMN GOOD JOB! PICKED UP AWESOME BALLOONS FROM WALGREENS THAT SAID "SALE" THEY WERE THEIR OWN PROMO BALLOONS BUT AFTER SOME BEGGING... THEY SOLD THEM TO ME!

MET DAVID HARPER FROM MULTIVERSITY COMICS AND HE TOLD ME HE DIDN'T SEE MY PIECE IN THE MONSTERS & DAMES BOOK. I CHECKED AND IT WASN'T IN THERE. IT HIT ME KINDA HARD. I GOT OVER IT EVENTUALLY BUT FELT BAD HIS INTRODUCTION TO ME WAS THAT...

ANGIE INTRODUCED ME TO BRANDON GRAHAM (KING CITY) AND WE ALL HUNG OUT... DESPITE MY PROTESTING HE RAN TO A STORE TO GET ME ADVIL FOR MY EYE PAIN / HEADACHE.

SAID HI TO JIM RUGG AND HE REMEMBERED ME FROM WHEN WE HUNG OUT WITH JOE AT THE ONE MODEL NATION PARTY LAST DEC. I GAVE HIM AN EMITOWN MINI AND HE GAVE ME THE AFRODISIAC!

SAW JOE TOO! HE COULDN'T TALK SO HE HAD TO WRITE!! IT WAS PRETTY AMUSING.

ECCC DAY 2

03.14.2010

SALE

SALE

THE CON WAS REALLY FUN. ONE OF THE BEST MEMORIES WAS WHEN JAMIE & JÖELLE CAME BACK TO THE HOTEL. RIDICULOUS ANTICS FOLLOWED. LAUGHED SO HARD

GAVE A KID THE SALE BALLOONS! KIDS LIKE BALLOONS!

I WILL ADMIT THAT I DON'T KNOW HOW TO PUMP MY OWN GAS. IN OREGON IT'S AGAINST THE LAW. LAST YEAR I MADE IT TO SEATTLE AND BACK BARELY ON ONE TANK OF GAS. TALLY SEEM WORRIED WHEN I TOLD HER MY PLAN AND THAT THE "EMPTY LIGHT" HAD COME ON. SOOOOOOO SUSPENSEFUL!

Z
DON'T WORRY!!! I'VE DONE THIS BEFORE AND I AM VERY VERY FAMILIAR WITH THE GAS GAUGE ON EMPTY!!! INTENSE!!!

P.S. WE DID MAKE IT ACROSS THE BORDER!

03.15. 2010
MADMAN
MADMAN GARGANTUA
MADMAN
KING CITY
KING CITY
KING CITY
KING CITY
AFRODISIAC
ANGIE WANG BUSINESS CARD!
BUTTONS FROM ANGELA MELICK!
SHARI CHANKHAMMA
SKETCHBOOK
TALLY'S MINIS!
SWAG
BEING BACK AT WORK FEELS SO DULL AND MUNDANE AFTER A WEEKEND OF COMIC CON FUN FUN·NESS. BACK IN THE OL' CUBICLE!
DO NOT LIKE
BANANA SANDWICH!?
MAYBE TIME TO REMOVE THE BANANA.

03.16.2010

ICE SHRIMP OPENS POSSIBILITIES FOR MOON SHRIMP.

OR SO I READ ON CNN TODAY. WONDER WHAT MOON SHRIMP WOULD TASTE LIKE! PROBABLY YUM!

HOLA

WENT TO THE POPEHOUSE TO CATCH UP WITH DOOX & JAMESTOWN. THEY WANT TO DO A MEXICO TRIP NEXT MONTH AND I REALLY WANT TO GO BUT THERE IS NO WAY. THAT SUCKS! I'VE NEVER BEEN ON A TRIP WITH MY FRIENDS AND I'VE NEVER BEEN TO MEXICO...

DRAT!

DELL

03.17.2010
WHEN I WENT TO THE BATHROOM AT WORK, SOMEONE HAD WROTE "I RULE POOPLAND" I THOUGHT IT WAS FUNNY...
OF COURSE
I RULE POOPLAND
TRIED TO DRAW BUT THE MOVIE WHIP IT SUCKED ME IN... AND I DIDN'T DRAW.
HELLO

03.18.2010

MARCH: ECCC
APRIL: MOCCA, STUMPTOWN
MAY: TCAF
JULY: SDCC*(NO TABLE!)
SEPT: SPX
OCT: APE
ALONE?!

I CAN DO IT...

I WAS ADVISED WHAT CONS I SHOULD TABLE OUTSIDE THE WEST COAST... SINCE I'M POOR IT WAS SUGGESTED THAT I PICK A NEW ONE EACH YEAR.

BELIEVE!

SOMETIMES (AND IT'S VERY RARE) I GET REALLY MAD. SO MUCH I FEEL LIKE I'M TURNING SUPER SAIYAN. OR SOMEONE HAD CAST BESERK ON ME AND I'M GLOWING RED, ON HASTE, AND AM UNPREDICTABLE WITH WHAT I'LL DO NEXT.

HAVE YOU HEARD NERDIER REFERENCES?! UGH.

LAST NIGHT I HUNG OUT WITH TALLY AND JAMIE. GOT HAPPY HOUR AT SILK AND TALKED COMICS. I LIKE TALKING COMICS!! ♡

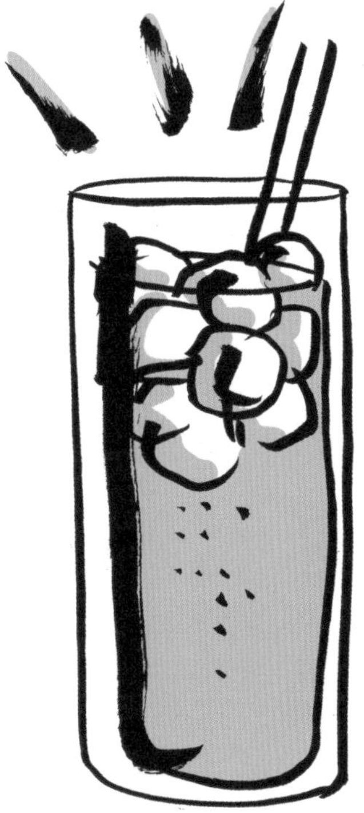

AFTER A MONTH OR SO... FINALLY HAD A MEDICINE FRI WITH CAT, RON, AND TALLY. THE BARTENDER REMEMBERED I ALWAYS GET A DOUBLE RUM & COKE! AW LIKE CHEERS! WHERE EVERYONE KNOWS YOUR DRINK.

BEST NEWS EVER!!! TODAY I GOT AN EMAIL FROM IMAGE SHOWING INTEREST IN PUBLISHING EMITOWN. OH SHIT!!!!!

03.20.2010

BOUGHT AN 14"x17" SKETCHBOOK. BIGGEST THEY HAD BUT I LOVE THE PAPER! I WANT TO DRAW COMICS ON IT...

THEN WENT TO PERISCOPE WITH TALLY, RON, AND CAT. ERIKA AND MATT STOPPED BY AND HEARD AN INTERESTING STORY ABOUT A GIRL THAT LICKS HERSELF LIKE A CAT...

WENT TO THE POPE HOUSE WITH JAMESTOWN. BOTH OF US FEELING EXHAUSTED. FOR SOME REASON THE BARTENDER GAVE US THESE SHOT GLASSES! DON'T KNOW WHY BUT

THANKS!

BULLET BOURBON

I SHOULD DO THIS, HUH... I HAVE TO DO THIS NOW...

yes

DETONATOR

THIS BE A DIFFERENT BATTLE FIELD!

03.21.2010

WELL THEN... I GUESS WE GO HOME......

I FELT SO TIRED... AFTER BEING UP UNTIL 4AM DRAWING...AND THEN STILL WAKING UP AT 9AM. AH WELL. IT WAS WORTH IT. YIKES I USED TO STAY UP ALL THE TIME DRINKING AND PARTYING...

HAD SKETCHGROUP WITH MY GIRLIES AT COFFEETIME AND THEN SAW JAMESTOWN AND DOOX AT SILVER DOLLAR... GOT HOME AND FELT SUPER TIRED. BEEN PRETTY BUSY LATELY... LOTS OF SOCIAL STUFF... IT'S FUN AND I LOVE THEM BUT A COZY BED AT THE END OF THE DAY RULES!

GOT THE FRESH PRINCE
OF BEL-AIR
FROM NETFLIX AND IT WAS STILL FUNNY!
I LOVED HOW HE DID RANDOM DANCES ALL THE TIME IN THE FIRST DISC OF THE FIRST SEASON
THEN I SAW THAT TARGET HAD IT FOR $16.99! A FIRST AND SECOND SEASON TWO IN ONE SET!
BOUGHT
!

03.23.2010
WHAT
WHEN I WAS 13
I HAD MY FIRST LOVE
I KNOW LUDACRIS SAYS THAT PART.
I WAS APALLED TO FIND OUT LAST NIGHT THAT JUSTIN BIEBER IS THE GIRL THAT SINGS THE "BABY" SONG. AND THAT HE'S ONLY LIKE THIRTEEN! WHAT-IN-THE-WHAT? MY WORLD... I CAN'T TRUST IT ANYMORE.
I LOSE CHAPSTICK ALL THE TIME. I DOUBT I HAVE EVER GONE THROUGH A WHOLE TUBE! I JUST LOSE THEM.
CHAPSTICK
RADIO! ♡
BABY, BABY, BABY OOH! BABY, BABY, BABY NOO! THOUGHT THAT YOU'D ALWAYS BE MINE. MINEEE
COMIX
COMICS ARE MY LIFE COMPLETELY RIGHT NOW!
AND I LOVE IT!

03.24.2010

WHEN I SKIM THROUGH THE NEWSPAPER DURING LUNCH, I ALWAYS LOOK THROUGH THE OBITUARIES. GRIM? I LIKE READING ABOUT THESE PEOPLE AND THE LIVES THEY HAD. SOME ARE INCREDIBLE! AND THESE WERE PEOPLE YOU COULD SEE ON THE STREET. EVERYDAY
HEROES

HEARD ON THE RADIO THE BROADWAY PLAY CATS IS COMING BACK. I ACTUALLY SAW IT WITH MY MAMA IN NEW YORK WHEN I WAS LIKE 14. I THOUGHT THE PLAY WAS FREAKY. GROWN PEOPLE DRESSED AS CATS FREAKED ME OUT. (MORE THAN CLOWNS!) AND THEY BRUSHED BY MY LEG WHEN THEY RAN THROUGH THE AISLE.

MAMA

URK!

GAP

SCAMPER

03.25.2010

I FELT LIKE JUST DRAWING ONE PICTURE TODAY.

ITS US. YES, WE'RE BACK AGAIN. HERE TO SEE YOU THROUGH UNTIL THE DAYS END. AND IF THE NIGHT COMES AND THE NIGHT WILL COME. BUT AT LEAST THE WAR IS OVER.

03.26.2010

I'MA BE QUICK, SENIORS!

DROVE TO CHEMOWA AND PARKED IN A "SENIOR PARKING" SPOT. IN ALL FAIRNESS THAT SIGN IS NEW AND I WAS A QUICK IN AND OUT TO GET MY PILLZ.

GOT THE MOST AMAZING TREAT! SOME KIND OF RHUBARB PASTRY. I ATE IT ON THE WAY TO KAIZER AND GOT CRUMBS EVERYWHERE. RHUBARB IS SO GOOD BUT LOOKS LIKE IT WOULD TASTE LIKE LETTUCE

MY GRANDMA MAKES THE BEST RHUBARB PIE! ♥

HUNG OUT WITH TALLY AND EXPLORED THE POSSIBILITIES FOR STUDIO AND LIVING TOGETHER.

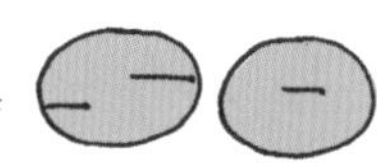

I THINK WHENEVER SATURDAY ROLLS AROUND I CATCH UP ON ALL THE SLEEP I LOST DURING THE WEEK. I SNOOZED AND SNOOZED AND SNOOZED. I ALWAYS HAVE THE STRANGEST DREAMS ON SATURDAYS...

AND

DESPITE SLEEPING FOR A ZILLION YEARS, I STILL NEEDED COFFEE TO FUNCTION. THEN JAMESTOWN PICKED ME UP AND I SHARED THE FRONT SEAT WITH A DIAPER CAKE (FOR A BABY SHOWER) AND WENT TO LAURA'S IN THE SUBURBS.

ON THE WAY HOME, JAMESTOWN KILLED A BUG WITH HER BARE HAND! I SCREAMED.

HOW YA DOING?

*# GROAN *#

EEEEE

SQUISH

I HATE BUGS. THANKS JAMIE ♥ !!

03.28.2010

RIPPED BUM (HE'S BUFF!) HAS BEEN USING MY APARTMENT'S AWNING TO KEEP DRY... IT'S NOT FUN GOING IN AND OUT TO TAKE HENRY POTTY. ACTUALLY, IT'S KINDA SCARY.

DOESN'T HELP THAT HENRY LIKES TO SAY "HI" TO EVERYONE...

UGH.

TROUBLE

WITH MY LAPTOP AGAIN! NOW IT WON'T LET ME LOG INTO MY OWN COMPUTER THIS IS SO FRUSTRATING! IT'S LIKE NOTHING BUT ISSUES WITH THIS THING LATELY! IT REEEALLY REALLY MAKES ME WANT TO RIP MY FACE OFF. I NEED TO BACK UP MY STUFF! AT THIS RATE, I'M SURE MY COMPUTER WILL HAVE PROBLEMS VERY SOON! HMMPH!

TEARING FACE OFF IN LAPTOP →

WENT TO THE BATHROOM AT WORK AROUND NOON AND SAW I WAS WALKING AROUND WITH TOOTHPASTE IN MY HAIR...

I WAS THAT PERSON. WHERE EVERYONE SEES IT BUT DOESN'T SAY ANYTHING... AND I MAKE THEM UNCOMFORTABLE...

THERE WAS A PROTEST TONIGHT IN DOWNTOWN PORTLAND ORGANIZED BY ANARCHISTS TO FIGHT AGAINST POLICE BRUTALITY. THERE WAS AN INCIDENT LAST WEEK WHERE A COP SHOT A MAN WHO DIDN'T COMPLY AND WAS BLOODY HOLDING AN X-ACTO KNIFE. THE MAN DIED. THIS WAS THE SECOND KILLING THIS YEAR. BUT THE PROTESTERS CAUSED PROPERTY DAMAGE AND THREW ROCKS AT THE POLICE WHO WERE TRYING TO CONTAIN THE PROTEST.

OK. LETS PROTEST VIOLENCE WITH

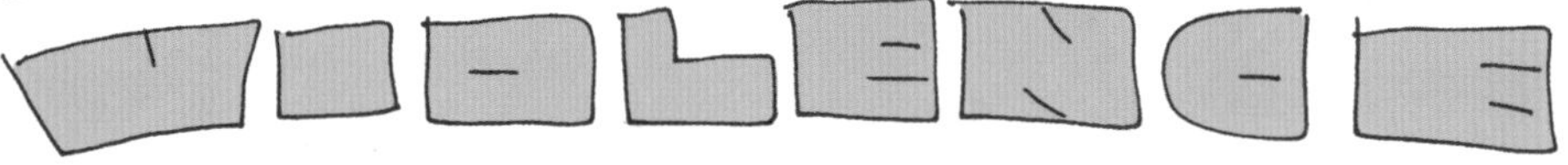

PSHHHH. THAT SHOULD SEND A GOOD MESSAGE.

03.30.2010
PrADA
MY FRIEND JOE CALLED US THE "PRETTY ARTIST DETECTIVE AGENCY" I GOT CARRIED AWAY.

03.31.2010
BE CAREFUL FOR THE SNOW IN THE PASSES. LIKE SHASTA AND THE SISKIYOUS... YOU SHOULD HAVE CHAINS...
WHAAAAT? NO WAY. BUT IT'S APRIL!!!

MY COWORKER CAUTIONED ME ABOUT A LOT OF THINGS FOR MY DRIVE TO S.F. TOMORROW. ONE OF WHICH WAS TO PREPARE FOR SNOW ON THE WAY DOWN. OH MAN, I HOPE THERE IS NO SNOW. I DO NOT OWN CHAINS! SUCH DEADLY BEAUTY. SNOW.

I FLY UP IN THE AIR AND FIRE PEOPLE'S ASSES AROUND THE COUNTRY. I LOVE MY JOB.

WATCHED UP IN THE AIR WHILE I WAS PACKING FOR MY TRIP. MAYBE IT WAS BECAUSE I WASN'T REALLY PAYING ATTENTION BUT I FOUND MYSELF NOT PARTICULARLY ENTERTAINED BY THIS MOVIE

GEORGE CLOONEY IS SO WEATHERED.

?

FREE COMIC
IF YOU HAVE
PAIN MEDS!!!
COMIS $5
BUTTONS $1
SKETCH $20
JULY
AUGUST

APRIL 2010

4/12 "BELIEVE IN WHAT YOU WANT"
-JIMMY EAT WORLD

ON THE FREEWAY I PASSED A GUY AND IT LOOKED LIKE HE WAS FLIPPING ME OFF! TURNED OUT HE WAS JUST RESTING HIS ARM LIKE THAT. SERIOUSLY THOUGH, DON'T DO THAT GUY. I WAS STARTING TO THINK I HAD DONE SOMETHING WRONG!!

IN OREGON YOU CAN'T PUMP YOUR OWN GAS. I ALWAYS MANAGED TO GET OUT OF WASHINGTON IN TIME WHEN I'M THERE. FOR THE FIRST TIME IN MY LIFE OF 26 YEARS, I PUMPED MY OWN GAS!

I DID IT!

IF I OWNED TONS OF LAND, I'D PUT DINOSAURS ALL OVER THE PLACE!

OH! IT'S A DRAGON!

TALLY

ON THE DRIVE THROUGH NORTHERN CALIFORNIA THERE WAS A DRAGON WE WERE TOLD TO KEEP AN EYE FOR. AT FIRST I THOUGHT IT WAS A DINOSAUR... AND I THOUGHT IT WAS HIDDEN IN THE HILLS TO BE TRICKY TO FIND...

04.02.2010

IN S.F. I SHOW TALLY MY OLD STOMPING GROUNDS FROM WHEN I LIVED THERE IN 2003/04. A LOT OF THE STORES I REMEMBERED ARE GONE. IT MIGHT BE BECAUSE IT WAS ALL RAINY AND DREARY LOOKING TODAY, BUT IT STIRRED UP SOME ICKY SEVEN YEAR OLD FEELINGS OF HOW LONELY AND SAD I WAS THERE. AND AS I TOLD TALLY MORE STORIES IN CONNECTION TO CERTAIN LANDMARKS, I FELT PATHETIC. RELIVING PATHETIC TIMES. LIKE TELLING HER HOW I WALKED EVERYWHERE FOR FUN ALONE. DRINKING A 40 AT THE PARK IN FRONT OF GRACE CATHEDRAL AT NIGHT... ALONE. I FEEL BAD THAT I WAS DISTANT WHILE HANGING WITH TALLY. BUT THAT ICKY GUT FEELING WOULDN'T GO AWAY...

WE DID GO TO JAPANTOWN AND TOOK SOME PURIKURA PICS. NEVER DONE THAT BEFORE. I CAN SEE WHY IT'S SO POPULAR! IT IS FUN! PLUS THE CAMERA GIVES ME AWESOME COMPLEXION!

TUMMY

LOOK AT THAT! OH... MY... GOD!
THE SKETCHES... THE MODELS...

MY FRIEND MATT GOT TALLY AND I A TOUR OF PIXAR! WE MET THE COOLEST GUY JOSH COOLEY WHO DOES STORYBOARDING. HE WAS SUPER NICE AND GAVE US AN AWESOME TOUR. I AM VERY THANKFUL!

LETS TALK COMICS

TALKED TO ERIC FROM IMAGE ABOUT EMITOWN AND IT'S REALLY HAPPENING! MY FIRST PUBLISHED BOOK! POSSIBLY OUT BY OCT/NOV! SO SO EXCITING!!

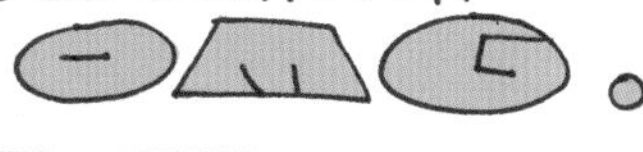

OVERALL, WONDERCON WAS OK. NOT MY FAVORITE CON BY FAR. TALLY AND I GO TO SOME TEA PLACE ACROSS THE STREET FROM THE CONVENTION CENTER. WE THOUGHT WE COULD GET $2 TEA OR SOMETHIN. NO... IT WAS LIKE A BILLION DOLLARS FOR TEA. I DON'T KNOW ENOUGH ABOUT TEA FOR THAT TO EVER MAKE SENSE. WE HAD $5 RICE PUDDING INSTEAD. AND

WATER...

MY FRIEND MATT GOT US TICKETS TO ROLLER DERBY. IT WAS MY FIRST TIME GOING TO ONE OF THESE THINGS. FROM WHAT I SAW, IT WAS PRETTY AWESOME. MAYBE I SHOULD CHECK OUT THE PORTLAND SCENE.

LIKE MY COWORKER HAD WARNED ME, I FACED A SNOWSTORM ON MY WAY BACK NORTH. NEVER DROVE IN ONE BEFORE. DON'T GET THAT MUCH SNOW IN PORTLAND. WHEN WE DO I NEVER DRIVE IN IT! TALLY CALLED HER FRIEND MOLLY WHO CHECKED ONLINE AND SAID WE SHOULD BE ABLE TO MAKE IT. AND WE DID!! PHEW! I NEED CHAINS. JUST IN CASE, YAH? BE PREPARED!! I'M SO NOT...

HOW FAST DO YOU THINK YOU WERE GOING?

GOT A SPEEDING TICKET. MY FIRST ONE! MY FIRST TIME EVEN BEING PULLED OVER! I THOUGHT I WAS DOING 75 IN A 70 ZONE. TURNED OUT I WAS DOING 81 IN A 65 ZONE. OH SHIT... THERE ARE NO ZONES IN OREGON OVER 65. WHA- I GUESS I SHOULD'VE KNOWN THAT. I JUST NEVER DRIVE ANYWHERE. I AM IMPRESSED THAT I DIDN'T CRY. ESPECIALLY WHEN I HEARD HOW MUCH THE FINE WAS. SIGH~

AFTER 10 HOURS OF DRIVING... A SNOWSTORM... TRAFFIC... SPEEDING TICKET...

I COULD NOT SLEEP...

04.05.2010

WITH ALL THE THINGS THAT WENT WRONG IN THE PAST WEEK, I DID NOT CRY... BUT THE TIRE WAS THE LAST STRAW. I FINALLY BROKE DOWN. AND THOUGH IT WAS SET ON CUE, IT STARTED TO RAIN ON ME TOO.

YOU WIN UNIVERSE.

04.06.2010
MAYBE WE CAN GET ONE OF HER LEGS TO BREAK... THAT WOULD MAKE HER CRY... OR ANOTHER FLAT TIRE? A BREAK IN? UUHH...
NO...NO, WAIT... WE GOT HER. SHE'S CRYING NOW.
I THINK THE BAD LUCK IS OVER. I FEEL LIKE THE UNIVERSE WAS WAITING FOR ME TO BREAK DOWN. I WAS SO BURNT OUT, I CRIED A LOT.
WAAA AAA AAH!

04.07.2010
HI FLOWERS! ♡
HELLO TREE!!
THE THING ABOUT HAVING A STRING OF BAD LUCK
IS WHEN IT'S ALL OVER AND THINGS ARE NORMAL ... EVERYTHING IS AWESOME.
THIS COFFEE IS PERFECT
ALL THE SMALL THINGS I NORMALLY WOULDN'T BE EXCITED ABOUT, I WAS THRILLED TODAY. I THINK THE BREAKDOWN WAS REALLY GOOD. IT WAS A RELEASE OF ALL THE STRESS AND ICKINESS THAT HAD GROWN FROM THE PAST WEEK. I FEEL FRESH AND NEW! THE WEIGHT IS GONE.
CONQUER

04.08.2010
LAST WED. 3/31
YOU SHOULD GET THE FLUIDS IN YOUR CAR TOPPED OFF. IT'S FREE AT HENRY'S IF YOU HAD AN OIL CHANGE RECENTLY. DO IT BEFORE YOUR TRIP TOMORROW.
← COWORKER DAVE
MON 4/5
DID YOU GET YOUR FLUIDS TOPPED OFF?
NO...
WHY NOT? IT'S ONLY A BLOCK FROM HERE. YOU SHOULD DO IT! IT'S FREE. ESPECIALLY AFTER YOUR TRIP TO SAN FRANCISCO.
← COWORKER DAVE
WED 4/7
DO YOU GET YOUR CAR TAKEN CARE OF YET?
NO...
WHAT? SERIOUSLY. GO ON YOUR LUNCH! IT'S A BLOCK AWAY. I'M GONNA BUG YOU ABOUT IT LATER THIS WEEK YOU KNOW...
← COWORKER DAVE
SO I WENT TO OIL CAN HENRY'S TODAY AND GOT MY CAR'S FLUIDS TOPPED OFF...JUST SO I CAN SAY I DID WHEN HE ASKS. I GUESS CONSTANT NAGGING DOES WORK!

PLAYED WIZARD AT THE POPE HOUSE WITH JAMESTOWN & DOOX. THERE, WE SAW OUR FRIEND BEN'S DOPPLEGANGER. IT WAS TRUELY EERIE. HOPEFULLY, THE GUY DIDN'T NOTICE HOW WE KEPT LOOKING ~~ANG~~ AND GIGGLING AT HIM. CAUSE THAT CAN'T BE FUN...

TOOK THE MAX TRAIN TO A TIKI BAR FOR CORN'S BIRTHDAY. IT WAS LIKE, ELEVEN-O-CLOCK A NIGHT AND THERE WAS A DOG ON THE TRAIN WEARING SUNGLASSES, HANGING OUT ON A SEAT. I LAUGHED... EXPLAINED WHY TO A STRANGER NEXT TO ME. "IT'S A DOG... WITH SUNGLASSES!"

CHILLIN!

I HEAR THAT SOME OF MY FRIENDS AREN'T DOING SO WELL LATELY. ONE GOING BACK TO SOME DARK TENDANCIES
I'M VERY WORRIED

04.10.2010

OH SHIT...

COOOOL

flop!

I HAVE HAD MY ARM FALL ASLEEP BEFORE BUT NEVER TO THE POINT WHERE I HAVE "DEAD ARM" I SLEPT ON IT AND WHEN I WOKE UP I HAD NO CONTROL OF MY FOREARM. I WAS AMAZED. I FLOPPED MY ARM AROUND A BIT. NOW I KNOW WHAT IT'S LIKE TO HAVE A LIFELESS LIMB. IT WAS

STRANGE!

BRO'S B·DAY BBQ AT THE PARENTS. TOOK ADVANTAGE OF YARD AND SUNNY DAY TO WASH HENRY

WENT TO JOHN'S B·DAY PARTY. DIDN'T DRINK. DRANK ICED COFFEE. DRANK TOO FAST... IT MESSED ME UP! MY HEAD HURT. BOOZE WOULD HAVE BEEN EASIER TO DEAL WITH. A LITTLE!

04.11.2010
2:02
IT SUCKS WHEN YOU HEAR ABOUT A GOOD FRIEND IN DARK TIMES DOING DARK THINGS AND THERE IS NOTHING YOU CAN DO TO HELP. YOU CAN'T EVEN TALK TO THEM OR SEE THEM. THIS IS A BLOWFEST. UGH...
WORRY WORRY WORRY!
SNIFF
ITCHY EYES
LAST NIGHT AT JOHN'S I PET HIS CAT ♥. BUT I REALIZE I AM A LITTLE ALLERGIC. I REMEMBER WITH WEENIE (MY DECEASED CAT. RIP 2008) I WOULD GET ITCHY EYES EVERY NOW AND AGAIN... I GUESS I LOST WHATEVER IMMUNITY I HAD WHEN HE DIED... NOOO! I WANT A CAT AGAIN SOMEDAY!
WTF
I WATCHED 2012 TODAY... IT WAS FUN BUT ALSO "WTF" AND "OH GOD, COME ONNN."

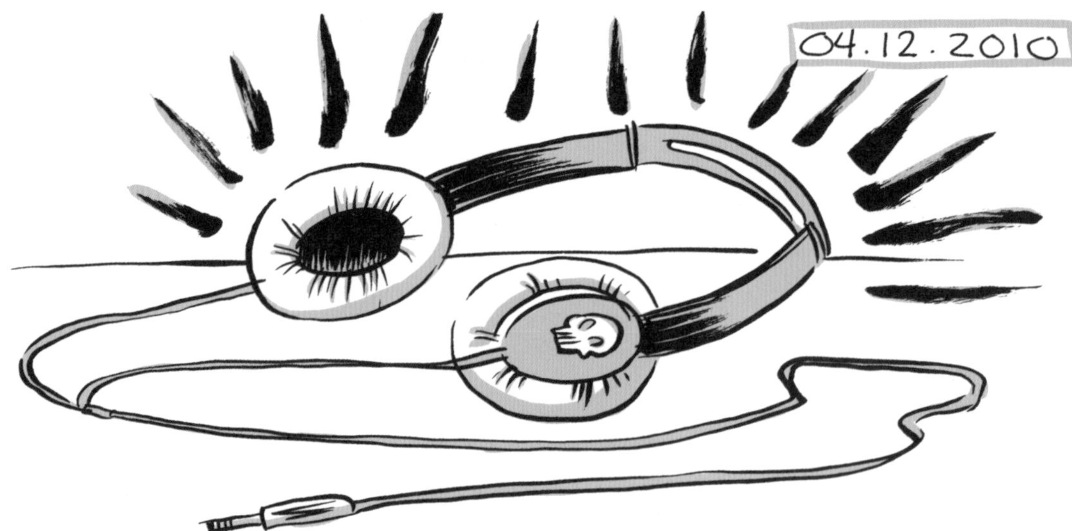

FORGOT MY HEADPHONES AT HOME TODAY. I MISSED MY POPPY RADIO JAMS AT WORK...NO JAMS... MAKE FOR A LONG DAY.

SPINNING AND SPINNING, DO YOU BELIEVE IN WHAT YOU WANT?

TAXES ARE DUE IN TWO DAYS. GUESS I SHOULD DO THEM NOW. I DO THEM BY HAND. DON'T TRUST THE WI-FI FOR IMPORTANT MONEY THINGS...

04.14.2010

I HAD TO DECLINE A TICKET TO SEE **CONAN O'BRIEN** IN SPOKANE, WASHINGTON FRIDAY. BUT ONE PARKING TICKET, SPEEDING TICKET, AND NEEDING TO BUY A PLANE TICKET FOR SDCC... AND LEARNING THIS IS THE LAST WEEKEND TO PREPARE FOR STUMPTOWN...UH...YEAH. CAN'T GO. I SHED A SINGLE TEAR. *SIGH* IT'S OKAY.

DECAF COFFEE IS STUPID.

GROANNN NNNNNN GROANNN NNNNN

THEY HAD RUN OUT OF **REAL** COFFEE AND I WAS IN A RUSH SO I GOT DECAF. IT WAS A WASTE OF DOLLARS. WHY BOTHER? WHY? WHY? WHY? HA.

04.15.2010

HUNG OUT WITH BEN! I HAVEN'T SEEN HIM SINCE NEW YEARS. IT WAS NICE TO CATCH UP AND HEAR HOW HE IS DOING. HE'LL ALWAYS BE A GOOD FRIEND AND IT'S AWESOME WE CAN STILL TALK LIKE WE SEE EACH OTHER EVERYDAY. THAT'S THE STUFF OF A DARN GOOD FRIEND. TAKE CARE OF YOURSELF!

BEN GAVE ME HIS BURNED COPY OF SUFJAN STEVENS' "SEVEN SWANS" YAH! I REALLY DO LOVE ME SOME DEPRESSING TUNES SOMETIMES.

I GET REALLY WORKED UP WHEN I HEAR ABOUT PEOPLE TREATING GOOD PEOPLE LIKE CRAP. I WANT TO JUMP IN AND SAVE THEM... BUT I CAN'T. IN THE END, THEY HAVE TO SAVE THEMSELVES. THAT DOESN'T MAKE IT ANY EASIER THOUGH.

04.16.2010
ONE
PEA
I HAVE BEEN REMINDED THAT I AM JUST ONE PEA IN ONE POD. AND AFTER ALL THE DATES I HAD LAST YEAR, I WORRY IF I'LL EVER HAVE THAT "CONNECTION" AGAIN. BEST FRIEND.
I HARDLY THINK ABOUT THIS STUFF BUT YESTERDAY REMINDED ME AND IT HIT ME HARD FOR SOME REASON.
SO STUPID.
GOOD THINGS WILL COME! I KNOW IT. DON'T THINK ABOUT IT.
NOT EVERYONE GETS THAT DREAM RELATIONSHIP. JUST ON THE T.V.

04.17.2010
PINEAPPLE IN A CAN
GREEN ONION
SOMEN NOODLES
PINEAPPLE CHUNKS
EGGS
VANILLA YOGURT
YOGURT
BERRIES
BEEF
TOMATOES... ALSO SPAM, MANGO, JUICE, SALAD, AND TOOTHPASTE. SHOPPING TRIP = SUCCESS!
JAMESTOWN GOT ME INTO A TV DRAMA ABOUT FOOTBALL! I CAN'T BELIEVE IT. WE BOTH THINK COACH TAYLOR IS HUNKY THOUGH. IT'S A REALLY GOOD SHOW! I LIKE IT.

04.18.2010

REAL WORLD WASHINGTON D.C.
HA, HA, HA. SILLY REALITY TV PEOPLE.
DELL

WENT TO PERISCOPE TO MAKE MORE BUTTONS IN PREPARATION FOR STUMPTOWN. I TOOK AN HOUR TO FIGURE OUT THE PRINTER AND THEN ENJOYED DUMB TV ONLINE THAT I MISS OUT ON AT HOME. I HAVE NO CABLE AND SLOW WI-FI.

DREW THE PORTLAND CITY SCAPE FROM MY FIRE ESCAPE ON A SUNNY DAY. IT WAS PRETTY FUN. DID I TAN. NO. DARN.

SAW JAMESTOWN BEFORE SHE LEFT FOR MEXICO (SO JEALOUS!) DIDN'T GET TO SEE DOOX... DANG, I'LL SURE MISS THEM ALL WEEK! :(

MADE CARDS FOR BUTTON SETS TO SELL. USED WATERCOLOR PAPER ← I BOUGHT FROM A SCRAP BIN 6 YEARS AGO. EACH HAND DRAWN AND COLORED. THINGS YA GOTTA DO WHEN YOU'RE POOR. THEY LOOK DECENT!

04.19.2010
BEFORE
WHAT TO EAT? SUSHI?
HANG OUT WITH... FOOD...
BOY FRIEND... TV...
PROJECT ONE
THUMBNAILS
MINIS
EMITOWN
PITCHES
BUTTON SETS
SAN DIEGO
STUMPTOWN
SKETCHES
PROJECT 2
I WAS SITTING AT WORK TODAY MY MIND CLUTTERED WITH THINGS I HAVE TO DO FOR THE LOVE OF COMICS, AND I WONDERED... WHAT DID I THINK ABOUT BEFORE I DECIDED TO TRY COMICS?
NOW
I'M A BUSY BEE!

04.20.2010

PUT IN AN ORDER TO PRINT ANOTHER RUN FOR MY MINIS. I HAVE TWO NIGHTS TO FOLD AND STAPLE... AMONG OTHER THINGS I NEED TO DO TO BE PREPARED...

BUT I **DO** HAVE A FRIEND WHO WANTS TO HELP! AW. I'M SO LUCKY.

TOMORROW MY WONDERFUL FRIEND WILL BE HERE! YAY!

BATTLE NUN
COMETH

04.21.2010

MY FRIEND BATTLENUN (AKA GONZ) CAME TODAY FROM CHICAGO! I ONLY GET TO SEE HER LIKE, ONCE A YEAR! THIS YEAR: TWICE! WE WENT TO SUSHILAND AND ATE LIKE HEROES. SUSHI!

GONZ CAME OVER AND HELPED ME FOLD MORE MINIS. I SHOWED HER FRIDAY NIGHT LIGHTS AND TOGETHER WE SWOONED OVER COACH TAYLOR.

04.22.2010

I READ ABOUT A FUNGUS THAT IS KILLING PEOPLE IN OREGON. IT WAS FRIGHTENING. IT SAID YOU CAN GET IT SIMPLY BY BREATHING IN AND THERE WAS NO CURE.
I FREAKED OUT A LITTLE.
BUT THEN I WAS TOLD THAT LIKE THE SWINE FLU, IT ONLY KILLS PEOPLE WITH PRE-EXISTING HEALTH ISSUES.
DOGS CAN GET IT TOO! SYMPTOM IS RUNNY NOSE! WTF. HIS NOSE IS RUNNY MOST TIMES!

04.23.2010

TALLY AND I ATTENDED THE

LADIES DRINK AND DRAW WEST

IT WAS PRETTY AWESOME MEETING FOLKS IN PERSON! ANGELA MELICK WAS THERE TOO! TONS OF COOL LADIES.

I GOT TO MEET THESE AWESOMES!

KATE BEATON

LUCY KNISLEY

HOPE LARSON

MEREDITH GRAN

AFTER THE DRINK & DRAW, MET UP WITH JAMIE RICH, JOELLE JONES, NICO HITORI DE, AND OTHERS AT O'BRIEN'S PUB.

04.24.2010

I HAD A SLIGHT HANGOVER FOR THE FIRST DAY OF STUMPTOWN. NOBODY HAD ADVIL AT MY TABLE, SO I MADE A SIGN THAT READ "IF YOU GIVE ME ADVIL, I GIVE YOU A FREE COMIC"

IT WORKED! I WAS SO HAPPY. WHEN I LATER TOLD A CO-WORKER THIS STORY HE SAID "PILLS? FROM A STRANGER?! MAN, YOU LIVE LIFE ON THE EDGE."

AFTER STUMPTOWN COMICS FEST (SAT), I WENT WITH ANGIE, TALLY, GONZ, CAT, RON, SEAN, LEIGH AND THE NEW TOP SHELF INTERN TO A GERMAN RESTAURANT. I TRY SAUSAGE... I WASN'T DIGGIN IT.

THEN WE ALL GO TO THE COSMIC MONKEY AFTER PARTY. THAT WAS PRETTY AWESOME.

THEN

WENT TO AN AFTER-AFTER PARTY AT THE TOP SHELF HOUSE. I LOVE THE TUBBY KITTY THERE! I HUGGED IT A LOT.

JACK!!!

A PUBLISHER CAME UP TO MY TABLE INTERESTED IN HEARING A PITCH FROM ME! HOW EXCITING AND SCARY AT THE SAME TIME! I'VE NEVER PITCHED BEFORE. TIME TO ORGANIZE SOME IDEAS! OH BOY!

THE BOX WAS HEAVIER AFTER THE CON! TOO MUCH SHOPPING! ALL GOOD THO.

WAAH!

COMIX

DESPITE HOW INCREDIBLY TIRED I WAS, I STAYED UP LATE READING "SMILE" BY RAINA TELGEMEIER IT WAS COOL MEETING HER AND I LOVED THE BOOK!

SMILE

04.26.2010

SECOND & THIRD VOLUMES OF OCTOPUS PIE BY MEREDITH GRAN

"SMILE" BY RAINA TELGEMEIER

ALSO GOT BABYSITTERS CLUB #1

"MERCURY" BY HOPE LARSON

"MAKE YOURSELF HAPPY" BY LUCY KNISLEY

ALSO GOT "RADIATOR DAYS" AND A BATMAN & ROBIN PRINT! ♥

"TIGERBUTTAH" BY BECKY & FRANK

"OTTO ZEPLIN" BY BT LIVERMORE (ALL 4 VOLUMES)

"OUIJA INTERVIEWS" BY SARAH BECAN

AND FROM THE TOPSHELF HOUSE:

- "THE 120 DAYS OF SIMON" BY SIMON GARDENFORS
- "UNDELETED SCENES" BY JEFFREY BROWN
- "HEY PRINCESS" BY MATS JONSSON
- COMIC DIORAMA BY GRANT REYNOLDS

HUNG OUT WITH JAMESTOWN! I ALSO HAD TO RETURN FRIDAY NIGHT LIGHTS. SO SAD! I MISS COACH TAYLOR ALREADY!

04.27.2010

HAD DINNER WITH GONZ & ANGIE BEFORE GONZ LEAVES TO GO BACK TO CHICAGO TOMORROW. I FELT SO TIRED. I FEEL BAD I WAS SO BLAH...

BURG
HOOD
GONZ HAD THE COOLEST JACKET. THE HOOD GOES ALL THE WAY OVER HER HEAD! LIKE A GHOST!

BUM WATCH 2K10

HE BITES BUM. I MEDICATE. I WATCH TO MAKE SURE HE DOESN'T. BITE.

OMG

PLUS I FEEL A COLD COMIN'

CAN I BUILD IT?!!!

YES...

YES I CAN...

04.29.2010
(I DREW THIS IN BED BEFORE PASSING OUT. CAN YOU TELL? SO BAD!)
PLEASE
DON'T BE THE FUNGUS!
PLEASE?
SICK AGAIN !
TOILET PAPER
TYPE TYPE
PJS
DELL
JAMESTOWN CAME BY AND HELPED ME WITH MY "WRITTEN APPEARANCE" FOR MY SPEEDING TICKET. SHE'S SO GOOD AT MAKING THINGS SOUND . . .
GOOD

04.30.2010

I HAVE TO PARK ON THE STREET NOW. THIS IS HARD SINCE I CAN'T PARALLEL PARK! I PARK FAR AWAY FROM MY APT SOMETIMES BECAUSE OF THIS. I NEED TO LEARN...

TODAY, JAMESTOWN PLAYFULLY CHOKED ME. WHAT SHE DIDN'T KNOW WAS THAT I COMPLETELY FREAK OUT. I BUCKLE UP AND START MAKING A GURGLING SOUND. I EVEN CRIED A LITTLE. I HATE IT IF ANYONE TOUCHES MY NECK. EVEN AN EX BOYFRIEND I HAD DATED FOR ALMOST FOUR YEARS COULDN'T. YOU WOULD THINK I HAD A TRAUMATI CHOKING INCIDENT BUT I DIDN'T... THAT I COULD REMEMBER. I WONDER IF IN A PAST LIFE, I WAS CHOKED TO DEATH... I DUNNO... I THINK IT'S WEIRD... THERE HAS TO BE SOME

REASON, RIGHT?

THANK YOU FOR VISITING EMITOWN

BY EMI LENOX

THIS PAST YEAR HAS BEEN QUITE POSSIBLY ONE OF THE MOST EXCITING YEARS OF MY LIFE.

FOR THE LONGEST TIME, MY FRIENDS HAVE HEARD ME WHINE ABOUT WANTING TO DO ART, BUT NOT DOING A LOT TO MAKE IT HAPPEN. HOWEVER, IT'S BECAUSE OF THESE FRIENDS I'VE GROWN MUCH MORE CONFIDENT. IT'S STILL A CONSTANT BATTLE, BUT I'VE NEVER FELT LIKE THE FUTURE HAS EVER BEEN BRIGHTER. AGAIN, I'M STILL ABSOLUTELY FRIGHTENED AT THE POSSIBILITY OF FAILURE, BUT FOR THE FIRST TIME IN MY LIFE I FEEL I CAN DO IT.

THEIR SUPPORT AND ENCOURAGEMENT GOT ME TO PUT EMITOWN ONLINE AND IN ZINES. THEY INSPIRED ME TO GET MY FIRST EVER TABLE AT EMERALD CITY COMIC CON. IT'S THERE I FIRST MET MY PUBLISHER ERIC STEPHENSON.

AND NOW WE HAVE A BOOK.

EMITOWN BEING OUT IN THE WORLD WILL BE A NEW EXPERIENCE AS WELL. I'M LEARNING SO MUCH AND I HOPE FOR THE BEST AND WILL CONTINUE TO WORK MY BUM OFF.

THIS WOULD NEVER HAVE COME TOGETHER IF NOT FOR THE SUPPORT AND LOVE OF MY PARENTS AS WELL AS MY CLOSE FRIENDS, JAMESTOWN AND LAURA. I'M FOREVER THANKFUL.

I WANTED TO ESPECIALLY THANK ALL THE READERS AND FRIENDS WHO DONATED SO THAT I COULD EVEN PRINT OUT MY FIRST MINI-COMICS FOR EMERALD CITY COMIC CON. WITHOUT THAT SORT OF SUPPORT OR GENEROSITY, I DON'T KNOW IF ALL THIS WOULD HAVE HAPPENED.

I'M ALSO VERY LUCKY TO HAVE MY FELLOW PRETTY ARTIST DETECTIVE AGENCY STUDIO-MATES, NATALIE NOURIGAT AND ANGIE WANG. DRAWING WITH THEM ALWAYS KEEPS ME INSPIRED.

I TRULY APPRECIATE THE SUPPORT AND GUIDANCE FROM PERISCOPE STUDIO, TOP SHELF AND EATPOO.COM. A SPECIAL THANK YOU GOES OUT TO JEFF LEMIRE, JOE KEATINGE, JAMIE S. RICH, THE ALLREDS, BRANDON GRAHAM, AND DEREK HUNTER FOR THEIR GUIDANCE AND SUPPORT. AN EXTRA SPECIAL THANK YOU IS DUE TO ERIC STEPHENSON, DREW GILL, BETSY GOMEZ, AND ALL THE AWESOME PEOPLE AT IMAGE COMICS.

I KNOW I'M FORGETTING PEOPLE, BUT YOU ALL KNOW WHO YOU ARE AND THAT YOU ARE AWESOME!